Bombay's People, 1860–98

Bombay's People, 1860–98

Insolvents in the City

Asiya Siddiqi

OXFORD
UNIVERSITY PRESS

OXFORD
UNIVERSITY PRESS

Oxford University Press is a department of the University of Oxford. It furthers the University's objective of excellence in research, scholarship, and education by publishing worldwide. Oxford is a registered trademark of Oxford University Press in the UK and in certain other countries.

Published in India by
Oxford University Press
YMCA Library Building, 1 Jai Singh Road, New Delhi 110 001, India

First Edition published in 2017

ISBN-13: 978-0-19-947220-8
ISBN-10: 0-19-947220-3

Typeset in Adobe Jenson Pro 10.5/13
by The Graphics Solution, New Delhi 110 092
Printed in India by Replika Press Pvt. Ltd

Every effort has been made to trace the copyright holders of Figure 1.2. The publisher would be pleased to hear from the copyright owner so that proper acknowledgement can be made in future editions.

For my husband,
Obaid Siddiqi

Contents

Figures and Tables

Figures

Tables

Abbreviations

BBCIR	Bombay Baroda and Central India Railway
DSI	Amounts due as a result of decree of suit against insolvent, judgment obtained by creditor
ETC	European trading company
GIPR	Great Indian Peninsula Railway
IND	Individual
IOB	Interim order for protection granted
IPP	Amounts due for interest/premium, money borrowed, promissory notes, balance of account
ITC	Indian trading company
KNB	Bank
LOR	Losses in trade/business other than redrafts
MRK	Mark
MRW	Marwari
MSC	Others

OTH	No signature
RAC	Goods purchased, running account, goods supplied
RDC	Redrafts and amounts due on shipment of goods
SGO	Signatures in Script Other than Roman
SGR	Signatures in Roman
SOL	Solicitor, lawyer
SSS	Share speculation and share transaction

Foreword

In this study, Asiya Siddiqi, one of the leading economic historians of South Asia, illuminates the social and economic history of Bombay (now Mumbai) in the latter half of the nineteenth century by scrutinizing in minute detail records of the Bombay High Court pertaining to insolvency proceedings. These records have not been explored earlier. By setting out the circumstances that led the key protagonists of her story to approach the courts for protection from creditors under the provisions of relevant statutes (particularly the Acts of 1828, 1848, and 1865), Siddiqi vividly depicts the ways in which money and credit figured significantly in the lives of Bombay's inhabitants. On the one hand we get to know, for example, of the transactions of prominent entrepreneurs such as Premchund Roychund and Jamshedji Tata, and on the other, of problems that petty loans accumulated by a butcher's family created for his unlettered widow, Ayesha, who demonstrated considerable resourcefulness in successfully availing of the shelter offered to poorer insolvent debtors by the state. In the process we get glimpses of many of the hitherto inadequately explored aspects of Bombay's history between the 1860s and the end of the century, precisely the decades in which it emerged as the foremost urban centre of the British Indian empire and as a major industrial city. These aspects include: the relationship between old money and newly acquired wealth; diverse sources of credit; financial swindles; the ability of artisans to sign their names as an indication of their level of literacy; and the place of borrowing and lending in the everyday lives of 'Bombay's people'.

The phenomenal growth in seaborne exports of Indian cotton and opium to China from the mid-1780s was a major factor that led to the rise of Bombay as an important port city. Bombay was the main outlet in western India for these exports. In a brilliant article published in 1982, Siddiqi probed the complexities of Bombay's China trade.[1] Her discussion was based mainly on the letter-books of a key participant in the China commerce, Jamsetjee Jejeebhoy. Siddiqi highlighted the difficulties faced by Bombay traders in transferring their earnings from China to Bombay, which led to a crisis by the end of the 1840s. Profit margins were reduced due to losses on account of unfavourable rates for the bills of exchange sent to them by their China agents. As opium was a banned substance in China, the drug was clandestinely sold to wholesale dealers through an elaborate smuggling network. This factor added to the uncertainties of securing regular payments. Jardine and Matheson was the principal firm in China handling Indian commodities and it went on to play a crucial role in the First Opium War (1839–42), providing vital information and logistical support to the British government. Even though the defeat of China in the war did not lead to the legalization of the opium trade, it did make it increasingly difficult for the Qing authorities to restrict the inflow of the drug.

A partial solution to the problem of remittances was provided by transmitting the earnings in the form of Chinese silver ingots called 'sycee silver'. Transporting silver was not very safe and the prices at which sycee silver could be sold in the Bombay market did not allow the realization of value equivalent to the sums being remitted. Siddiqi gives details of the various expedients that Bombay traders had to resort to for transmitting profits from Canton to Bombay, emphasizing their difficulties.

The important point is that the position of Indians in the trade was extremely precarious, the more so as it was a risky venture since it involved clandestine transactions at several points. Further, the China trade was geared primarily to serve the interests of Britain, and the presence of Indians in it was barely tolerated. Profits from opium (the chief commodity in the trade by the early nineteenth century) and cotton were mainly used to purchase tea for the British market. During the first half of the nineteenth century, tea became an article of mass consumption in England. The earlier generation of traders such as Jamesetjee Jejeebhoy, who had dominated the commerce in the second quarter of the nineteenth century, were edged out by the 1840s. They were soon replaced by a new set of traders. Nevertheless, a large number of Bombay merchants from various communities continued to participate in the China trade for most of the century. Some of the earnings from this commerce were invested in the cotton textile industry and cotton mills came up in Bombay around the mid-nineteenth century.

At the same time, some quantities of raw cotton from western and central India began to be exported to England via Bombay by the end of the 1850s. The Lancashire cotton 'famine' caused by the American Civil War of 1861–5 (when cotton grown in the southern states of the United States of America almost ceased to be exported to Lancashire) dramatically increased Britain's dependence on Indian cotton. From supplying 16 per cent of the raw cotton consumed by Lancashire at the outbreak of the war, India was supplying three-fourths by 1862.[2]

These were the years of a cotton boom in Bombay. Huge investments, often speculative in nature, were made in the commodity in the expectation of large profits from rapidly rising cotton prices. A new breed of Indian entrepreneurs, who were mainly financial operators, came to the forefront in this period. Premchund Roychund is the most well known of them, and typifies the brash speculators of these years who engaged in large-scale gambling transactions. In the words of a perceptive historian of the city, Premchund Roychund 'had a sharp eye for the loophole and the regulatory grey area.'[3] It is not surprising that many of these transactions, often rather dubious, required access to credit on a similar scale. This was made possible, as Siddiqi shows, through official connivance. Indian capitalists in Bombay had very close links with colonial officialdom. The dramatic implications of such dealings are the focus of two chapters in the book.

The cotton boom ended suddenly in 1865, leading to a financial crash in which a substantial number of speculators were ruined. Several banks and insurance companies that had been established during the boom were liquidated. Premchund himself became insolvent in 1866. His bankruptcy has perhaps given him greater fame than his speculative ventures (even as it is difficult to separate the two); he invariably figures in scholarly accounts of the early financial history of the city in this context.[4] Nonetheless, as a class, Indian capitalists in Bombay commanded sufficient resources to be able to survive the crisis. They already controlled part of the city's financial infrastructure, dominated the trade in raw cotton, and were substantial owners of real estate.

Premchund Roychund made a comeback after a few years, though his later career was not as spectacular as that of the early 1860s. Even though Jamshedji Tata too suffered losses, his business survived partly due to his access to some of the wealth of Kahandas Narandas, who, as Siddiqi notes, 'belonged to the traditional business elite who did not have the advantage of colonial support' and never recovered from the shock. Needless to say, Tata went on to create a huge business empire. The details of the careers of Jamshedji Tata and Premchund Roychund in the years following the 1865 crash are glossed over in their biographies, which generally tend to be hagiographical. This study sheds light on that critical phase in the history of Indian entrepreneurship.

Then from the mid-1850s, Indian capitalists established the first cotton textile mills in Bombay. The first cotton (spinning) mill, set up by Cowasjee Nanabhoy Davar in 1854 (the mill began functioning in 1856), was entirely owned by Indians. Within half a century, the city had more than a hundred mills, the overwhelming majority of which were the result of Indian capital investment. Bombay, thus, grew into a great industrial centre with a conspicuous local presence. This resulted in extensive building activity, a necessary concomitant of urban expansion. The insolvency records contain useful information about artisans engaged in construction work—carpenters, stonemasons, bricklayers, stonecutters, and tile-makers. Siddiqi has used information available in these records to give us some idea about the incomes of artisans, besides those of clerks, petty shopkeepers, and others, as noted in the insolvency proceedings. In other words, the study is not confined to the world of high finance but also looks at the manner in which skilled workers and the labouring poor (including dancing girls and courtesans) coped with problems of money and credit within the framework of colonial law. Significantly, ordinary people were not untouched by the 1865 crisis.

By the end of the century, Bombay was a working-class city in which class solidarities were replacing, though not entirely, ties of the village, ties of religion, and ties of caste. In the early twentieth century, these class solidarities were to provide the basis for nationalist mobilization as well. The picture that emerges from this book is of a city with a strong tradition of cosmopolitanism, wherein relationships maintained across communities sustained everyday life notwithstanding the practices of colonial governance, which emphasized community identities. Yet Bombay managed to retain for long an inclusiveness that accommodated considerable diversity, thereby marking out its specific path to modernity.

Amar Farooqui
Professor
Department of History
University of Delhi

Notes and References

1. Asiya Siddiqi, 'The Business World of Jamsetjee Jejeebhoy', *Indian Economic and Social History Review* 19 (July 1982): 301–24.
2. Sven Beckert, *Empire of Cotton* (New York: Alfred A Knopf, 2014), p. 255.
3. Naresh Fernandes, *City Adrift: A Short Biography of Bombay* (New Delhi: Aleph Book Company, 2013), p. 52.
4. See Dwijendra Tripathi, *The Oxford History of Indian Business* (New Delhi: Oxford University Press, 2004).

Acknowledgements

So many friends, teachers, colleagues, and members of my family have helped me make the long journey from the beginnings of this book to its publication that it is impossible to do justice to them all, but I would particularly like to thank the following.

I was remarkably fortunate to have in my tutor, Christopher Hill, and my PhD dissertation director, May McKisack, extraordinary scholars and teachers, and I am happy to be able to acknowledge my debt to them.

Many people aided me in my research for this book. The chief justice of the High Court of Bombay Shri Chittatosh Mukherji gave me access to the records. I thank him for his kindness. The prothonotary and senior master, Ms Bharucha, was most helpful throughout, while the official assignee, Shri Tamanawar, and the insolvency registrar, Sri Bathena, provided space and the service of their staff, especially Shri Anand and Shri Govind, who brought the records out for use. I thank them all.

I thank the late Dharma Kumar who helped me in framing the project and getting it off the ground. I gratefully acknowledge the help I received from the late Sukhamoy Chakravarty and the late V.M. Dandekar as well as from Keshub Mahindra, S. Ramani, and P. Sadanandan.

Sneha Narvekar and Smeeta Suvarna painstakingly extracted the dates from the records, making their way untiringly through manuscripts that were often fragile and difficult to read. Without their dedicated endeavours the work could not have been done. I warmly thank them. Vaishali Naik and Sujata Rao spent much time feeding the data into the computer. Anil Gupta very generously gave his time and expertise in preparing the initial manuscript.

I owe a very special debt to Mythili Ranga Rao, who organized all the computer work, the data entry, processing, analysis, and retrieval. Her contribution was especially significant for the method she devised to construct a basic income file from micro-level data, namely, each of the income entries for each insolvent for the entire period.

Many thanks to the editorial team at Oxford University Press for its terrific editorial guidance and critical comments throughout the revision process. I would like to give a special thanks to Amar Farooqui for his meticulous attention to the Foreword.

My daughters Diba Siddiqi and Yumna Siddiqi edited and helped rewrite sections of the manuscript.

I am also grateful to the anonymous reviewers of the manuscript.

At the University of Mumbai Library, where I did most of the research for this book, I was lucky to have a cohort of talented scholars and friends, and would particularly like to express my gratitude to Ruchira Banerji and the late Usha Hemmadi for their encouragement.

Many scholars and friends have taken an interest in this work and I thank them for discussions and valuable suggestions. They include Chris Bayly, Raj Chandavarkar, Ila Chandrashekar, Indira Chowdhury, Mariam Dossal, Irfan Habib, Jim Masselos, Janaki Nair, Majid Siddiqi, and A.R. Vasavi.

An enormous thanks finally to my family—Obaid, Imran, Yumna, Kaleem, and Diba Siddiqi, and to Imrana Qadeer, Jyotsna Dhawan—and the rest of my extended family for their constant love and support.

Asiya Siddiqi
Bangalore, 2017

Introduction

While exploring historical material on the lives of Bombay's citizens in the nineteenth century, I came across the mention of the insolvency of Premchund Roychund, the famous broker.[1] He had petitioned the Bombay High Court for protection and had supplied the court with information on his affairs. This led me to the records of nineteenth-century insolvents in the High Court. Among the old manuscripts stored at the High Court of Bombay is a set that contains a wealth of information on the lives of the citizens of Bombay in the nineteenth century. It consists of the petitions of insolvents and accompanying documents. This material helped me to reconstruct aspects of the early colonial history of Bombay as reflected in the lives of insolvents.

In Indian society, imprisonment for debt had not generally been used as a means of enforcing payment. An early nineteenth-century commentator remarked, 'Confinement in jail for default in paying debts was not practiced under the Mahratta nor under Tippoo's Government.'[2] Various customary methods for inducing debt payment were in vogue in which the influence of caste elders and personal moral pressure often played a prominent part. For instance, when payments from sirdars (leaders) and military chiefs were required, it was usual 'to plant at their houses 10 or 15 Sipahees and demand daily on their account 25 to 150 Rupees, according to the circumstances of the debtor, but not to prevent his taking food although themselves remained fasting'.[3] It is not very clear when state machinery, in particular the confinement of debtors in state prisons, began to be employed as a means of coercion for the settlement of private debt. But by the early nineteenth century, this practice had certainly come into existence in Bombay. Such confinement was odious not only for those who had to suffer it but often also for those who resorted to it in order to put pressure on debtors. In many instances caste rules prevented a prisoner from eating his meals in the polluting premises of a jail. His creditors were responsible for taking him to an appropriate place for the purpose or else, if any harm came to him, be subject to very great censure. From the point of view of the colonial government, moreover, since borrowing and lending played so large a part in normal urban life, the confinement of large numbers of people, and their not being able to earn their livelihood, served little purpose.

Not surprisingly, the earliest insolvency legislation had as its primary objective not to book debtors but to provide them with relief. Although this legislation did not altogether replace existing practices in the relations between debtors and creditors, the setting up of an official referral authority for regulating debt had a subtle influence on social relations. Insolvency documentation reflects this influence.

The first insolvency courts in the Presidency towns, called 'Courts for the Relief of Insolvent Debtors', were set up by Statute 9 Geo. 4, c. 73, passed in 1828.[4] Any person aggrieved by an order of the Court for the Relief of Insolvent Debtors had the right to make a petition to the Supreme Court, and the Supreme Court had the power, after hearing the parties, to make an order on the petition. The order was binding upon the parties and upon the Court for the Relief of Insolvent Debtors.

The Act of 1828 prescribed the initial procedure and infrastructure for the adjudication of petitions. Officers of the Courts for the Relief of Insolvent Debtors were to be appointed by the Supreme Court. The most important officer was the 'Common Assignee'. If a petition was presented by a creditor and an order for adjudication was made, the property of the insolvent vested in the Common Assignee. The Common Assignee, or Official Assignee as he later came to be called, assumed control of the property with the object of managing it and discharging the debt. The power that the Official Assignee exercised and the material resources that he commanded could be very considerable.

Closely connected with the admission of a petition was the provision for an interim order by the High Court, which protected the insolvent from arrest at the instance of his creditors until the petition had been finally adjudicated. This provision occupied a central place in the social impact of the insolvency law.

In Bombay the earliest insolvency petitions that are found in the records of the High Court were filed in the 1830s, we presume under the law of 1828. With minor changes this law held until 1848, when a more elaborate and modified legislation was introduced.

Acts 11 and 12 Victoria c. 21 of 1848 repealed earlier enactments. Courts for the Relief of Insolvent Debtors established by the Act of 1828 were continued, but the court was to be held before a judge of the Supreme Court. Debtors who petitioned the High Court for protection were required to submit a complete statement, or schedule, of their assets and expenses for the period during which the debt had been contracted. When a petition had been presented, or an act of insolvency had been adjudged, and the schedule required by the Act had been submitted, the High Court had the power to make an interim order for the protection of the insolvent from arrest or detention in prison for any debt or liability to which the order should apply. The order was to apply within the limits of the towns of Calcutta, Madras, and Bombay (at present Kolkata, Chennai, and Mumbai), or any other place within the territories of the East India Company.

Following earlier practice the Act of 1848 required insolvents to hand over to the Official Assignee all their possessions except personal articles of a maximum value of Rs 300 that belonged to them or to their families. For the first time women were specifically admitted to the benefit of the Insolvency Act. They had to be married and the value of the personal belongings they were permitted to keep was Rs 200.

Insolvency assumed altogether unprecedented proportions in the mid-1860s, when, upon the ending of the Civil War in America, the booming export of cotton to Great Britain from Bombay came to an abrupt halt. Once again Lancashire began to source the bulk of the cotton from the southern states of America. Scores of persons who had invested in the trade found themselves ruined. Countless others not directly involved in the export of cotton were swept up in the crisis that engulfed the city. Among those who became bankrupt were some of the European trading houses, such as Finlay Scott and Company, as well as Indian exporters and financiers, many of them associated with the European firms of the city. The latter, organized as the Bombay Chamber of Commerce, took the initiative in inducing the government of Bombay to pass a special law for the management of the estates of insolvents.[5] This law, entitled 'An Act for the More Speedy Liquidation of Insolvent Traders' Estates in Bombay', came into force on 27 September 1865 as Act XXVIII of 1865.

The Act provided for the winding up of insolvent traders' estates carrying a debt exceeding Rs 5 lakhs (a lakh is equal to a hundred thousand) by trustees under the control of the High Court. The word 'trader' was defined as a 'person or partnership not being a Joint Stock Company, carrying on trade or mercantile operations within the local limits of the Ordinary Original Jurisdiction of the High Court of Judicature at Bombay'.

A trader unable to pay his debts, or one who had committed an act of insolvency under the meaning of Acts 11 and 12 Victoria c. 21, or one or more of his creditors could call a meeting of his creditors, at which a majority present or represented was empowered to resolve that the estate be wound up under the management of trustees and that an application be made to the High Court for the purpose. Upon the resolution being adopted, those who met could nominate three or more trustees to liquidate the estate and to fix the salary or remuneration to be paid to them, and the amount of security, if any, to be given by the trustees.

The Act of 1865 prescribed the procedure to be adopted for the appointment of trustees and for their functioning. The meeting of creditors had to be presided over by a chairman who exercised the crucial right to determine which persons present at the meeting had the right to vote on the matters before the meeting, namely whether the estate should be wound up by trustees and, if so, which persons should be appointed trustees and what their remuneration should be.

Once these resolutions had been filed in the High Court, the chairman or any other creditor nominated by the meeting for the purpose could apply to the High Court for an order to wind up the estate. The High Court had to satisfy itself that the resolutions of the meeting had been observed and that their terms were reasonable and were calculated to benefit the general body of creditors. It could then make an order giving instructions concerning the management of the estate. Upon the passing of such an order, all the possessions of the trader and all his interests and rights to any estate, both present and future, would be vested in the trustees and would be deposited with them, until the final order with respect to the liquidation of the estate had been passed by the High Court. In the interim the trustees were to administer the estate in the same way as the Official Assignee managed other insolvents' estates, investing the assets and declaring the dividend to be paid to the creditors from time to time.

Insolvents whose estates were under the management of trustees were protected from legal action and arrest at the instance of their creditors. If they did not concur with the trustees on any matter concerning their estates, they could apply to the High Court to set aside any action of the trustees.

The trustees were empowered, with the sanction of the High Court, to pay to the trader, out of the funds in their hands, a reasonable monthly allowance for maintenance. The trustees themselves were to receive a salary as well as sums to cover the expenses incurred in winding up the estate. These were to come out of the assets of the estate, were to have priority over all other claims, and were to have the sanction of the High Court.

Act XXVIII of 1865 was a great boon to insolvents who had some of the largest debts such as Premchund Roychund as well as to other prominent insolvents such as Tata Sons. Both Premchund and the Tatas, with connections in the European trading community, were able to put their estates in the hands of trustees. This saved their affairs from exposure. They were able to carry on business and to emerge from the crisis relatively unscathed. It is possible that since the fortunes of such important and wealthy persons were at stake in the largest insolvencies payments may have been made to prospective trustees in order to win their support. This law, it would appear, was intended to favour important merchants, especially those with European connections. Those traders and merchants who had succeeded in obtaining trustees do not come into view in the insolvency proceedings and are excluded from this study. For the rest Acts 11 and 12, c. 21 of 1848 applied. The law prescribed the format of the petitions that were entered into by insolvents in order to protect themselves from their creditors. This format enables us to make a number of analyses and to observe certain economic and social indices. Among these are literacy, incomes, occupations, and religion.[6] We study the number and distribution of insolvency petitions in terms of economic status, occupation, and religion. What was the economic status of insolvents? From which occupations and religious groups were they drawn? We hope to examine the working of the insolvency law and also to draw more general conclusions on economic developments. Another part of the study looks at the petitions of the larger traders and merchants and focuses especially on the structure of mercantile credit.

Insolvency Documentation

A person who sought the Court's protection submitted a petition that stated his name, religion, occupation, and place of residence in the city. Along with this he was required to file a 'schedule' that contained a full account of his material position. The schedule noted the total amount of the petitioner's debt. Its principal contents were a 'balance sheet' and lists of those to whom he was indebted, his creditors, as well as of those who were indebted to him, his debtors. The same, of course, held for women.

The balance sheet was drawn up in double entry form and covered the period over which the debt had been contracted. It stated the total value of the person's earnings, receipts, and assets such as jewels or cash in his possession and the property he owned. The other side of the balance sheet noted his expenditure itemized as, among other things, 'maintenance' or food, house rent, medicines, amounts spent on marriages, deaths, and so on. Together with the schedule the petitioner submitted his account books and valuable belongings to the Official Assignee of the High Court. The latter were listed in his schedule. So also were the personal belongings he was allowed to retain and their value. The petitioner signed the petition, or if unable to do so, he or she appended a mark.

Once the schedule had been submitted, the High Court considered whether it was in order and determined whether prima facie evidence existed to show that the petitioner could be deemed insolvent under the law and his petition could be considered for protection. Where this was the case, the High Court passed an 'interim order for protection'. If there were indications that the person had not disclosed all his wealth, or if his accounts had not been properly drawn up and submitted, or for other specified reasons his conduct had been improper, the petition could be rejected. For all intents and purposes, the interim order amounted to the petitioner being granted protection. We take the presence of the interim order in the file to mean that the petition had been admitted and protection given to the petitioner. We note the number of people who had petitioned and obtained an interim order and the number of cases where it had been withheld, as well as those schedules in which the interim order was missing, in order to observe how the insolvency law operated to provide relief to hundreds of debtors. In the majority of cases, the files of individual debtors do not contain evidence of follow-up proceedings, such as court orders on the management of the estate and distribution of returns from it or its final winding up. In effect, therefore, the interim order was tantamount to the petitioner getting continued protection. The story goes that in Bombay protected debtors would often frame the interim orders and display them in their workplaces. The institution may, in some way, have promoted the popularity of the government. At the same time, it may have been unpopular among creditors, who were equally numerous. In any case, it probably did serve the purpose of limiting the numbers in jail on account of debt.

Demography, Trade, and Industry

This study covers the period from 1860 to 1898. It attempts to relate the results of the analysis to events in the social and economic history of the city. The year 1860 was chosen as the initial date in order to serve as a baseline for viewing the significant changes that took place in the trade of the city during the period of the American Civil War. The study was not extended beyond 1898 partly because by this year, the quality of paper deteriorated drastically. The sturdy paper made of cloth fibre that had been used earlier gave way, towards the end of the century, to paper made from wood pulp. This was very brittle and fragile, and it became increasingly difficult to handle it.

The period 1860 to 1898 saw, first, a great boom in the trade of the city as a result of the American Civil War, when the cutting off of raw cotton supplies from the American south to Lancashire stimulated exports from India. Raw cotton from the Deccan and Gujarat had already begun to be exported from Bombay to Great Britain from the early 1850s. Credit and managerial mechanisms for the conduct of this trade already existed. The war gave it a great impetus. However, the end of the war abruptly checked this trade.

The less thorough censuses taken in the earlier years of the century recorded a population of 180,000 in 1814, 229,000 in 1830, and 566,000 in 1846. Later, the city's demographic fluctuations appear to have been influenced considerably by the course of commerce. In the years of the American Civil War, the population in Bombay increased. The first comprehensive census of the city taken in 1864 indicated an increase to 816,562. The census of 1872 revealed a fall to 644,405. This may have been a consequence of the slump when, upon the collapse of the cotton export trade, traders and working people[7] may have withdrawn from the city. Thereafter, the population rose to 773,196 in 1881 and to 821,764 in 1891. In 1901 it stood at 776,006. Epidemics and famines must also have affected the migration to and exodus from the city. It has been remarked that the increase recorded in the 1881 census was 'due to the general progress of trade, particularly of the cotton spinning and weaving industry, the extension of railway communication, and the advance of urban administration'.[8] Although the mill industry rapidly expanded in these years, at least a part of the population swell noticeable in 1881 may also have been a consequence of the devastating famine of 1877–8, when stricken rural people flocked to the city for relief. Indeed, it is not easy to disentangle the push and pull factors that affected urban population. The low figure of 776,006 recorded in the 1901 census, it was believed, was mainly the result of the plague epidemic that broke out in the city in 1896 and following years. Not only was there high mortality, but large numbers of people left the city in order to escape the disease.

In the second half of the nineteenth century, while there were some conspicuous fluctuations in the city's population, the overall picture was one of stagnation. Against this fact must be placed the growth of the cotton spinning and weaving industry. By 1865 there were 10 mills employing an average of 6,500 workers daily. Between 1871 and 1875 another 17 mills had been established, taking the total to 27. They employed over 13,500 workers daily. By 1898 the number of mills had increased to 82. By this year, the average number of workers employed daily was 70,728. If we take the figures of the total population from the censuses of 1864 and 1901 respectively, the workforce engaged in mills is seen to have increased from 0.8 per cent of the total population in 1865 to 9.1 per cent in 1898.[9] The increase, in other words, had been spectacular.

Prices and money supply must also have affected trade and industry as well as the living standards of people. It is difficult to monitor the possible effects of such crucial measures as in 1893 a stop was put to the free coinage of silver in the Indian mints (Figure I.1).

The most obvious consequence of the measure was to turn the rupee into a token coin. Did it also affect the bullion trade, prices, and trading capital? Did it, among other things, accentuate the fall in the price of silver? The export of opium to China, balanced by imports of silver, had been a flourishing trade for a hundred years. In the last decade of the nineteenth century, this trade suffered a serious and lasting dislocation because of a fall in the price of silver.[10]

The Records of Insolvents

The records of insolvents for the period are an unusually large data set. They consist of manuscripts that, at the time this study was undertaken, were housed in cupboards that ran along the walls of a room of the High Court in which the court sat when it was in session. Many of these cupboards, it seemed, had not been opened for a very long time. Individual schedules were found folded, along with the accompanying documents such as the petitions, interim orders, and, occasionally, affidavits and tied with a string. The schedules had then been grouped and tied together in bundles of ten. It is possible that some of these documents had not been handled for a hundred years or more.

Of course, the archives of the High Court are not set up for the use of researchers. The retrieval of the material was not altogether easy. The bundles were not always arranged in order and were full of dust. Some had come loose and the individual schedules had been scattered. In many cases the paper was damaged or extremely brittle and difficult to handle. Moreover, the documents could be accessed only in the short intervals of the day when the room was not being used for a court session. We received the utmost help of the Official Assignee and his staff, especially the peons, who brought out the bundles for us each morning and took them back at the end of the day.[11]

Up to 1878 the schedules had been numbered in the records in continuous serial order. Thereafter they were numbered serially for each year. By examining the numbers of the schedules for each year and the dates of filing of the first and last petitions in that year, we could work out the total number filed in each year, including those that were missing. This number is presented in Table 3A.1. Apart from the total number of petitions, this table also lists the total number of petitioners, the total number of petitions missing in each year, those who obtained an interim order for protection, and those who were in jail at the time of petitioning.

The total number of petitions from which we have captured information is 19,195. The remainder, namely 3,010, were missing or, less often, irretrievably damaged. Of the total number of petitions, 17,195 were admitted for interim protection.

In many cases more than one petitioner was represented on a schedule. Where the income or, more specifically, net receipts of co-petitioners were given in a schedule, we have entered that individual separately for analysis. The total number of petitioners, therefore, exceeds the number of petitions. Where no separate income was noted for co-petitioners, no detailed information concerning them was entered. All the same, the names of all co-petitioners were entered in our overall list. The total number of individuals entered was 20,980.

On the data sheet we first noted the number and date of the petition, together with the name, occupation, religion, gender, and place of residence of the petitioner, the amount of the debt, and the period over which it was contracted. Where the petitioner was in jail, the fact is mentioned in the petition and is entered on our data sheet. The large number of petitions submitted by persons in jail for debt indicates the severity of debtors' law and brings home the ameliorative function of the insolvency law in providing debtors with a way out of the worst consequences of indebtedness.

Our principal index for economic status is the figure of the net receipts noted in the individuals' balance sheets. Except for the bigger merchants and traders, we use this figure to reckon economic status. For the latter we use the figure of the debt itself on the assumption that the magnitude of the debt reflected in a general way a person's perceived creditability. The declared income of an insolvent merchant was often a poor indicator of his erstwhile economic status.

The main component of net receipts, we reckon, is salary or profits or earnings from a person's trade. We use net receipts as surrogates for income even though in certain cases this figure incorporates such items as sums received from creditors and those laid out in a firm, as well as the value of assets sold or amounts received as costs and benefits from a court decree.

We have classified occupations according to a thirty-six-point code. Information about women is presented separately. In another part of the study we examine the accounts of those whose debts ran into five-digit figures or more for the years 1860–6. They comprise mainly the bigger merchants, brokers, and traders. Here we are particularly interested in noting sources of credit and the nature of the debts (Tables 3A.19 and 3A.20).

The Insolvents

At the outset we present the number of petitions and petitioners year-wise, together with a count of those that were, in effect, given protection, and of those who were in jail (Table 3A.1). Here we are concerned mainly with the function of the law in providing protection to debtors. As more than 85 per cent petitioners got protection, we do not identify them separately. Further, we classify the petitioners in terms of occupation and income in order to see what kinds of people gained protection as well as to observe certain economic and social indices, notably fluctuations in incomes and literacy levels. While doing this we must first define the limitations of the data.

In absolute terms, the database is small, with an average of about 500 per year out of a total population of about 700,000. If out of the latter figure even half were minors and non-earners, that still excludes a very large number of persons. Moreover, the cases were not randomly picked but were selective for insolvency. Despite these limitations, it seems worthwhile to use these data for historical analysis. It has several merits and several special features.

One of the more remarkable features of our data is that they embrace almost every kind of occupation and every religion as well as a wide range of incomes. The one limitation as to religion is that Buddhists and Jains are not noted separately but are included among Hindus. The data contrasts with the records of bankrupts in England who were generally 'traders'.[12] Even if 'traders' is interpreted in the wider sense of persons engaged in a trade or calling, the insolvents of Bombay were more diverse, a fact which should be evident from our occupation codes. Among the larger clusters in terms of occupation were artisans of different kinds, clerical and managerial workers, service people, and traders and merchants. Overall the number of insolvents recorded is but a small proportion of the population. Nevertheless they are numerous enough to encourage us to use the information in order to study trends over time.

Were insolvents, by virtue of being insolvent, a socially marginal category or were they not all that different from other citizens? Although this is a question that we cannot categorically answer, our impression is they were not intrinsically different from others in terms of economic status. This was particularly true of those who engaged in trade, which was invariably financed out of borrowed capital. Craftsmen too, carpenters for instance, functioned on money borrowed from their clients. Even otherwise borrowing and lending were widely prevalent in urban society as normal activities. Those who petitioned the court as insolvents were persons who for some reason—for instance, trade losses occasioned in many cases by a commercial crisis—were not able to honour their debts or those who were particularly hard-pressed by their creditors. They may also have included those, perhaps not many, who took refuge in the law in order to evade their creditors. Almost certainly they included others who could scarcely be described as being down and out or socially and economically marginal. For instance, in 1882, the sheriff of Bombay, General William Selwood Hewett, petitioned as an insolvent.[13] The famous broker and merchant Premchund Roychund was heavily in debt in the crisis of 1865, and managed to survive mainly because of the support of influential persons in the European commercial community, one of whom became his trustee. Continuing to be active in business throughout the following years, he petitioned for protection as an insolvent in 1886.[14] His principal creditor was a fellow Jain merchant and banker, Dalpatbhai Bhagubhai, grandfather of Kasturbhai Lalbhai (Kasturbhai Lalbhai and his father Kasturbhai Dalpatbhai were prominent industrialists and mill owners from Ahmedabad). Perhaps among the poorest petitioners there were more who were in indigent circumstances. But even they cannot be counted as being simply at the bottom of the social scale; the very fact of their having been able to borrow was a token of their creditors' perception that they were creditworthy. In short, we may not be wrong in considering the petitioners as being representative of Bombay's population.

We present aggregate data together with tables, diagrams, and comments. A separate chapter deals with women. Two other chapters deal respectively with connections between religious affiliation and occupation on the one hand and with the credit structure and the kinds of debts of a selection of bigger merchants on the other hand.

This study has four life stories that bring forth the social and cultural context of Bombay in the mid-nineteenth century. The incidents depicted here represent different strata and religious and occupational orientations—aspects that will be the focus of our inquiry in Chapters 2 to 4 of this book. The first life story is an episode from the early history of Jamshedji Tata, a prominent Parsi merchant. The second is an account of Tata's partner, Kahandas Narandas, a once wealthy Vaishnav jeweller. The third is a piece on Premchund Roychund, the famous Jain broker. The fourth is the story of a humble Muslim woman, Ayesha, mother of an illiterate butcher. These stories provide a window into the lives of a spectrum of Bombay's citizens and into some of the changes that were taking place in the commercial and social history of the city. On the one hand, we have the enhanced role of brokers in garnering credit and export of commodities for trade and on the other, the ways in which the people themselves responded to these challenges.

Notes and References

1. I am grateful for access to the records of the Bombay High Court and the Maharashtra State Archives and to the Indian Council of Historical Research for support. I thank the many friends who have commented on earlier drafts of the chapters of this book.
2. Arthur Steele, *Summary of the Law and Custom of Hindoo Castes within the Dekhun Provinces Subject to the Presidency of Bombay, Chiefly Affecting Civil Suits* (Bombay: Courier Press, 1827), p. 205.
3. Steele, *Summary of the Law and Custom*, p. 205.
4. It may be noticed that it was at this very time that courts of bankruptcy were first set up in England. In 1831 an Act was passed (1 and 2 William IV, c. 56), described as 'An Act to Establish a Court in Bankruptcy'. (Sheila Mariner, 'English Bankruptcy Records and Statistics before 1850', *Economic History Review* 33 [1980]: 351–66.)
5. *Report of the Bombay Chamber of Commerce 1864/65* (University of Mumbai Library), pp. 21–6. 'Estates in Bombay' came into force on 27 September 1865 as Act XXVIII of 1865.
6. The data relating to expenditure and assets have not been presented in this study.
7. 'Working people' refers to the subordinate classes generally and includes smaller traders, artisans, and service people.
8. *Gazetteer of Bombay City and Island* [hereafter *Bombay Gaz*] 1 (1909): 164.
9. *Bombay Gaz* 1: 488. For population figures, based on the censuses, see Morris David Morris, *The Emergence of an Industrial Labor Force in India: A Study of*

the Bombay Cotton Mills 1854–1947 (Berkley: University of California Press 1965), p. 20.

10. *Bombay Gaz* 1: 436–8.
11. We devised a one-page data sheet for all schedules other than those of the bigger merchants and brokers, and a two-page one for the latter. Research assistants entered the information on these sheets, working through the entire corpus, spreading out each bundle and each schedule, and reassembling them afterwards. They also entered the simpler codes, such as those for literacy. The author checked each data sheet that had been filled in, and also entered those codes that involved conceptual criteria, notably, the ones for occupation. We often had to get back to the originals for verification. In order to do so, we generally met on the two Saturdays of the month when the court was not sitting and we could use the room for a longer time. The information on the data sheets was then fed into the computer under the supervision of Ms Mythili Ranga Rao. Afterwards, she checked the entries for errors.
12. See Mariner, 'English Bankruptcy Records'.
13. Insolvency schedule 402, 1886. (All insolvency schedules refer to the records of the Bombay High Court and are cited by number and date.) Hewett had been borrowing from Marwaris and others for his personal expenses. One of his creditors was the Parsi attorney Shapurji Hormasjee. Fear of being sued in the Court of Small Causes and the High Court, declared Hewett, induced him to petition as an insolvent.
14. Insolvency schedule 285, 1886.

1 *Business and Social Relationships in Nineteenth-Century Bombay*

The stories of four people in Bombay around the same time tell us how some people coped with the consequences of the commercial crises that racked the city in the 1860s. This chapter consists of three narratives of people who became insolvents. Each is about the circumstances of particular merchants and brokers. Jamshedji Tata was an emerging entrepreneur. His proximity to representatives in the colonial order enabled him to overcome the crisis in his business. Premchund Roychund, a prominent broker who became insolvent, also had close ties with the colonial bankers whose support helped him survive. Kahandas Narandas belonged to the traditional business elite who did not have the advantage of colonial support; he was totally ruined. The fourth and the last story is that of Ayesha, the mother of an insolvent butcher, who was different from any of these men. She was a humble woman who fashioned her life relying on traditional sources of support, and eventually the law, to overcome the difficulties of her family. Her story appears in Chapter 6 of this book.

Jamshedji Tata and the Jewels

The portrait of Jamshedji Tata with which we are most familiar is that of the industrialist in his old age, represented as a patriarchal figure. There is also a much older photograph (Figure 1.1). It is dated 1861, when Tata was twenty-one years old. It was taken in China, where he spent several years taking care of his family business, which to a large extent consisted of opium shipped from India. The photograph is interesting for several reasons. It shows him managing a complex business at a young age, that too in a foreign environment fraught with conflict. With the backing of the British Indian government and that of the British home government, Indian merchants were at the time exporting large quantities of opium to China. China was devastated both by the human degradation this caused and by the drain of silver that was being used to pay for the opium. The Chinese eventually tried to stop the inflow of opium and this led to several years of conflict with the British. Tata was in China during a part of this critical time and joined the British forces as a volunteer. The photograph shows him in military uniform, and the accompanying text says he experienced some 'soldiering' at the time. It proclaims his support for the British government that was fighting to maintain the opium trade.[1]

The massive opium trade, as indeed trade in general, drew on Indian financial resources. The commercial economy of pre-industrial India was one of the most developed ones of its times. Did rising entrepreneurs like Tata draw on indigenous sources for support? We try to answer the question by looking at Tata's connection with his partner, Kahandas Narandas. Tata's biographer, Harris, does mention that Kahandas, whom he calls 'Kaliandas', was Tata's partner but he tells us nothing about the details of his relationship with the Tatas.

Kahandas was a member of an old business firm of Ahmedabad whose principal trade was in jewellery. The firm also traded in other staples and had trade links with Iran, Penang, and Siam. Kahandas was considered one of the wealthiest men in Bombay until his collapse in the mid-1860s. His was a laid-back style of functioning. He did not acquaint himself with the details of business, leaving these to his *mehta* or manager.

The 1860s were momentous for Bombay. The American Civil War cut off supplies of raw cotton from the American south to the mills of Lancashire. Bombay, drawing on the cotton-producing hinterland, became an important source of cotton to Lancashire. There was a great boom in the trade of the city, in which many fortunes were made. Then the war unexpectedly ended, and prices of cotton in England crashed. There followed a spate of bankruptcies that especially affected those exporters whose shipments were on the way and those who had borrowed capital.

There were two laws that provided relief to insolvents. The earlier law, passed in 1828, made it possible for an insolvent to petition the High Court for protection from his creditors. If the petition was accepted, he could not be sued by his creditors and put in jail. Then, at the height of the depression that followed the end of the war, with so many heads rolling, another law was passed that enabled the bigger merchants to assign their estates to be administered by trustees. This was a great boon to insolvent merchants. It shielded their affairs from public view and enabled them to carry on business. Often an insolvent merchant would offer a prospective trustee a gift, perhaps a jewel, in order to win him over.

Both Kahandas and Tata went under in the crisis. Kahandas appealed to the court for protection. The papers relating to Kahandas's petition are to be found among the records of the High Court of Bombay. Jamshedji Tata was a witness at the hearing. Much of our story comes from the horse's mouth, namely Tata's evidence. Kahandas appeared to be remarkably innocent of the law; he did not know that as one who had been judged to be insolvent he could not part with his property. In order to support himself, he sold some of his jewellery after he had been declared an insolvent. He was ignorant too of the precipitous fall of the cotton market in England and continued to believe he would regain his wealth, having made large exports. When he did realize his fortune was lost, he was utterly distraught. In the meantime his trusted mehta had fled to Daman in order to escape a writ against him for not honouring a contract to buy certain shares. Kahandas was unable to explain his accounts to the court. He kept saying, 'I have lost my money, I have lost my memory.'

In the course of the hearing, Tata declared that Kahandas had joined the Tatas in August or September 1864. Tata said, 'He brought in altogether to the firm several lakhs, I believe.' Here was a clear statement of the financial backing Kahandas had provided when he joined the firm.

Tata went on to say, 'I became bankrupt on the 25th July, 1866.' He seems to have read the writing on the wall well before that date. The war ended on 9 April 1865. Five days later, on the 14th, Tata was on a ship bound for England. On his person, he said, he carried jewels worth Rs 80,000 or Rs 1 lakh that belonged to Kahandas. He did not have a list of these jewels. Once he arrived in London, he engaged two jewellers, Block and Martin, and Jacob, to have the gems cut and reset. He declared he then sent all the jewels he had brought back to Kahandas, except for some diamonds, which he returned through a person he named. He said Kahandas had acknowledged having received the jewels. There was much discussion about a certain oval diamond ring that Tata said he had given to Jacob to be cut and afterwards returned through one Nusserwanjee Kutruck, asking him to give it to his father, presumably to be given to Kahandas. This was in December 1865. Two days later, Tata said, he wrote to Kahandas. When Kahandas was asked to produce Tata's letter he said he could not find it. Tata said this ring was mentioned in a letter Kahandas wrote to him in January 1866. While the hearing was still on, Tata asked the court for permission to go and look for this letter. He returned to say he had found the letter but he did not mention the ring. Later in the hearing, when Kutruck was questioned, he said he had given it not to Tata's father but to his partner Hormusjee Nowrojee. The evidence is particularly ambiguous in places where the answer is noted but not the question that had been addressed to the witness. Tata may have been pressed to say what he had paid to the trustees. It may have been in answer to this that he said, 'I had assets in England.... My trustees got other property.... It was at the beginning of 1866 he [Kahandas] gave me the credit of two lacs.' Tata was asked for the bills of the jewellers. His answer was, 'I have not the bills of the jewellers here. They are with my trustees in England.'

The answer affirms that he had trustees in England. What happened to the diamond ring is not clear. When Kahandas was eventually convicted, one of the grounds of his conviction was that he had not accounted for this ring. The evidence raises certain questions. Tata declared he did not have a list of the jewels he was carrying. This was surprising. He also said that he was not receiving any commission for having Kahandas's jewels worked. This too was surprising. Further, it raises the question of why the bills should have been with his trustees unless they were in some way connected with the jewels. Was Tata being paid in some other way?

The end of the war signalled the end of the trade boom. Tata may have foreseen that the financial position of his firm was threatened and he may have been anxious to get trustees. Kahandas's jewels were Indian uncut gems which were no longer fashionable. Tata may have had an agreement with him that he would take them to England and have them re-cut and reset, thereby enhancing their value. Since he was not charging a commission, a part of the understanding may have been that he be allowed to have an item of the jewellery, which he could offer to a prospective trustee. While we do have clear evidence of the financial assistance Kahandas had given to the Tatas, the question of Jamshedji Tata having appropriated any of his jewels remains speculative.

Tata's Partner, Kahandas Narandas

A view of the innate conservatism of Indian society persists in historical writings on India. Paradoxically, this bias often occurs in the study of processes of change, such as the emergence of the modern industrial sector. Thus, while questions concerning capital formation in India have scarcely been seriously addressed, we nevertheless encounter notions about the 'under-developed system of credit'.

'Capital tended to be immobile,' writes Morris David Morris, 'both because of uncertainty and because of the lack of appropriate capital-mobilizing institutions.'[2] Biography, which could help us understand entrepreneurial history, is often hagiographic. The most well-known biographies of Jamshedji Tata are those published by Frank Harris in 1925 and the two volumes published more recently by R.M. Lala. These biographers ignore a significant historical question. India had one of the most highly developed commercial economies of any country in the pre-industrial world. This was particularly true of the western region, especially Gujarat, which had a high level of urbanization at least as far back as the seventeenth century. Did aspiring merchants and entrepreneurs such as Tata draw on indigenous sources?

A Changing Business Environment

Tata's partner, Kahandas Narandas, was a native of Ahmedabad. When Kahandas became insolvent, he appealed to the court for protection. The papers relating to his insolvency are to be found among the records of the Bombay High Court. This material enables us to reconstruct the structure of an old-time firm and its part in providing material help to the Tatas in the early stages of their business. In sketching the career of Kahandas Narandas, in part, we touch on the tragedy of a man who was ruined when the boom in the cotton trade of Bombay crashed with the ending of the civil war in America. At a human level, it is perhaps not difficult to see the root of Kahandas's failure. It was that of a man born to wealth based on old-time trade, who was not sufficiently wise to the ways of the emerging world of financial deals geared to the export trade or to the pitfalls of the law and the law courts—one who was no match for artful brokers and clever entrepreneurs better able than he was to exploit the colonial resource base. We see glimpses of the encounter between different lifestyles and different styles of doing business.

'An Old Established Firm', a Traditional Lifestyle

Kahandas's case is particularly interesting because of his close association with some of the most prominent men of business of his time—Premchund Roychund, Jamshedji Tata, Dinshaw Manakji Petit, and Cawasji Nanabhai Dawar. At the base of this association was his status as a man whose great wealth derived from old-time trade. So well known was he as a very rich person that the president of the Bank of Bombay coupled his name with that of Sir Jamsetjee Jejeebhoy as men to whom, in normal times, the bank would not hesitate to lend as much as Rs 5 lakhs on personal security.[3]

Kahandas Narandas was a member of the firm of Motichund Ragoonathdass, described by contemporaries as a 'famous firm',[4] one that 'had a large business and was an old established firm'.[5] Motichund Ragoonathdass was Kahandas's 'grandfather by adoption'. He and Kahandas's father were both jewellers—not 'working jewellers', but dealers in precious stones.[6]

Jewels play a prominent part in Kahandas's story. There is mention of jewels he had bought and sold, and of fabulous jewels he had presented to his bride—tokens of his high status. Indeed, his jewels had an important symbolic presence: they signified his wealth and enabled him almost limitlessly to draw on credit in the market. There were jewels, moreover, that called into play a cultural encounter: those set, it seems, in the traditional *kundan* style—for which Banaras was famous—stood devalued, while Western-style faceted gems were more sought after. Also kundan jewels often used crystal instead of gems. Kahandas was accused of substituting glass in place of precious stones in the jewels he had had to surrender to the court. He had to suffer the indignity of having to declare, 'I did not take the stones out and substitute glass.... It is the custom of natives to put in false stones. I swear that is the custom.'

The firm had countrywide connections in the jewellery trade. Kahandas's possessions included 'ancestral jewels made at Banaras'. Not only did the firm buy jewellery in distant places, but it also sold it in the cities of Gujarat and in Bombay. The sales included items supplied to a jeweller in Jaura and others sold in Baroda and Ahmedabad. The sales also included items sold in Ahmedabad and sent to Baroda.[7] High living standards in Gujarat, of which we get glimpses in the nineteenth century, supported luxury consumption.

While retaining its base in the jewellery trade, Kahandas's firm had large investments in other traditional staples, a fact that shows the range of possibilities within the reach of successful premodern mercantile firms.

The firm of Motichund Ragoonathdass had an old business of piece-goods export to Siam (Thailand). These may have consisted of the highly decorated painted cloths, often worn as hip wrappers, which were being exported to Thailand from India from at least the seventeenth century. Made in Thai patterns by Indian craftsmen, the wrappers, worn at court, were then decorated with gold by craftsmen in Thailand.[8] Along with goods, textile designs, and techniques, ideas concerning ways of trading and raising credit may also have travelled on the trade route. The firm's total receipts from the Thailand trade during the period when the debt in question had been incurred, that is, from October 1864 to November 1867, was Rs 375,003.[9]

Among Kahandas's trading arrangements was a partnership with two Irani merchants of Bombay, the brothers Haji Mohammad Tucki and Agha Abdul Rasul. We can learn little of the details of this connection, but the brothers are entered as creditors in Kahandas's schedule for an unadjusted balance of Rs 632,089 on their partnership trade. The connection must have been an old one as Haji Mohamed Tucki was one of the executors of Kahandas's father's will.

In the insolvency papers of another Irani merchant, Agha Ally Akbar bin Haji Jafar, who traded with Iran and Penang, Kahandas's name appears as a creditor for tea and sugar he had sold to the insolvent. Elsewhere in Kahandas's own papers, we have the large figure of Rs 32,946 received from the trade in sugar during the period of the debt, as well as Rs 565,496 debited to 'Eran cotton account'. Kahandas had, besides, a five-eighth share, amounting to Rs 46,000, in the ship *Faiz Alum*.

Elusive though this information is, it is possible that it indicates Kahandas's participation in an older area of trade, still prevalent at the time, which linked Bombay with the Persian and Arabian gulfs and with the Malay peninsula.[10]

Yet another substantial item of profit was the sum of Rs 38,855 earned in the opium trade in partnership with Premchund Roychund. In addition, Kahandas had shipped, in March and April 1866, 314 chests of Malwa opium, costing Rs 762,011, through Nusserwanji Ratanji Tata, agents of Jamshedji Nusserwanji Tata at Hong Kong and Shanghai. The account of this shipment had not yet been received, but the agents had given Kahandas an advance payment in the form of bills to the tune of Rs 844,650. These figures indicate the enormous profit expected from the opium trade. Advance payment made to exporters of cargo by agents amounted to a fraction of the cost price, generally two-thirds. In this case, it exceeded the cost price.[11]

The names of Premchund Roychund and Jamshedji Tata feature prominently in Kahandas's dealings, as we shall presently note.

A salient feature of the firm's financial structure was the large amount of trading capital invested by the women of the family. Among them was Bai Jaicoor, the second wife of Kahandas's father and heiress of Bai Jumna, daughter of Motichund Ragoonathdass. She 'used to pay sums of money into the firm of Motichund Ragoonathdass', declared Kahandas. Hers was an old account that commenced long before his brother's death in 1851. Thereafter, he had taken over the account. In the list of Kahandas's creditors Bai Jaicoor's name appears three times. The first and largest item is described as 'balance of running account for money deposited with the insolvent on interest'. This probably represented the principal amount Bai Jaicoor had placed with the firm. Kahandas remarked he had re-entered her in his schedule as a creditor 'for three lacs and odd'. In addition, there were two smaller sums, each described as 'balance of an account for money deposited with the insolvent for interest'. There are hints that some of Bai Jaicoor's capital may have been used for the 'Siam' piece-goods trade. The holdings of Bai Jaicoor are suggestive of the custom of inheritance among women. In the first and largest item against her name, she is described as 'heiress of the late Jumna, daughter of Motichund Ragoonathdass'. This probably indicates her matrilinear inheritance. Against the two subsequent entries, she is designated as 'widow of the late Narrondass Hurribhoy'. This, together with the reference to her habit of paying sums of money into the firm, suggests that she probably earned an interest on her deposit, a part of which she used to reinvest. Thus, we get a view of wealthy women with an independent income over which they exercised control and which they could bequeath to their daughters. Of course, it is an open question as to what extent they were in a position of real control over their money, which was managed by the men.

Besides Bai Jaicoor, other women of the family had also invested in the firm, as had Kahandas's maternal uncle, Tulsidas Ramdas. The names of a number of individuals, from Bombay and other cities including Jamnagar, Surat, Uran, and Ahmedabad, also feature among those who had deposited money with the firm to run on interest.

The items of credit designated as money deposited with the insolvent for interest, we infer, served as the fixed trading capital of the firm. The total amount was Rs 406,434. This included Rs 524 presented to Navivahu, the new bride of Kahandas at the time of her marriage. Of the total the amount that belonged to women was Rs 367,439, or more than 90 per cent.

The character of the business as a family firm is conspicuous, one managed by the men of the family, with the women holding a very large portion of the trading capital in the form of deposits. Not only was this freely available for investment in trade but, as it was borrowed money, it was not accountable for the debts of the firm. The institution of deposits by members of the family, in particular women, probably influenced family relations as much as family ties defined the character of the trading firm.

Of course, deposits did not constitute the entire trading capital of the firm. In addition, there was the capital that belonged to Kahandas himself. A part of this, as we have mentioned, was invested in partnership trade such as that with Haji Mohammad Tucki and Agha Abdul Rasul. Presumably, in this and other such arrangements, the partners each provided a portion of the capital. The total capital of the firm, exclusive of the borrowed and partnership funds, was Rs 19 lakhs.[12]

It was not only wealthy women, such as those belonging to Kahandas's family, who deposited their money on interest with traders and merchants. There are many instances in the insolvency records of small sums, including those that belonged to 'wives' or 'widows', being invested in this way. Small savings being channelized into commercial credit may have been integral to the mercantile culture of this region.

An assumption of ease and affluence is reflected in the way Kahandas managed his business and in his style of living. There were many entries in the accounts of sums that had been written off. These included not only business losses, but the liabilities of relatives on account of share speculation and interest. Such, for instance, was the sum of Rs 244 owed by Lullooshah Hurjeevandas, whose brother was married to Kahandas's sister. A large figure of Rs 21,577 had also been written off. Lalubhai Volubdas, who owed it, was not a relative, but he was dead, and the survivors—his wife and son—were not in business. Although they owned a house, Kahandas had been advised that he could not recover the debt as it was time-barred. Then there was a sum of Rs 4,986 against Jumnadas Gellashah, his wife's brother. 'We got him married and expended this amount on his marriage', declared Kahandas. 'So far as I know he is not able to pay so I wrote it off.'

It would seem Kahandas did not closely concern himself with the accounts that were written down in his books. His mehtas would ask him before doing anything on his behalf and before writing anything. But he declared he 'was not in the habit of looking at the books. I relied on my mehtas'. Then, more emphatically, he told the court that he was 'not well up in books, my mehta can tell you about this. I know nothing of accounts how the item(s) are credited and how debited ... I have no knowledge of account'.

On the surface, these remarks may suggest a casual, perhaps even inefficient style of management. But it is possible they carried another meaning. A scrutiny of the accounts may have been construed as mistrust in the mehtas. Leaving bookkeeping to them may have been a part of the convention of trust that was crucial to a successful business.

Trust and a personal mode of functioning were characteristic also of the way in which Kahandas paid the mehtas. He would give them small sums when they required the money. At the end of the year these sums would be written off. Thus the mehtas, especially those who were most trusted, were more like privileged retainers, a part of Kahandas's household, than like employees on fixed wages.

Kahandas's head mehta, and the one on whom he relied the most, was Wittuldas Doolubdas. It was Wittuldas whom Kahandas sent to Baroda in August 1865 or 1866—he remembered the month but not the year—to sell several of his jewels. Among these, he seemed to recollect, was a necklace worth Rs 49,000, but he was not sure. Wittuldas had also taken other jewels to Baroda but Kahandas could not remember which. Then, in January 1866, Kahandas sent jewellery to Ahmdedabad, which was sold for Rs 63,112. By this time, he may have begun to experience some financial pressure. 'I sold jewellery to keep up my reputation', he said.

'All these things, [that is, the sale of jewels] was done by Wittuldas', said Kahandas. Again, it was Wittuldas who made the statement of the value of the jewels noted in the insolvency schedule. 'Either he valued them or called someone else to do it ... I believe I saw the statement. I approved of it because I had confidence in my mehta', declared Kahandas.

At the peak of the crisis, Wittuldas, who had a writ against him for failing to honour his commitment to buy certain shares, fled to the Portuguese enclave of Daman.[13] Without his help, Kahandas was unable to explain the details of his accounts to the court.

Largesse and a lavish lifestyle were subtly related to commercial culture. They affirmed a person's creditability and were particularly significant in a commercial culture where loans were negotiated on personal security, that is, simply on the word of the borrower without resort to material security. The unwritten conventions of commercial relations were influenced by perceptions of a man's character and his wealth. His status was proclaimed by such things as the magnificence of his son's wedding, the lavish alms he gave to priests, or the splendour with which he celebrated Diwali, perhaps also by the number of wives he himself married. Such symbolic gestures became integral elements of behaviour.

'My two elder wives and my children are minors', declared Kahandas. Late in 1865, he married his 'third and present wife'. Her name was Gulab, 'Rose'; she was thirteen or fourteen years old. She was generally referred to as 'Navivahu', 'new bride'. He did not go to the girl's home for the wedding, nor did her father, Purshotum Bhagwandas, bring her to Bombay. Instead, he sent her to Bombay to the house of one Hurgovind Nuthoo. The wedding took place in Bombay. Kahandas paid Hurgovind Nuthoo a thousand rupees for the expenses.[14]

The procedure may have reflected deference to a person of Kahandas's high social status, for the normal custom would be for the bridegroom to go to the bride's house. But it may also be that the bride's father, whom Kahandas mentions in another context, had become insolvent. The spectre of bankruptcy, entailing the fear of arrest, may have prevented Gulab's father from coming to Bombay.

Among the jewels Kahandas gave to Navivahu was a diamond necklace worth Rs 1.5 lakhs, the same, it seems, that he had earlier sent to Baroda through Wittuldas to be sold.[15] Two years later, Navivahu bore him a son.

New Business Ventures

Besides trading in the older staples, Kahandas branched out into other business towards the middle of the century. This included the Bassein Sugar Company managed for him by Tulsidas Ramdas, his maternal uncle. Tulsidas lived at Bassein and made purchases for him on behalf of the company. Kahandas used to pay him from time to time and debit the sums to Tulsidas's account. They both may have contributed the capital. We learn very little about the details of this business other than the fact that there had been a considerable loss that had had to be written off. This was in 1865. We have no way of knowing if the loss was a consequence of the widespread commercial crisis of that year.

Conspicuous among Kahandas's investments in the modern sector were 8 shares in one of the earliest textile mills in Bombay, the Oriental Spinning and Weaving Company, and 134 shares in the Bombay Coast and River Navigation Company, a pioneer steam navigation venture sponsored by Indian merchants. At the time of the great spurt in the share market in the 1860s, Kahandas invested in a large variety of shares. The cost value of his shares amounted to about Rs 5 lakhs. Apart from this, Kahandas's major new investment was in the shipment of raw cotton to England.

The Friendship of Premchund

In the business milieu of Bombay in the mid-nineteenth century, personal relations, especially those cemented by a common language, principally Gujarati, and a shared business culture, again predominantly Gujarati, must have been an important element in the easy communication that existed between such men as Kahandas, Cawasji Nanabhai Dawar, Jamshedji Nusserwanji Tata, and Premchund Roychund. These relations helped to channellize wealth from one of the richest regions of the country into trade and industry.

Kahandas must have been a friend of the pioneer industrialist Cawasji Nanabhai, in whose house in Bombay he stayed in 1868.[16] We have noted that Kahandas was a shareholder in Nanabhai's mill, the Oriental Spinning and Weaving Company. Kahandas's most extensive, and ultimately most ruinous involvement, was with Premchund Roychund. In the web of favours and obligations exchanged by the two men as tokens of friendship and as a part of joint trading ventures, we may trace some of the pathways along which credit travelled to support the cotton export trade.

The main structure of the cotton trade took shape in the great expansion of exports in the 1830s. In order to encourage shipment of produce to England, the East India Company as well as private trading houses advanced to the shippers a portion of the value of the cargo, generally two-thirds, while the shippers themselves furnished the remainder. The Company stopped making these advances in the early 1850s. In the following years, as cotton exports grew in volume, and especially in the boom of the early 1860s, it was the agency houses of Bombay that handled these shipments.

This burgeoning activity required the services of middlemen on a scale hitherto unknown. At the initial level these men acted as brokers who attracted prospective shippers. In order to do this they often had to raise capital that would enable the shippers to procure the cargo and the agency houses to make the advances. Every link of the chain that made up a transaction called for trust, often cemented by personal friendship or by a perception of the status of the parties involved, and eventually affirmed by the success of the venture. Confidence, moreover, had to be sustained over a considerable period since it took four to six months for the cargo to reach its destination and for accounts to be finally settled in Bombay.

Premchund's strength in the world of business was rooted in the many-pronged resources that he seemed to be able to command (Figure 1.2). His father, Roychund Deepchund, was broker to the Presidency Bank of Bombay, the principal official bank in the city.[17] He himself was not simply a broker but, as he was quick to point out, a 'guarantor' to the leading agency house, Ritchie Stuart and Co.[18] In other words, he did not, as ordinary brokers did, simply arrange the shipments that the house handled; he performed the important function of 'guaranteeing' the company's shipments. This meant that he both procured shipments for Ritchie Stuart and Co. and raised the credit required, guaranteeing its repayment. His position in Ritchie Stuart and Co. and that of his father in the Bank of Bombay placed them in the select circle of Indians who could communicate with Europeans in the city with ease.

Premchund's English, as his letters indicate, was not flawless.[19] All the same, he could read, write, and converse comfortably in English. He could also handle accounts, and credit and share transactions with a facility that gave him great scope at a time of expanding trade and abundant money. Of course, he was also a consummate commercial organizer.

At some time in the early 1850s, Premchund and Kahandas began to engage in partnership trade. We have noticed their joint investment in opium. They also traded jointly in cotton exports to England. It was in the financial organization of this trade that we see Kahandas occupying a pivotal position. Premchund had built a network of agents in the countryside who procured raw cotton for him, a substantial portion of it paid by means of *hundis*—inland bills of exchange—drawn on Kahandas. The network extended to Dhollera, Belgaum, Surat, and Broach.[20] It may have included other inland centres of the cotton trade such as Barsi. 'Hoondies were drawn on me by Premchund's agents in the Mofussil,' said Kahandas.[21] Clearly it was Kahandas's reputation as a wealthy man which ensured the acceptance of his hundis in the cotton-producing interior. The joint transactions must have been profitable. Premchund became a trusted friend. 'I had confidence in Premchund,' declared Kahandas, 'and friendship for many years with him, and therefore I allowed him to manage my affairs.' He did not pay Premchund a commission. 'In many of my transactions,' he added, 'he was interested as a partner to the extent of one half.' It seems it was Kahandas who supplied all the capital. In short, his managerial ability in the trade enabled Premchund to obtain from Kahandas free capital to cover his own share of the shipments.

Kahandas had begun to rely on Premchund also in his personal arrangements. Among these was a trust he instituted in 1863 of a part of his property consisting of a bungalow in Cumbala Hill and a range in Kalbadevi. The trustees were Premchund Roychund and at first Tulsidas Ramdas then Ardeshir Bomanji Kaka. They were supposed to make available the rent from the property, Rs 850 a month, for the maintenance of Kahandas's two older wives and their children. Kahandas later rued the arrangement as the trustees failed to honour it.

For fifteen years or so, the trading relations seemed to work smoothly, with export capital being replenished and high prices of cotton in England piling up as profit. During this time Premchund amassed a considerable fortune both from trade on his own account and from his commission as a broker to Ritchie Stuart and Co., through whom, in the main, the shipments were made. No doubt Kahandas too was happy with the transactions.

Two developments changed the situation and precipitated Kahandas's ruin. With financial cover from Kahandas, Premchund began to borrow money for a number of speculative ventures. At the same time, the end of the war in America checked the boom in the cotton market. What made Kahandas particularly vulnerable was that he was liable both for his own investments in cotton and for those of Premchund, since it was he who had provided all the capital, the partnership arrangements between them being private ones.

Ritchie Stuart and Co. appears as a large creditor to Kahandas. It is very likely that Kahandas's debts to the firm were linked to cotton shipments and perhaps other purposes in which Premchund had a hand.

As late as 1866, Kahandas did not realize Premchund was under financial stress. He declared, 'I signed accommodation notes for Premchund in 1866 to the amount of 36 lacks, and did not receive one pie in consideration.'[22] In 1865 and 1866, Premchund had helped Kahandas obtain loans from the Bank of Bombay. With Premchund's help, Kahandas also borrowed Rs 11 lakhs from several other banks. He used most of the money to pay for hundis or bills of exchange drawn on him by Premchund's agents in the interior on account of their joint cotton transactions. Then, in April 1866, Premchund persuaded Kahandas to become security for him for a loan of Rs 25 lakhs from the Bank of Bombay. Towards the end of 1866, Kahandas's debt to the Bank of Bombay stood at Rs 255,717.

In response to writs of attachment from two of the banks, the High Court of Bombay adjudicated Kahandas an insolvent first in October 1866 and again by a second order in December 1866. Kahandas seems not to have been aware that the cotton market in England had crashed and that he was hopelessly ruined. He declared, 'I was adjudicated insolvent but I did not consider myself insolvent. I had 21000 bales of cotton unsold in England. I had an advance of £15 per bale. I don't know what they realized. I have not got the account.' Not being aware of the provisions of the insolvency law, he sold some of his jewels and other property to support himself after he had been adjudicated insolvent. He openly admitted to the court he had done so. He said, 'I can't say why I did not hand over all my property at once to Official Assignee on my being adjudicated insolvent. I did not know the law which required me to do this.'[23]

Meanwhile, Premchund had stopped seeing Kahandas and was unresponsive to his letters. When Kahandas did realize what had happened, he was utterly traumatized. He visited one cotton district after another, first spending about a month in Barsi, then moving from place to place in a vain attempt to recover his money from the dealers, distributing charity, giving money to Brahmin priests and asking them to pray for him. To the court that was conducting the hearing on his insolvency case, and to the commission investigating the failure of the Bank of Bombay, his words were, 'I have lost my money, I have lost my memory; having lost my money I am not well in senses.'[24]

The Tata Connection

Premchund, who was well acquainted with the position of almost all the wealthy traders in cotton and opium in the city, may have introduced Tata to Kahandas. According to Tata, Kahandas joined the firm in August or September 1864. Tata declared, 'He brought in altogether to the firm several lacs. I believe he was then a wealthy man. Up to April 1866 I thought he was a wealthy man.' Another witness, the acting Official Assignee of the High Court, had the same view. He said that in 1864 Kahandas's firm was doing profitable business and that his subsequent losses were the result of his joint cotton transactions with Premchund.

While Tata admitted Kahandas had brought several lakhs into the firm when he joined it, elsewhere in the hearing he declared, 'I am not aware I am down as a debtor to Insolvent to the amount of 12 lacs.' He was quick to turn the tables. He said, 'I became bankrupt on 25th of July 1866. I had then accepted Insolvent bills to the amount of nearly lacs 30. The bills were accepted as advances on cotton.... It was in consequence of accepting these bills I had to stop payments. Candass owes my estate about £6000 or £7000.' It is evident Kahandas had provided capital to Tata's firm both in the form of the amount he had initially contributed to it, perhaps Rs 12 lakhs, and in the form of the bills he had endorsed as advances on the firm's cotton exports. These bills were so substantial that when Kahandas was unable to honour them, Tata's firm too failed.[25]

The Visit to England

While both Tata and Kahandas had been hit by the commercial crash, unlike Kahandas, Tata had been clever enough to secure his position. The American Civil War ended in March 1865 with the defeat of the southern states. Within a month, Tata was on his way to England. He declared,

'On the 14th of April 1865 I left Bombay for England.' He may have anticipated the impending commercial collapse, for one of the objectives of his trip seems to have been to procure trustees for his company—a task in which he appears to have succeeded. He referred many times subsequently to his trustees in England.

The recourse to trustees—generally creditors or friends of the insolvent, who would take over the management of the affairs of a bankrupt firm or individual—was the surest way for them to escape the worst consequences of bankruptcy. When trustees were procured, generally something had to be paid to them.

What was perhaps the primary objective of the trip to England, one in which Kahandas was involved, was disclosed by Francis Xavier Pereira, who was employed by Kahandas. Pereira declared, 'I left India April 1865 ... Insolvent [i.e. Kahandas] sent me and Nusserwanjee [i.e. Jamsedji] Tata to open a firm in England and gave us Rs. 500 till the firm was opened. The firm was opened.'

Indian exporters often experienced disquiet from the manner in which their cargo was handled by importing firms in England; hence the endeavour to have their own offices in England. Tata, who already had the experience of agencies in Hong Kong and Shanghai, may have taken the initiative of opening an office in Liverpool. Kahandas, it appears, bore the expense.

Tata undertook yet another task, a somewhat unusual one. He declared, 'I took jewels from insolvent to England.... I believe the jewellery I took away from Bombay was worth Rs 80000 or one lac.... I took the jewels on my person. I paid no duty, was not aware I had to pay duty.'[26] He was under instructions from Kahandas to have the gems cut and reset, a task he declared he agreed to carry out without charging a commission. He had the work done by two jewellers in London. He claimed he returned all the jewels to Kahandas, except a parcel of diamonds which he gave to Pereira for Kahandas. In the course of the hearing, there were often conflicting statements about individual items of jewellery. As mentioned earlier, the questions put to Tata are not recorded, but his answers are often suggestive. The counsel seemed anxious to have a full account of the jewels. Surprisingly, Tata, who had carefully preserved Kahandas's letters and copies of his own letters to him, declared, 'I have no list of those jewels.' Asked about the bills of the jewellers, he said, 'I have not the bills of the jewellers here. They are in England with my trustees.' Tata may have been asked what had been paid to his trustees. His answer was, 'I had assets in England. I handed over £10000 in cash. My trustees got other property.' The nature of that property was not disclosed.

Kahandas had sent Tata a cash credit of £20,000 at the beginning of 1866. He alleged that Tata had not accounted to him for this money. When questioned, Tata answered, perhaps a little casually, 'Candass gave me a credit for £20000. I believe my trustees have sent him an account. I drew I believe to the amount of £14000.'[27]

All in all there is convincing evidence that Kahandas provided substantial support to the Tatas in the early stages of their business. As to Kahandas himself, he tried in vain to come to terms with his creditors. In the end, the insolvency court convicted him for making away with and concealing several items of property: a pair of carriage horses, jewellery, and furniture retained by him and sold after he had been adjudicated an insolvent, and a diamond ring. Kahandas's total liability was Rs 16,408,276. He was sentenced to two years of imprisonment. It seems he did not actually go to jail. He appears, at least for a time, to have fled to Daman. At this point he passed out of history.

Kahandas's case reveals significant aspects of the functioning of the insolvency law. While the court passed the sentence, the Official Assignee of the High Court exercised the authority to carry it out. He could delay implementation indefinitely. There seems to have been immense scope for the Official Assignee to accept favours, especially when wealthy insolvents such as Kahandas were involved. Until April 1886 no moves had been made to implement the court order. At that date, on the application of a new Official Assignee, the court passed an order for the execution of the judgment to a part of Kahandas's property. By this time Kahandas was perhaps not living, for it was Navivahu and others who opposed the order, on the plea of the judgment being time-barred. The case eventually went up to the Privy Council, which rejected the plea that the judgment was time-barred. In the end, Kahandas's family may have lost a substantial part of the property remaining with them.

By contrast, Kahandas's friend, Premchund Roychund, one of the biggest of all insolvents, was able to get trustees and soon bounced back into business like Tata. Premchund had amply demonstrated his ability to raise credit in the market. His trustee was George Ramsay Wilson, a member of the European commercial community of Bombay.

Premchund Roychund

In the brightest days of his career, his friends lionized Premchund Roychund. Accompanying him on his walk to his office in the Fort, they would hold an umbrella over him, honouring him as a prince might be honoured.[28] Many years after his death, he was acknowledged to have been the leader of the brokers of Bombay.[29] From humble beginnings, Premchund Roychund attained this exalted position at an exceptionally eventful phase of Bombay's commercial history.

Premchund's father, Roychund Deepchund, had been a dealer in wood in Surat. When they first come into view, Roychund is the broker of the Bank of Bombay, the prestigious official bank in the city, while his son Premchund is a guarantee broker to the leading commercial firm Ritchie Stuart and Co., the largest exporter of cotton in the city. In this capacity, Premchund procured cotton up-country and arranged its shipment through the company, at the same time guaranteeing the company for any loss it might suffer on account of loans given to the dealers. We do not know how father and son achieved the transition from modest traders to these prominent positions. The key to their success lay partly in the vital function they performed in garnering resources in the indigenous market and making them available for European commercial activity. While Premchund's relations with the European commercial community provided access to the city's export trade, his links with the vast and scattered nodes of indigenous credit and supplies made him an effective agent for linking the two. In his account of the early years of Premchund's career, Dinshaw Wacha emphasizes the boom in the cotton trade of Bombay when the American Civil War cut off supplies from the American south and Bombay became an important supplier of Indian cotton to the mills of Lancashire.[30] It was at this time that Premchund forged links with Ritchie Stuart and Co. The latter provided him with the latest information on prices in England. As they soared, so too did the incentive to export cotton. The profits of the trading community, dealers, brokers, and export houses scaled dizzy heights.

The times were propitious for Premchund's extraordinary entrepreneurial talents. He traded not only on his own account but also in partnership with innumerable individuals. So complicated were these partnerships that when Wacha had occasion, at a later date, to examine Premchund's accounts, he found it almost impossible to unravel them. The very fact of their number proves Premchund's ability to harness resources from a large number of modest investors. Premchund's agents were spread in the cotton-producing districts of Kattyawar and Gujarat. They facilitated the flow of supplies to Bombay. This was not all. Premchund had the support of one of the wealthiest persons in Bombay, his friend Kahandas Narandas, who endorsed his hundis.

Sales were effected on the spot as well as on consignments of cargo to England with an advance paid to the shippers by the export houses. Premchund, Wacha tells us, had familiarized himself with the financial position of most of the wealthy traders in cotton and opium. He was, therefore, in a unique position to advise Ritchie Stuart and Co. about the persons to whom advances might safely be made.

The activation of capital was reflected in an increase in the number of brokers. 'The brokers under their acknowledged leader, Shet Premchund Roychund, became possessed of great influence, authority and wealth.'[31] Between 1840 and 1850, there were no more than six brokers in stocks and shares. In the 1860s, they numbered between 200 and 250. Although their number decreased at the time of the crash of the late 1860s, the trend persisted. In 1921 the number was 478 while in 1924 it was 225–50. The majority were Gujaratis: Hindus, Jains, and Parsis. In drawing brokers to the central financial market of Bombay, Premchund made a lasting contribution to the commercial culture of the city. The steps taken under his leadership eventually led to the setting up of the Bombay Stock Exchange.

The boom years of the cotton trade enabled Premchund to strengthen his connections with members of the European trading community. Eager as anyone to amass wealth, Chapman, a leading member of the European commercial community and a government director of the Bank of Bombay declared, 'Undoubtedly, he [Premchund] was the greatest speculator in Bombay, but he had been courted by all classes of society. His position was far above that of an ordinary speculator, and I should call him the keystone of the commercial prosperity of Bombay.'[32]

One of Premchund's steadfast friends was Michael Scott, of Ritchie Stuart and Co. Premchund handled his share transactions and did not charge him a commission. When Scott left Bombay Premchund threw a banquet in his honour and presented him with a diamond necklace worth Rs 30,000. Another intimate associate was Tracey, member of Ritchie Stuart and Co and a director of the Bank of Bombay. Tracey was jointly engaged with Premchund in so many speculative ventures that at one time he owed Premchund more than Rs 2 lakhs. This balance was afterwards reduced. Nevertheless, as a result of their continued joint speculations, Tracey came to owe Premchund Rs 386,836, a sum which Premchund wrote off. Tracey borrowed Rs 4.5 lakhs from the Asiatic Bank in his firm's name for Premchund. On 19 April 1866 he gave the Bank of Bombay a guarantee for Premchund's overdrawn account amounting to Rs 3 lakhs. When the matter came before the board of the bank, the secretary, Robertson, declared that this was a guarantee by the firm of Ritchie Stuart and Co, of which Tracey was a member. Both he and Tracey knew this was untrue. So close was the connection between them that Tracey continued to seek Premchund's advice on investments even after he had left Bombay.[33]

Even more significant was the fact that Premchund was hand in glove with Blair, secretary of the Bank of Bombay, until the latter left for England on 29 April 1865. He had borrowed large sums from Premchund's father, Roychund Deepchund, and was engaged in extensive share speculations, constantly buying and selling shares. Premchund managed these transactions and did not charge him brokerage. In some of these speculations, Premchund was his partner. Besides these persons, Premchund was on intimate terms with the managers of other banks in the city. Among them was Anthony Morrison, manager of the Asiatic Bank.

Although the Asiatic Bank was started out of local resources, it was registered in London with a view to engage in the exchange business. It was promoted in 1863, the promoters being Michael Scott, Gavin Steel, and Cowasji Jehangir. Its prestige was enhanced when it obtained a royal charter and at the same time its capital was doubled. The directors were in England. Michael Scott, Gavin Steel, and Cowasji Jehangir acted as the local consultative committee. Its exchange business, that is, dealings in foreign exchange, made it a serious competitor of the other exchange banks in the city. The bank acquired a prestige that placed it next only to the Bank of Bombay in the public eye. By a quirk of fortune, when Cowasji Jehangir retired and Michael Scott left for England, Premchund Roychund came to have a prominent position in the affairs of the Asiatic Bank. Premchund's connections not only gave him easy access to the resources of the two leading banks of the city, but also helped him at a critical moment in his career.

It is not surprising that Premchund acquired great influence at the Bank of Bombay, whose directors were, for the most part, members of the city's European commercial firms. On 28 July 1864, he was elected a director of the Bank of Bombay, a position he resigned on 12 September 1864. Then, he was to declare, his 'friends', Hannay, Michael Scott, and Tracey, pressed him to become a director once again. He was re-elected on 12 December 1864; he resigned on 29 June 1865.

A few weeks before Premchund first became a director, a branch of the bank had been opened at Kalbadevi in the heart of the Indian town, the centre of indigenous trade and finance. This may have been done on Premchund's advice. He was certainly all in favour of the measure. When Blair told him that a branch was to be opened at Kalbadevi, Premchund said 'It would be a very good thing', and that there would be 'plenty of deposits there ... from the bazaar people and Marwarees.'[34] The opening of the Kalbadevi branch invited considerable censure when, upon its failure, the affairs of the bank came under scrutiny. Act III of 1840, by which the bank was constituted, disallowed the opening of another branch in Bombay. In their eagerness to tap the indigenous market for business, the directors had ignored this provision.

Perhaps almost inevitably the extension of business in the indigenous market led the way to significantly less stringent terms on which the bank began to give loans. Act III of 1840 did not allow granting of loans except on the security of government paper, bullion, or imperishable goods. It laid down a number of other restrictions. All these restrictions were set aside by Act X of 1863, which allowed the discount of any negotiable security. Consequently, it permitted the discount of a promissory note signed by one person. The remark of Hannay, the president of the bank, may have reflected this practice when he named certain very wealthy persons to whom the bank would readily give a loan of as much as Rs 5 lakhs on 'personal security', or in the form of a promissory note, that is, simply on a promise of repayment without security. The surprising fact is that most of the directors giving evidence before the enquiry commission seemed not to have been aware of the changed terms and appeared to assume that loans continued to be given in the old way. How far the restrictions laid down in the earlier law were observed is not clear, but from 1863, loans began to be given in a remarkably unrestricted manner. Blair surreptitiously began to grant loans on personal security only, that is, on a promissory note signed by one borrower or by joint borrowers, without additional security. In effect this amounted to a tacit endorsement of indigenous convention. The first of such loans, termed cash credits, was of Rs 1 lakh granted to Premchund's father in August 1863.

As loans were not protected by material security, the only safeguard was the financial viability of the persons to whom they were granted. Premchund was considered to be the best judge of the financial status of those applying for loans. Blair gave Premchund a book of forms of promissory notes which Premchund would fill up with the names of the parties applying for loans. At other times, Premchund would write to Blair recommending applications for loans. On certain occasions, the money was handed over to Premchund instead of to the applicants. While this was the situation at the main branch of the bank, the agents at Kalbadevi, Broach, and Surat had all been instructed to go by the advice of Premchund or his agents while considering applications for loans.

As the war progressed large amounts of gold and silver were imported into Bombay—mainly the earning of the cotton that had been exported. Wacha reckoned that in the years 1861–2 to 1864–5, this amounted to a value of Rs 51.78 crores (1 crore is equal to 10 million). Never before had the city experienced such bounty. The banks were flush with funds. Traders had amassed wealth. Premchund had made a considerable fortune speculating in cotton. He used a part of his wealth in making a number of endowments to the universities of Bombay and Calcutta. To the University of Bombay he donated Rs 2 lakhs for the elegant clock tower that was named Rajabai Tower after his mother, which still holds its own amidst the city's many modern structures. He gave another Rs 2 lakhs for the magnificent library building. To the University of Calcutta he gave Rs 2 lakhs, which was used to institute five scholarships bearing his name.

The cotton textile industry had made its appearance in Bombay with the establishment of the first mill in 1853. But Premchund's soaring ambition looked to altogether spectacular instant gain. The accumulation of wealth signalled the mushrooming of a large number of companies. Wacha has listed seventy-eight companies that were started in the boom years. They ranged, among others, from land reclamation companies to cotton-pressing companies, to those whose declared agenda was banking.

Premchund was so influential that his name and support were considered essential to the launching of companies. Even if he was not the promoter of a company, he was still allotted a large number of shares in it. The promoters consulted him and allowed him to participate in the distribution of the allotments.[35] So rampant and widespread was the speculative drive that no sooner was a company floated than its shares were at a premium, which could be immediately realized. Wacha calculates that while the paid-up capital of a number of companies was about Rs 30 crores in the period from March 1864 to March 1865, the total premia on these companies was almost Rs 38 crores. Being able to allot shares put Premchund in a position of immense power and influence. He distributed the shares among bank managers, promoters and their friends, himself.[36]

It was, of course, well within the bounds of indigenous commercial culture to buy cheap and sell dear. That was the obvious way of making profit. From this strategy there was but a step to influence prices, something which Premchund could do, given his command of the funds of more than one bank and of the choice he exercised in the distribution of shares. While he had a hand in the allotment of shares in many of the prized companies, his favourite hunting ground was the Back Bay Company.

Of the companies that were floated, perhaps the most substantial was the Bombay Reclamation Company, also known as the Back Bay Company. The company projected an ambitious scheme to reclaim 1,500 acres of land along the foreshore of the island. Of this, 300 acres were to be gifted to the government. Its promoters were Michael Scott, Cowasji Jehangir, Premchund Roychund, Walter Cassels of Peel Cassels and Company, and Gavin Steel of Grey and Company. The Back Bay Company chose to bank with the Asiatic Bank. The prestige of the company was enhanced by the fact that it enjoyed official patronage. The government gifted it wasteland amounting to 140 acres in Elephanta Island and 66 acres in Andheri Hill. The company was registered in September 1863, but the formal right to reclaim the foreshore land was not granted by the government until 24 June 1864. On this date a wave of speculation swept the city like wildfire.

Premchund fanned the flames. In the latter part of 1864, he was particularly active in peddling shares of the Back Bay Company. Thus, for instance, he urged Sorabjee Jamsetjee Jejeebhoy, son of the baronet Sir Jamsetjee Jejeebhoy, to buy Back Bay shares. When Sorabjee told him he was short of money, Premchund said 'Take my word, Sorabjee, and do not trouble yourself about money. I will get you as much money as you require. But do not go in for less than one hundred shares.' Premchund said, 'He could procure 10 lakhs of rupees in a twinkling. He said he would get the money from the Asiatic and the Bombay banks.'[37] Thereupon, he sent Sorabjee two notes, one addressed to Morrison of the Asiatic Bank, the other to Blair of the Bombay Bank, asking them to lend Sorabjee Rs 5 lakhs each. They would give the money 'with pleasure', they wrote. Sorabjee settled for forty-three shares. As the Rs 10 lakhs were insufficient, he gave Premchund cheques amounting to another Rs 60,000, to be deposited with the two banks. This was in July 1864.

In August 1864 Premchund masterminded a transaction which may have been designed to boost the price of Back Bay shares. He said to Kursondass Madhowdass that the Bank of Bombay was at a loss about what to do with its money and that he, Premchund, had been asked to get it invested. He advised Kursondas to buy 100 Back Bay shares on the joint account of Kursondas, Premabhoy Hemabhoy, and himself, and to borrow the purchase money from the Bank of Bombay. Kursondas and the others accepted the proposal. Premchund then arranged to execute it. He suppressed his own name and that of Premabhoy Hemabhoy. Being a director of the bank at the time, he may not have wanted to disclose his participation in a speculative venture. He arranged for a loan of Rs 25 lakhs from the Bank of Bombay in the name of Kursondas and two others, each of them giving a promissory note for the amount borrowed. Thereupon, fifty-three shares were bought from Premchund and the rest from other brokers. Eighty of the shares were deposited with the bank as security.

Two months later, in October, Premchund called on a Mr Diver and told him that Back Bay shares were about to become very valuable and that the Bank of Bombay was prepared to advance money on them. Diver joined two others, George Taylor and Atmaram Madhowjee, in buying twenty Back Bay shares from Premchund, having obtained a loan of Rs 5.5 lakhs from the Bank of Bombay. The entire transaction was managed by Premchund. The buyers did not see the money or the shares which were deposited with the bank as security.

In another instance, on 28 December 1864, Premchund negotiated a loan of Rs 6.25 lakhs for Cursetjee Furdoonjee from the Bank of Bombay on the security of his promissory note and the deposit of ten Back Bay shares he had purchased from Premchund. These ten shares were purchased for Rs 5.25 lakhs. In other words, the bank had advanced Rs 1 lakh in excess of the price of the shares to Cursetjee. Premchund negotiated the loan.

Then, late in March 1865, Premchund initiated an arrangement whose objective, according to Hannay—the newly appointed President of the Bank of Bombay—was to support the price of Back Bay shares. In words which had the ring of a prophecy, he told Hannay and Morrison that because of 'influences at work' the price of all shares, including those of the Back Bay Company, were about to come down. It was agreed that Hannay, Morrison, Blair, Tracey, and Premchund should each buy five Back Bay shares in order to keep up the price and a loan for the purchase money should be obtained from the Asiatic Bank in the name of Premchund's manager, Dossabhoy Dhunjeebhoy. Accordingly, twenty-five Back Bay shares were bought through Premchund, who of course took the opportunity to sell some of his own shares.

On the other side of the globe, the war had become one of attrition. Did Premchund anticipate it would soon end, that American cotton would once again begin to flow to Lancashire and bring to an end the boom in Bombay, and that share prices would tumble?

Once launched, the Back Bay Company lost little time in proceeding with the project. Some equipment was imported from England. Being anxious to meet its obligation of delivering 50 acres of reclaimed land to the government each year, the company organized work on the site at night as well as in the day. Being solvent until June 1865, it was able to do so. The position altered drastically a year later, by which time the cash balance of the company was almost exhausted. Its fixed deposits of Rs 91,000 with the Asiatic Bank were not available as the bank, which had opened its coffers wide in the speculative spree, was on the verge of collapse and soon stopped payment.

The war ended on 9 April 1865. Before that fateful event, clouds had already begun to gather in the horizon. The news was received with alarm and set in motion a spate of bankruptcies in Bombay. In Liverpool cotton that had been selling for 20 pence a pound fell to 10 pence by the end of April 1865. Worse was to come a year later. In late summer that year, as Lancashire did not receive the expected supply of American cotton, Bombay's share market revived temporarily. Many took this as a sign of better days to come. But by the following year, every hope of a revival had vanished. By the spring of 1866, Premchund was strapped for funds. Wacha, who examined his accounts, reckoned he had drawn from the Bank of Bombay altogether Rs 1.38 crores on his own account and that of his friends, most of this sum having been used in speculation. Besides, he was indebted to other banks and to other persons. As the shadows of the financial crisis lengthened, scores of people were ruined. In the streets of Bombay, where but a while earlier Premchund had been all but deified, there were now throngs who held him responsible for their losses. 'People have filed suits against me,' cried Premchund, 'and I am bullied by small paltry debtors who don't allow me to sit down even quarter of an hour.'[38] The magic he had wrought seemed to have snapped. While being stretched, Premchund was aware of his strength. Even though he was heavily in debt to the Bank of Bombay, , he applied to the bank for a loan of Rs 25 lakhs on 26 April 1866, declaring that if the loan was not granted he would have to stop payment the next day, meaning that he would no longer be solvent. Robertson, the secretary, at once informed the new president, Lidderdale, who called a meeting that afternoon. Those present included not only the directors but also the managers of a number of banks in Bombay. In the discussion that followed, it became evident that all the banks were inclined to support Premchund. It also became evident that Morrison and Thomson had an interest on behalf of their banks in supporting him. Even though the amount for which he had applied was large, the consensus was that his failure would bring about an unprecedented financial crisis in the city. Nothing could better demonstrate the hold that he continued to exercise on the minds of the financial elite of the city. After some discussion it was decided that the loan should be granted after it had been established that the security Premchund was offering was adequate. To this end a meeting was called for the next day.

Early the next morning, the same persons, together with Muller of the Comptoir d'escompte de Paris and Beattie of the Commercial Bank, assembled once again, this time at Lidderdale's bungalow. While they deliberated within, Premchund sat monarch-like in the verandah, and Tracey carried messages between him and those engaged in the discussion. They first considered Premchund's liabilities and were shown a paper that contained statements of these. They found the paper to be unintelligible but Tracey, who Premchund admitted was helping him obtain the loan, assured the meeting that Premchund's difficulties were temporary and that he had a large sum locked up in the cotton districts of Dhollera, which would soon be released. Besides the support of members of the banking community, Premchund also had the benefit of the friendship of one of the wealthiest persons in Bombay, Kahandas Narandas, who endorsed his hundis.

The discussion centred on the question of how viable the security Premchund was offering was. This was considered to be quite inadequate. The landed property Premchund had pledged was said to have been valued at Rs 26 lakhs. Norman, a director of the Bank who had earlier been collector of land revenue in Bombay and was considered knowledgeable on property values, declared the property to be worth no more than Rs 14 lakhs. The issue provoked considerable discussion. Repeated references were made to Premchund at his perch in the verandah. At one point Premchund indignantly declared that if the directors were going to make so much trouble for him he would 'prefer stopping at once', meaning he would declare himself insolvent. This, of course, was something no one wanted. His own signature to the promissory note he was offering was of little value as he had evaded the payment of his debts and had fled to the Gaikwar of Baroda's territory. Another signatory, Kahandas Narandas, was deep in debt and had passed unsuccessfully through the insolvency court. This was true also of another signatory, Kursondass Madhowdass.

Although the directors of the banks and their associates seemed to expend considerable effort in trying to assess the value of the security Premchund had pledged, the exercise was in fact farcical. On the fateful afternoon of 27 April 1866, they agreed unanimously to grant Premchund a loan of Rs 25 lakhs for six months on the security he had offered. Of this amount the Bank of Bombay was to provide Rs 10.5 lakhs. The Oriental, Chartered Mercantile, Asiatic and Commercial Banks, and the Comptoir d'Escomte de Paris were to each subscribe Rs 2.5 lakhs, and the Bank of Hindustan Rs 2 lakhs towards the loan. It was also resolved that initially the Bank of Bombay would subscribe the entire amount of Rs 25 lakhs, later to be recouped from the other banks.

The directors' keenness to support Premchund may have been influenced by the fact that some of them were themselves involved in his dealings. They may have also partly believed that by assisting him they would save the Asiatic and Bombay Banks to which he was heavily in debt. But the loan did not see Premchund out of the woods. In September 1866, he declared he was insolvent. Once again, his friends in the European commercial community came to his rescue. They appointed one of their own number, George Ramsay Wilson, to be his trustee.

Premchund re-entered business with aplomb. Twenty odd years later he was once again insolvent. He applied to the courts for protection.[39] The petition was opposed by several creditors, prominent among whom

Figure I.1 The New Mint, Bombay. Original colour lithograph by Jose M. Gonsalves.
Source: Phillips Images, Mumbai.

Figure 1.1 Jamshedji Tata, as a Soldier; Taken in China, 1861
Source: Frank Reginald Harris, *Jamsetji Nusserwanji Tata: A Chronicle of His Life* (London, 1925).

Figure 1.2 Premchund Roychund at His Son's Wedding.
Source: Sharada Dwivedi, *Premchand Royc(hand) (1831–1906): His Life and Times.*

Figure 2.1 A Street Scene in Bhendi Bazaar, Bombay, c. 1880 (photograph by Raja Deen Dayal). The trees planted during Bhimdev's rule (towards the end of the thirteenth century) lent their names to various localities that developed on the islands. 'Parel' derived from the 'paral', the trumpet flower, 'Umerkhadi' was the fig tree creek and 'Bhendi Bazaar' was named for the 'bhendi' (Hibiscus populnea). By early to mid-nineteenth century, beyond the Esplanade, the bazaar localities emerged as the heart of the Indian town where residential, commercial, social, and religious activities were integrated into a tightly knit urban fabric as in a traditional Indian town. Temples, mosques, agiaries, churches, bazaars, and organic street patterns all coalesced in a vibrant world far removed from that which was evolving on the southern islands of Bombay. Local bazaars for daily provisions sprouted in and around densely inhabited residential localities, whereas specialized markets generally clustered together.
Source: Phillips Images, Mumbai.

was Premchund's fellow Jain, Lalbhai Dulputbhai, father of Kasturbhai Lalbhai, prominent industrialists and mill owners from Ahmedabad. The High Court postponed the hearing on the petition at least seven times while granting Premchund protection throughout the time. The record does not indicate how the matter was resolved.

The stories of the people recounted in this chapter reveal the activities and relationships that governed their lives. They illustrate the networks through which money credit and loans circulated in the world of business. These stories connect the economic trajectories to the social and cultural worlds of people and their lives. In contrast to the three life stories recounted here, the fourth story is that of Ayesha. While she was not herself an insolvent, her son's insolvency critically affected the family, as we shall see in the final chapter of the book.

Notes and References

1. See Frank Reginald Harris, *Jamsetji Nusserwanji Tata: A Chronicle of His Life* (London: Oxford University Press, 1925).
2. Morris D. Morris, 'The Growth of Large-Scale Industry to 1947', in *Cambridge Economic History of India*, vol. 2, *c. 1751–c. 1970*, edited by Dharma Kumar and Meghnad Desai (Cambridge: Cambridge University Press, 1983), pp. 556–676.
3. R. Hannay, president, to D. Robertson, director, Bank of Bombay, 13 August 1865. Copy of exhibit A148. Appendix to 'Final Report of the Commission on Failure of First Bank of Bombay, 1868' [hereafter Bombay Bank Failure Report].
4. A Parsi (anonymous), *Mumbaina Share Sattani Tavarikh* (Bombay: E&G Job Printing Press, 1867), pp. 303–4. (I am grateful to Prof. Martand J. Mehta for this reference.)
5. Evidence of Wilkes Hill, Acting Official Assignee, High Court of Bombay, 1868. Wilkes Hill was another witness in the case. He declared, 'I have examined the general character of the books and the insolvent's business. It had a large business and was an old established firm.... I should say in 1864 the firm was doing a profitable business. I should say a large proportion of the losses was in consequence of the joint shipment of cotton with Premchund.' (Notebook, 1868, witness examined by Macpherson, hereafter Notebook Macpherson.)
6. High Court Bombay insolvency. The Hon'ble Justice Tucker in the Court of Relief of Insolvent Debtors, 15 July 1868 [hereafter Tucker Notebook]. 'My father and grandfather were jewellers ... we only dealt in precious stones.'

7. 'I sold these jewels at Ahmedabad. I sent Wittuldass to Baroda to sell ornaments.' (Tucker Notebook.)
8. See exhibit 55.537, 'Hip wrapper, 18th century, cotton, gold, hand painted, madder dyed'. Museum of Art, Rhode Island School of Design, Providence. Rhode Island, USA.
9. Evidence given by Kahandas in High Court, Bombay insolvency records.
10. For the volume of this trade, see the introduction in Asiya Siddiqi, ed., *Trade and Finance in Colonial India, 1757–1860* (New Delhi: Oxford University Press, 1995).
11. For the terms on which goods were exported, see the introduction in Siddiqi, *Trade and Finance in Colonial India.*
12. 'I have dealings with the insolvent. I claim to be a creditor of the insolvent.... The insolvent owes me and Mohomet [*sic*] Tucker 6 1/2 lacs on account of that debt.' (Tucker Notebook, Aga Mahmood Abdool Russool, afforded by Macpherson.)
13. 'Most of my books are kept by Wittuldas who is gone to Daman. He has a writ against him to pay the call on two or three Mazgaon shares.' (Tucker Notebook.)
14. Tucker Notebook.
15. 'The necklace and pendant valued at a lac was the necklace I afterwards gave my wife.' (Tucker Notebook.)
16. 'I was living with Cawasjee Nanabhoy in his bungalow four months ago.' (Tucker Notebook.)
17. 'I am the son of Roychund Deepchund. He was the broker of the Bank of Bombay.' (Bombay Bank Failure Report, p. 71.)
18. Bombay Bank Failure Report.
19. See, for example, Roychund's letter. Bombay Bank Failure Report.
20. Premchund, minutes of evidence, Bombay Bank Failure Report, p. 87.
21. Kahandas, letter, Bombay Bank Failure Report.
22. Tucker Notebook.
23. Tucker Notebook.
24. Tucker Notebook.
25. Jamsetjee Nusserwanjee Tata, sworn and examined by Machperson.
26. 'I knew him at the beginning of 1865. On the 14th of April 1865 I left Bombay for England. I took jewels from insolvent to England.' (Macpherson Notebook.)
27. Macpherson Notebook.
28. Bombay's central business district is referred to as the 'Fort area' after the erstwhile British fortifications around the harbour that had been built in the seventeenth century.
29. Report of Provincial Banking Enquiry Committee, 1924.

30. Sir Dinshaw Edulji Wacha, *Premchund Roychund: His Early Life and Career* (Bombay: Times Press, 1913).
31. Report of Provincial Banking Enquiry Committee, 1924.
32. Chapman's evidence, Bombay Bank Failure Report.
33. Tracey, Bombay Bank Failure Report.
34. Premchund's evidence in Bombay Bank Failure Report.
35. Wacha, *Premchund Roychund.*
36. Wacha, *Premchund Roychund.*
37. Premchund's evidence in Bombay Bank Failure Report.
38. Premchund's letter to Kahandas, Bombay Bank Failure Report.
39. Insolvency schedule 295, 1886. All insolvency schedules refer to the records of the Bombay High Court and are cited by number and date.

2 *The Bigger Merchants*

This chapter is concerned with how some of the bigger merchants were adversely affected by judicial decisions concerning their commercial activity. As a result a change in the mores of business activities is noticeable after the 1860s. In the older culture that underpinned commercial activity, mutual trust played an important role.[1] The earlier personal element in business relations is evident in a letter that R.I. Tracey, a close associate of Premchund Roychund, wrote to him from England:

> My Dear Premchund,
>
> I have been disappointed at not hearing from you for the last few mails. Can it be press of work that prevents your writing? I hope not, for all who have been doing any business lately must have suffered from it. Poor Bombay is indeed paying dearly for its short dream of prosperity....
>
> I have to write this mail to Robertson about that overdraft of Yours which I guaranteed....
>
> What balance still remains unpaid?

> What are you doing now, and what do you think about future business? ... Remember me to your father and Dossabhoy.
>
> Believe me, & c.,
> R.I. Tracey
> London, December 3rd, 1867[2]

In this chapter we have made a separate analysis of the bigger merchants among insolvents, those whose debts were Rs 10,000 or more (Table 3A.19). The incidences of insolvency among these merchants reveal temporal trends similar to those of insolvency as a whole, in that there was a surge in numbers following the crash of trade in 1865, which continued in the following years and peaked in about 1870. Those under strain struggled to financially survive for several years but eventually had to seek the protection of the court. Most of them got protection.

A significant cause of instability in the export trade was the structure of the consignment system. Shippers of produce exported cargo on their own account through agents, most of them European firms in the city. They handed over their cargo to the latter and were paid a portion of the estimated value of the goods. Final accounts were settled only when the cargo had been sold in the markets abroad. This meant that the entire transaction took place at the risk of the shippers, who had little control over the foreign market and were exposed to great risk from price fluctuations and perhaps also from price manipulation. If the agents reported there had been a loss, the shippers were required to make good the deficit. These payments, termed 'redrafts', are often listed among the debts of insolvents. The manner in which credit was raised for the consignment trade and the motive of the European trading houses, interested more in their commissions than on the outturn of the commercial transactions, produced extreme instability in the market in Bombay. So unconcerned were these trading houses with the well-being of the shippers and so anxious that the payment of redrafts should be strictly enforced that they tried to initiate legislation to this effect, a move the Bombay government resisted.[3]

Loans to prospective shippers were readily guaranteed by the many guarantee brokers who worked for the trading houses. Those in need of money could obtain these loans on signing shipping documents, apparently not always aware, or so they later declared, that they were committing themselves to making consignments.

We have studied the structure of credit of the bigger merchants from 1860 to 1866 (Table 3A.20). From the list of creditors for all merchants in these years whose debts were Rs 10,000 or more, we picked and codified the four largest items of credit. The table deals only with the number of credit items and not the amounts involved.

Several indices rise conspicuously on the collapse of the trade. The number of debts arising from running accounts for the buying and selling of goods rises dramatically with the crisis. This means that many merchants were unable to settle their accounts. Redrafts on shipments also go up, as do losses from share speculation and loans.[4] The item 'IPP' (see Table 3A.19), we surmise, referred to debts mostly owed to individuals. A large number of them were in the form of promissory notes, that is, loans raised on personal security, or simply on a verbal understanding or promise to repay. In other words, they represent a truly indigenous type of credit, the so-called bazaar credit. The large number of these entries shows the abundance and importance of this type of credit. Contrary to the received view that there was a shortage of capital and of capital-mobilizing institutions in the Indian money market, in fact money for investment could generally be raised in the bazaar (Figure 2.1).[5] This also explains why Indian guarantee brokers who helped to raise money were so important to the European trading houses and to banks. The abundance of credit raised through promissory notes indicates the important place of trust in the indigenous money market. An increase in the prevalence of material security may have eroded this trust.

When we look at the list of types of creditors, debts owed to banks go up. So too do debts to Indian trading companies, and more so to European trading companies (Table 3A.20). Debts to individuals show a sharp increase. We were unable to extend our study of credit structure to the peak of the crisis, the early 1870s. Had we done so, some of these indices would perhaps have shown up in even sharper relief.

An undercurrent of disquiet over the terms on which trade took place and over the unequal position of Indian merchants is reflected in some insolvency proceedings. Conspicuous among those who voiced this disquiet were leading lawyer-politicians, many of whom acted as counsels for insolvents. The names of Kashinath Trimbak Telang, Rahimutullah Mohammad Sayani, and, above all, Badruddin Tyabji are especially noticeable. The cases of two insolvents, both of whom were defended by

Badruddin Tyabji, reveal something of the bitter sentiment that had begun to take shape in reaction to the conduct of the European trading houses.

Sunderdas Waghji, a merchant based in Bombay, had been making consignments since 1865 through Cardwell Parsons and Company, later to merge with the London Asiatic and American Company Limited.[6] Most of the goods shipped had been myrobalans. In 1872 and 1873 Sunderdas made particularly large shipments. When the goods reached England in 1872, the market fell. There was a huge redraft on the consignment. The representative of the firm alleged in court that were it not for the fall in the market, the redrafts would not have been so large, but he also declared that Sunderdas Waghji had made inferior, adulterated, and short-weight shipments. The firm insisted on the redrafts being paid and, in order to reinforce the demand, a member of the firm, Charles Benn, visited Sunderdas's house, searched it, and took away his wife's jewellery.

Tyabji argued that the firm had never before found fault with Sunderdas's consignments even though he had been shipping myrobalans since 1865. Earlier the prices had been good and if they had so continued, Sunderdas would not have lost money. But prices fell by 25 per cent. The firm, he declared, was culpable as it did not warn Sunderdas that his transactions were hazardous. Looking only to its commissions, it kept lending him more money and encouraged Sunderdas to ship instead of dissuading him. As for the weights, Tyabji said the firm knew that the weights were and always had been approximate.

Sunderdas was ordered to be imprisoned for one year. His conduct had been fraudulent, declared the judge. 'The court must mark its sense of such conduct by taking severe notice of it. This [was] requisite for the protection of society generally, and specially honest traders.'

The second case is that of Visram Govindji, who had consigned pearls to be sold in England through Peel Cassels and Company. The pearls had been valued and the shipper had been paid an advance. When they reached England, the agent declared that the value was much less than ascertained. The shipper was charged with fraud. Tyabji argued that the pearls had been lying with the company, that they had ample time to get them valued, that the prices of jewels often fluctuated, and that his client could not be charged with fraud. Besides, Tyabji hinted at the casual manner in which senior members of the company had handled the matter. While the case was on, Mr Peel had left for England. Tyabji enquired as to why Peel was not examined before he went to England. Visram Govindji's petition was adjourned without protection for one year.

Indian merchants suffered heavily from the collapse of the cotton trade, based exclusively on the consignment system. The literature often explains their ruin in terms of their propensity to speculate and trade recklessly. Even a thoughtful study such as Marika Vicziany's does not touch on the details of consignment trade, and the in-built hazards to which it exposed the shippers, arising principally from the fact that the trading houses through which the shipments were made had, above all, an interest in their own commissions. This itself, as the case of Sunderdas Waghji shows, was likely to lead to overtrading.

The rise of nationalism is often associated with the consciousness and activities of the middle-class intelligentsia. Our study amplifies this perspective by focusing on the commercial culture of Bombay. Persons other than merchants often engaged in trade. They, as well as professional merchants and traders, suffered from the peculiar hazards of consignment trade. Reaction to the iniquities of the consignment system and the way the European trading establishments exploited it to the ruin of Indian shippers may have been an important element in the sharpening of national awareness in the later years of the century. When Badruddin Tyabji pointed an accusing finger at the conduct of the European trading houses, it is likely his words were taken up in the corridors of the High Court and beyond. The system came under great strain during the commercial crisis.

In the years following the crash of the cotton trade, British merchants in Bombay tended to ship cargo such as cotton not on their own account but in response only to orders together with letters of credit sent out by the importers in England.[7] As compared to Indian merchants at the port, British merchants were better placed to assess the demand at home and to make these arrangements. Indian merchants, on the other hand, were not in so favourable a position to participate in trade on order; they continued to export goods on consignment, always a risky business. By the 1880s Indians no longer figured as large exporters of cotton, a commodity which, perhaps more than any other, had incurred losses.[8]

Notes and References

1. Tracey to Premchund, evidence in 'Final Report of the Commission on Failure of First Bank of Bombay, 1868' [hereafter Bombay Bank Failure Report], p. 86.

2. Bombay Bank Failure Report.
3. 'Annual Reports of the Bombay Chamber of Commerce', 1866–8, library of the University of Mumbai.
4. See Marika Vicziany, 'The Cotton Trade and the Commercial Development of Bombay, 1855–1875', PhD diss., University of London, 1973, p. 225.
5. See Morris D. Morris, 'The Growth of Large-Scale Industry to 1947', in *Cambridge Economic History of India*, vol. 2, *c. 1751–c. 1970*, edited by Dharma Kumar and Meghnad Desai (Cambridge: Cambridge University Press, 1983), pp. 556–676.
6. Insolvency schedule 9317, 1873. (All insolvency schedules refer to the records of the Bombay High Court and are cited by number and date.) Hearing, 17 June to 26 August 1874, recorded in Justice Pinhey's notebook entitled 'Notes by Justice Pinhey', Insolvent Court, Bombay, 1873.
7. See Marika Vicziany, 'Bombay Merchants and Structural Changes in the Export Community, 1850 to 1880', in *Trade and Finance in Colonial India 1750–1860*, edited by Asiya Siddiqi (New Delhi: Oxford University Press, 1995), pp. 346, 361–9.
8. Vicziany, 'Bomaby Merchants', pp. 346, 361–9.

3 *Reading the Records*

Literacy and Social–Occupational Stratification

In the previous chapters we explored the kinds of relationships that are manifest in the stories of Bombay merchants. In traditional society business and personal relationships were often intertwined. This was the case with Kahandas Narandas and his mehta and others whom he supported.

The marks and signatures of the insolvents recorded in the documents yields various kinds of information about them. In this chapter, we will discuss our investigation into these marks and signatures, followed by an analysis of the maze of data gathered from the insolvents' records.

Marks and Signatures

The schedules lend themselves to a study of literacy status. While there are well-documented accounts of the development of educational institutions in Bombay in the nineteenth century, we know little about actual levels of literacy. There is very little directly available information about the individuals in different occupations and their literacy levels. Data extracted from the records of the insolvents present a representative sample of the various occupations and help us understand the socio-economic backgrounds of the insolvents.

Marks

At the turn of the twentieth century, it was discovered that the patterns of lines on the fingers of each individual were unique. The discovery was useful both to forensic medicine and to documentation. It became the basis of the practice whereby individuals not able to sign their names used thumb impressions when required to affix their identity to a document. This ended an earlier convention whereby such persons would affix a 'mark' in place of a signature.

In India the occurrence of these usages increased greatly under British administration with the proliferation of administrative documentation. This was particularly true of legal records such as those where individuals had to identify themselves at the time of entering a petition or initiating a case, and often in the course of the proceeding as well.

The insolvency petitions of the Bombay High Court abound both in marks and signatures. A sample of the marks that were generally used has been given at the end of this section. The marks often reflect the tokens in terms of which people identified themselves. Of particular interest are such marks as, for instance, the circle, used by a very large number of women, regardless of their religion. The circle, an abbreviation for the pot, which is in turn a symbolic representation of the womb, has been and still is a fertility symbol in Indian art, ritual, and religion. Its use by women drawn from different strata and from many religions signifies the universality of a symbol that expressed society's recognition of the place of woman as the propagator of life (Figure 3.13).

Many insolvents used tools of trade as their marks. Thus, ironsmiths often used a pair of bellows, tailors scissors, carpenters a saw, and traders a pair of scales (Figures 3.6, 3.5, and 3.4). A sarangi player drew what resembles a bow (Figure 3.8). In some cases we notice a person using a mark that represented his earlier occupation. Thus, Rama bin Khundoojee, who was a *mocuddum* (a representative or agent of a company) in the Colaba Cotton Press, used as his mark a plough, an indication not only of his substantive calling but also of a lingering sense of identity with that calling (Figure 3.14). All in all, these marks prominently convey the place of a person's occupation in self-identity. It was but natural perhaps that where people could not state their distinctive individuality by writing their names, they would resort to symbols that represented their occupation. The usage may have been strengthened by the distinctive values that governed Indian society, in which not only was occupation a salient element in caste categories, but also those who were associated with labour, generally belonging to the less privileged castes, were often debarred from becoming literate.

Besides marks indicating occupation, we find some Muslim insolvents using as their mark the first two letters of the Arabic alphabet, in several instances written incorrectly with the dots in the wrong places. The Arabic alphabet, being the alphabet of the Quran, had a special significance for Muslims. One Muslim petitioner sketched what looked like the dome of a building. Perhaps he intended it to be a mosque (Figure 3.10). These marks, in other words, expressed a sectarian identity. Similar to this was the sign of the cross some Christians used (Figure 3.12). Occasionally, we also find the swastika being used (Figure 3.11). Perhaps this denoted a Hindu identity. Of course, most Muslims simply used occupational marks just like many other people did. In some cases where certain occupations were exclusive to Muslims, the persons who used marks representing those occupations were all Muslims. This was the case, for instance, with dyers, who were frequently also cloth printers, and who often used a square formed with dots. This may have stood for a printing block (Figure 3.6).

The use of marks in place of signatures may have been a long-standing practice. Eighteenth-century documents reveal seafaring traders using a boat or an anchor as their marks.[1] These marks were used also by sailors in our sample (Figure 3.7). Moreover, the practice of using marks for signatures was not unique to India. It was widespread also in preliterate European societies.[2]

The practice of using marks in place of signatures may well have had a subtle effect on group consciousness, binding in some way persons who used the same mark, whether on account of occupation, religion, or sex. One of our insolvents, a butcher, declared that his father, who could not write his name, used as his mark a pair of scales such as butchers used.[3] A large number of butchers in our data did, in fact, use scales as their mark (Figure 3.4).

While comparing marks with the Indus script characters, I have found that five marks are common to both. In the late nineteenth century, these marks represented specific occupations in the insolvency records. The marks were used by a gardener, a cart-man, a blacksmith, a tinsmith, and bricklayers. While we cannot make any conclusive statements about the meaning of these signs in Harappan times, we can only speculate that the symbols may have indicated an occupation.

Marks Used by Insolvents

The marks presented below are freehand copies of the original.

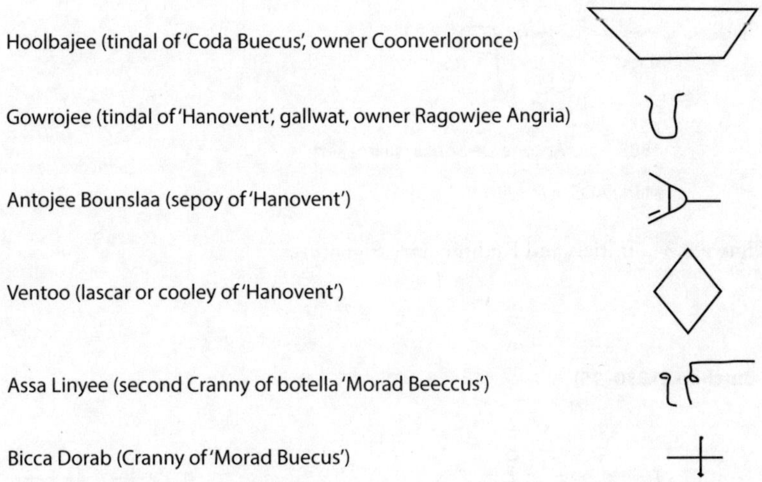

Figure 3.1 Marks of Ship's Crew, 1762

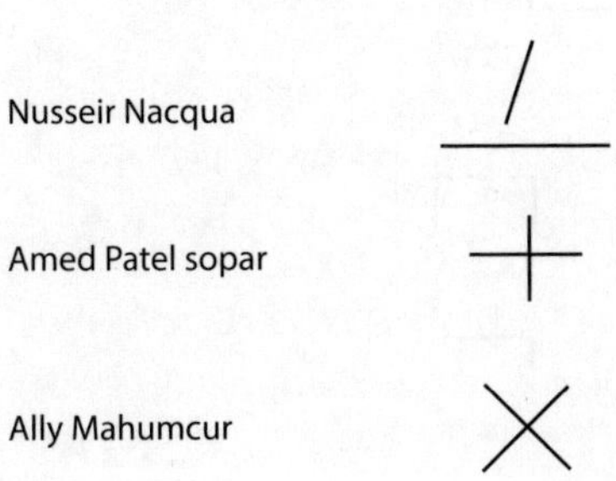

Figure 3.2 Marks of Merchants Importing Rice into Bombay, 1781

1830 Possiagaurea Koli (carpenter)

Signature in well-formed Devanagari followed by poorly formed and misspelt signature in English.

Possia Powria

Father fisherman

Mark: 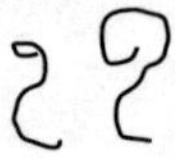

(Integrated by Mohammad Herahem Muckba)

1888 Feleciano Perecra (sailmaker)

Mark: 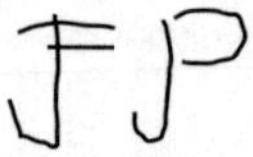

1888 Antone De Souza (sailmaker)

Mark: ADS

Figure 3.3 Initials and Rudimentary Signatures

Butchers (1830–95)

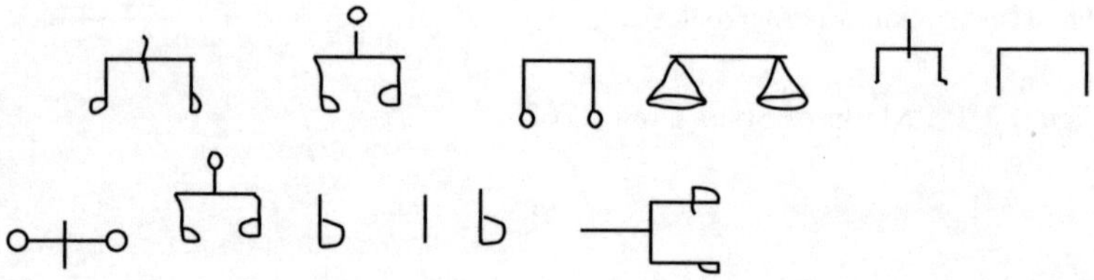

1830 Suttoo Ramjee 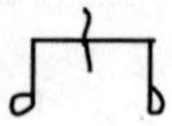

1880 Mohammad Dawood Dhangar 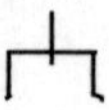

(Cont'd)

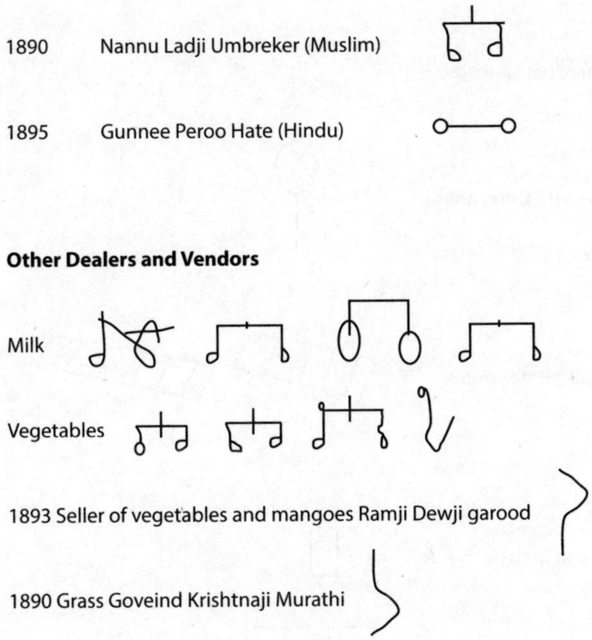

Figure 3.4 Marks Representing Insolvents' Occupation I

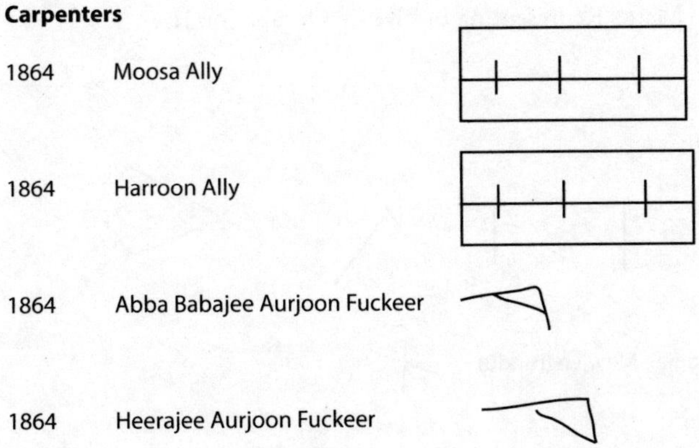

(Cont'd)

Barbers

1853 Ramjee bin Limbajee 

1889 Sukaram Santoo ghate 

Stonemason

1852 Sewajee Bin Ferfojee 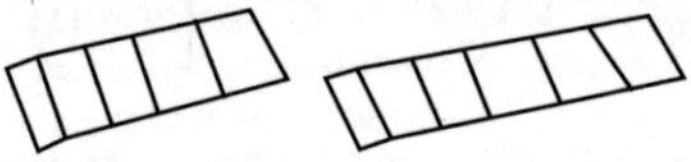

Bricklayers

1857 Dawood Moossa A 

1857 Geerungoo Ellapa 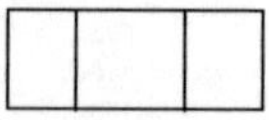

1884 Laxumon Hapa Kamate 

Figure 3.5 Marks Representing Insolvents' Occupation II

Blacksmiths

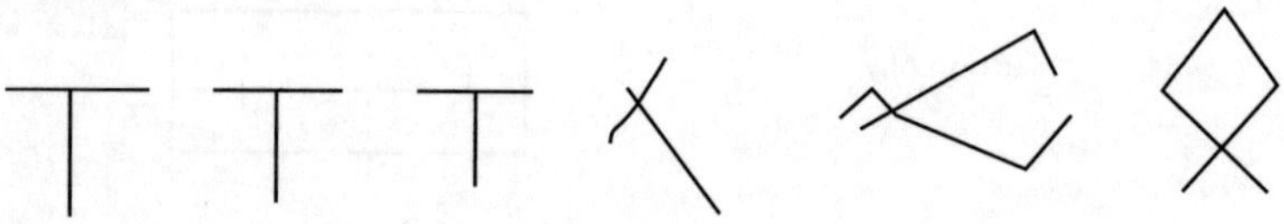

1872 Bhanjee Mowjee (Hindu) 

Dyers

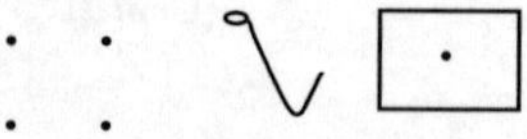

(Cont'd)

1868 Khutree jooma Vurea (Muslim)
('labourers', handles log poles, which are used to transport goods down a stream)

Tailors

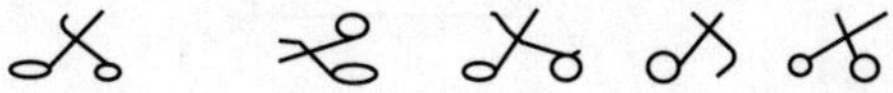

1893 Hari culla Merai 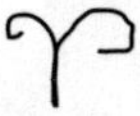

Washermen

1880 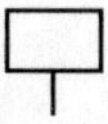

1893 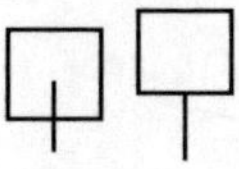

Figure 3.6 Marks Representing Insolvents' Occupation III

Sailors

1863 Mohammad Cassum (lascar) 

Dawood Zina (khallasi) 

1873 Fuckira Moheedin (sailor) 

1876 Dawood Cassum (sailor) 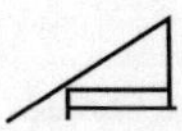

(Cont'd)

1883 Shaik Mahomed Machu (native sailor) 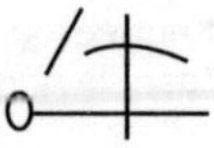

1884 Bagas Fakira (khalasi) 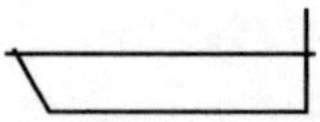

1890 Shaikally Khimji (sailor) 

1893 Sidia Mowji Kharwa (native sailor) (Hindu) 

Fishermen

1830 Gowria Dada Cooly 

1872 Possia Maya 

1872 Bhica Dhurmajee 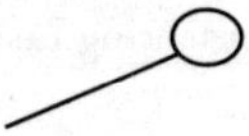

Figure 3.7 Marks Representing Insolvents' Occupation IV

Stonecutters

1864 Suggajee Shaik Halimjee 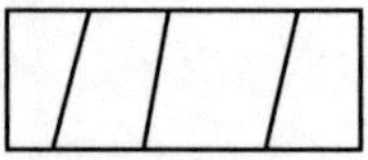

1864 Nama Hurrgba 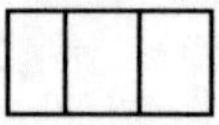

Tile-makers and Turners

1857 Pooja Ram 

1874 Govind Canjee 

(Cont'd)

1874 Asha Fuckira 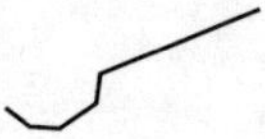

Embroiderers

1866 Mullick chand bin Mullick Noor 

1876 Nunnu Miya 

Musicians

1860 Dawood Khan Dildar Khan (fiddler) co-insolvent of Suckeena (courtesan) 

1870 Gunputee Ruckmajee (musician) 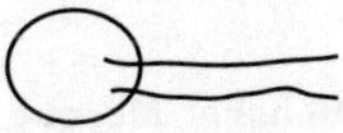

Figure 3.8 Marks Representing Insolvents' Occupation V

Cart Drivers, Cart-men

1847 Hurry Ranojee 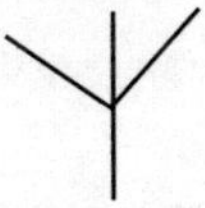

1868 Vuzeer Jamal 

1873 Ambia Mahadoo 

1873 Dajee Heer Gaoud 

1884 Vully Noora Momna 

(Cont'd)

Sweeper

1868 Munglee Ruta 

Weaver

1895 Pobux Hooseinbux soonthijamath 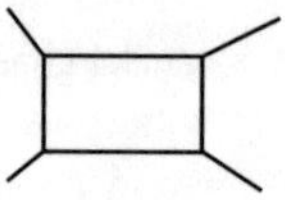

Farrier

1882 Shaik Ebnain Shaik Currim Nalband 

Figure 3.9 Marks Representing Insolvents' Occupation VI

Arabic Alphabet, Mosque ?

1860 Shaik Esmal bin Shaik Mohammed (vegetable seller) 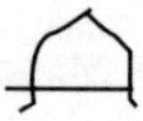

1863 Abdul Currim (sarang) 

1864 Dadoo Meya Abdool Cadur (sailor) 

1864 Shaik Mahomed Shaik Edroos (tindal) 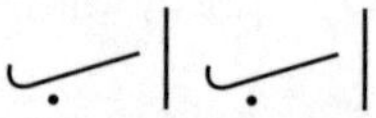

1887 Mumool Khan Ahmed Khan Mea (fitter) 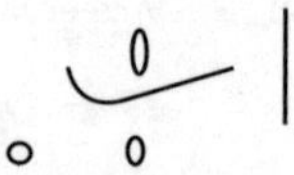

1888 Jaffer Sulam Mohidrri Dulvie (sailor) 

1896 Shaik Esmail Valud Shaik Nubi Sheb Dukni (boiler maker) 

Figure 3.10 Marks Representing Insolvents' Community I

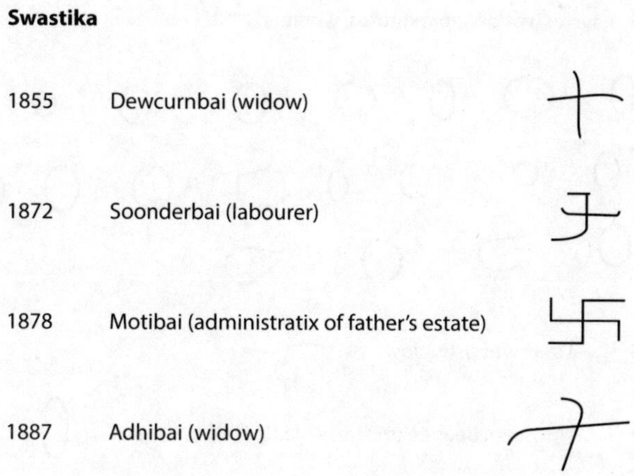

Figure 3.11 Marks Representing Insolvents' Community II

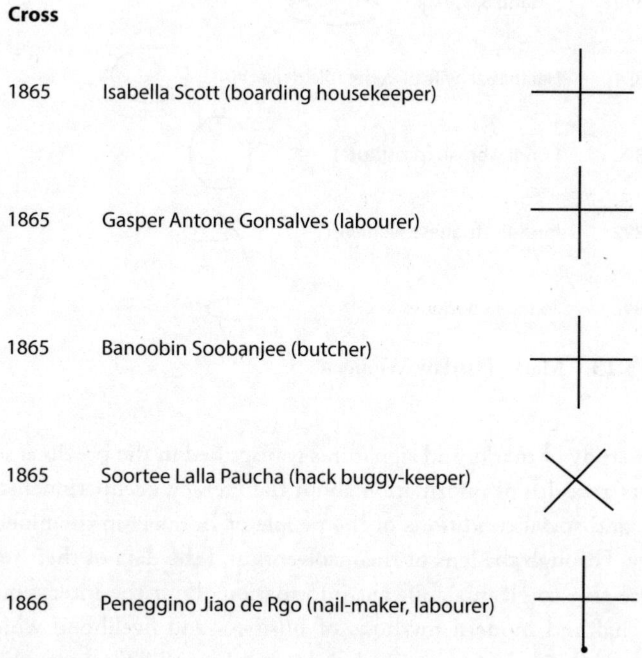

Figure 3.12 Marks Representing Insolvents' Community III

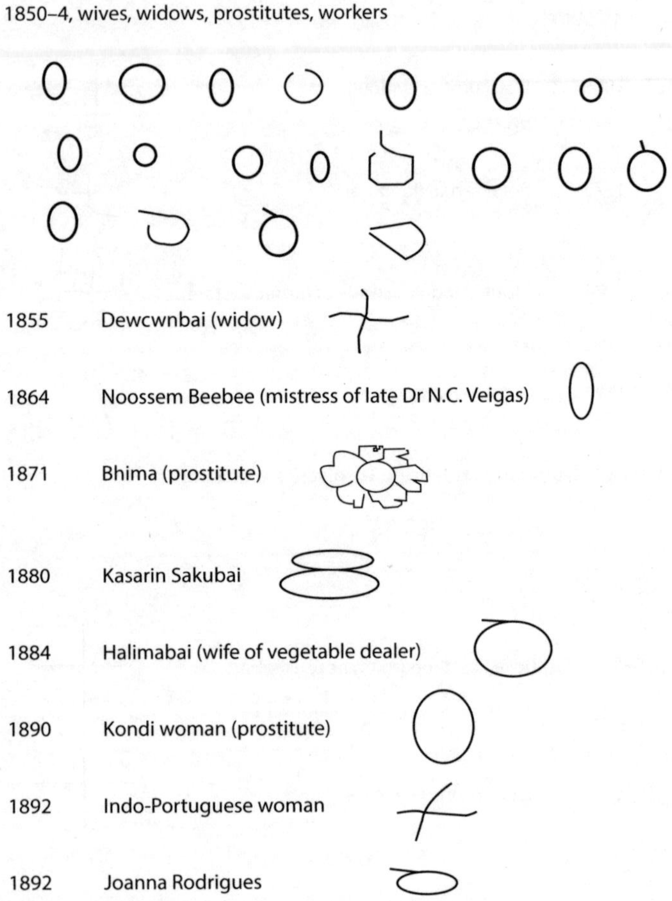

Figure 3.13 Marks Used by Women

The study of marks and signatures transcribed in the previous section presents a wealth of information about the literacy, occupational stratification, and social conditions of the people of Bombay in the nineteenth century. Through the lens of the insolvents and the data of their records, we were able to glean significant information about the intertwining of traditional and modern methods of business and livelihood which we have observed in the cases of Kahandas and Jamsedji Tata and which we shall see through the life of Ayesha. In the following sections, the discussion will be based on the figures given earlier. Another set of references

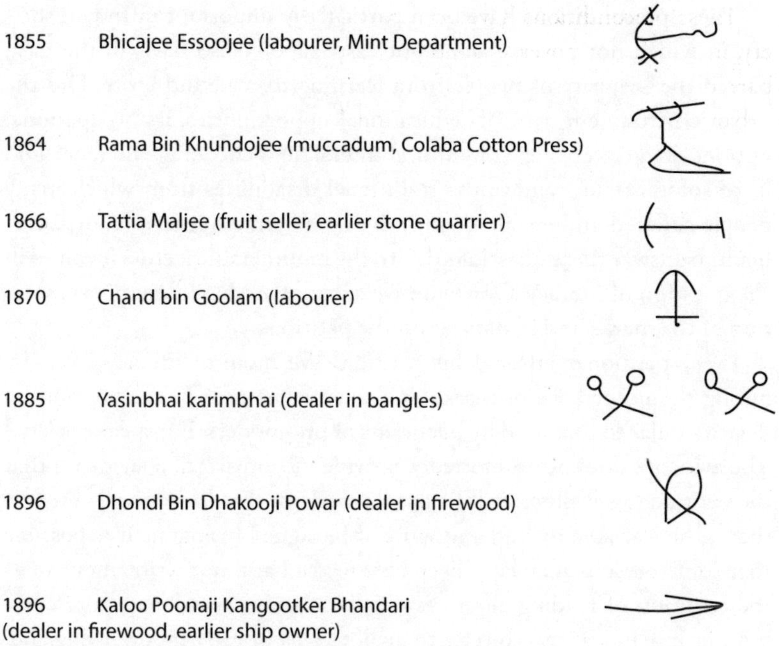

Figure 3.14 Marks of Insolvents' Former Occupation

will be used for the tables created from an analysis of the data. These have been placed in Appendix 3A.

Literacy

The lively convention of the employment of marks for attestation was replaced by the use of thumb impressions. We inquire whether the occurrence of marks may have declined with increase in literacy even before the use of thumb impressions had become widespread.

Literacy is considered to be one of the preconditions of development. Pre-industrial levels of literacy are sometimes looked upon as a significant index of the potential for change in a society. Yet different societies not only adopt different pathways in becoming literate, they also make different uses of literacy. Cultural preconditions often determine who is able to read and write in a given society, as much as they shape the options that are available to and are used by the literate.

These preconditions have been particularly important in Indian society, in which not poverty alone but caste taboos also have, in the past, barred the majority of people from learning to read and write. Did the urban environment, with its educational opportunities, its occupational options, its greater range of cultural interaction, encourage literacy? Did it, to some extent, remove the traditional disabilities from which many people suffered and enable them to become literate? It is, of course, difficult to answer these questions due to the innumerable factors involved in the question of literacy. Our tentative answers are based on an examination of the marks and signatures on the petitions.

Every petitioner attested his petition. We monitor literacy levels by noting the occurrence of marks as against signatures in the petitions, a device similar to that used by historians of pre-modern European society.[4] The evidence does not, admittedly, provide incontrovertible evidence that the petitioner was illiterate if he used a mark, or that he was truly literate, that is, he was able to read and write, if he signed his name. It is possible that some persons may have been able to read and not write, more so as the tradition of reading aloud, especially religious texts, was quite common in Indian society. To refer to analogies from early modern England, neither Shakespeare's father nor his daughter Judith could evidently sign their names. The same was true of Sir Isaac Newton's father, who was not able to sign his will and drew a bird as his mark.[5] It would be misleading to count these persons as being illiterate. Conversely, there may well have been people, like the butcher Ismail Subhan, who were barely able to sign their names and could write little else. Keeping this in mind, at first we classified signatures as well written and poorly written. But this introduced a subjective criterion, and we eventually decided to adopt a three-point code: MRK for marks, SGR for signatures in the Roman script, and SGO for signatures in all other scripts. The latter include Devanagari, Gujarati, Persian, and occasionally Hebrew, Chinese, Malayalam, or Tamil.

We assume that those who were unable to write used a mark. For the purpose of our analysis, we equate the use of a mark with illiteracy. We make another, perhaps more questionable, assumption. Given the status of English as the language of the rulers and the language of much of administration, it was almost certainly privileged. We assume that those who could would use it.

The next section of the analysis refers to the occupational codes and tables related to these. The codes and the tables have been provided at the end of this chapter. In the analysis that follows, we first chart the incidence of marks and the two kinds of signatures over the entire data (Table 3A.2). In the code, SGO stands for signatures in a script other than Roman, generally an Indian script, SGR for signatures in Roman, MRK for marks, and OTH for no signature.

In an endeavour to chart more general literacy levels, we have excluded merchants and clerks (Codes 6 and 7). We assumed persons in these categories could, because of the nature of their work, be assumed to have been literate. Our comprehensive list indicates that a surprisingly large number of petitioners, 56 per cent, signed their names in an Indian language and a considerable number, 28 per cent, signed in English (Table 3A.2). Further, over the period, the numbers of those who used signatures went up and so did the number of those who used English.

Of course, this analysis could be interpreted to mean that more people who were able to sign, and were perhaps literate, were generally more resourceful and had better command of credit and legal facilities, and that their literacy status, as indicated by the use of marks or signatures, does not represent the general level. The data are probably less representative than those based on marriage registers that Stone used for his study.[6] But it is possible that literacy levels themselves went up. There is no reason to suppose that people able to sign were less inclined to petition at the start of the period than was the case later.

Next, we look more closely at the signatures and marks of various artisans, as well as managers, food dealers, and other dealers (Tables 3A.3, 3A.4, 3A.5, 3A.6, 3A.7, 3A.8, and 3A.9). These occupations are quite numerous and correspond with the middle or lower range of incomes. They are, therefore, useful for reviewing literacy rates. We have recorded the number of insolvents in each of these occupations.

Artisans

In the analysis of all artisans, comprising workers in metal, stone, and brick (Occupation Code 13), textile workers (Occupation Code 15), carpenters (Occupation Code 18), mechanics (Occupation Code 19), and all other artisans (Occupation Code 20), it is found that while the majority signed in an Indian script, there was a considerable number using English (SGR) as well as marks (Tables 3A.3, 3A.4, 3A.5, 3A.6, 3A.7). Among carpenters, SGOs are considerably more numerous, while SGRs are fewer (Table 3A.4). Those using marks are more numerous than SGRs but fewer than SGOs. As for mechanics, the number of petitioners is conspicuously small, especially in the first ten years. Here MRKs are generally fewer (Table 3A.5). Among metal, stone, and brick workers, SGRs are altogether fewer and SGOs are conspicuously high. While MRKs are considerable in number here, they are fewer than SGOs. Towards the end of the period, MRKs appear to decline somewhat (Table 3A.6). Among textile workers, the position is similar. SGOs are high, SGRs are few, and MRKs are considerable (Table 3A.7). This group was probably quite varied. While it included many craftsmen and workers, it also contained successful dyers engaged in trade. This activity may have fostered literacy. From the records that I have examined, I have only looked at how the numbers of marks and signatures reflect literacy in different occupations. I have not examined other implications.

Service People

This group comprises domestic servants, miscellaneous service people, and labourers (Occupation Codes 10, 11, and 12 respectively). As compared to the comprehensive list, here we notice a more marked trend (Table 3A.8). SGOs are high throughout. The number of SGOs and SGRs go up and MRKs decline. This is significant as the number of petitioners is high in this group, while at the same time it comprises many people of comparatively humbler means.

During the period of the boom in trade, service people were able to negotiate better wages because of the increase in demand for their services. Perhaps being literate increased their bargaining power.

Food Dealers

In the list for food dealers, SGOs are distinctly more numerous than SGRs. MRKs amount to a considerable number as well (Table 3A.9). Here too, there appears to be a trend. SGOs increase, SGRs go up somewhat, while MRKs decline. Like service people, this is a large and heterogeneous group.

Other Dealers

Among other dealers (Occupation Code 26), SGOs are more numerous than they are among food dealers (Table 3A.10). SGRs increase and MRKs decrease over the period.

Managers

Managers are a heterogeneous group. The majority signed their names in an Indian script, about a quarter signed in English, while a very small number used marks (Table 3A.11).

As we have mentioned, being able to sign did not necessarily mean a person was truly literate. But it does distinguish the person who was able sign from those who used marks and were not able to write at all. The striking feature of our results is that those who signed were impressively numerous and that, taking signatures as an index of literacy, the curve seems to go up.

Official, private, and missionary institutions played a prominent part in breaking, to some extent, the traditional monopoly over literacy exercised by the upper classes. Indeed, the activities of the Bombay Native Education Society, founded in 1824 and later designated as the Elphinstone Native Education Institution, were resisted by some upper-caste persons such as Dadaji Dhackji, who opposed the admission of lower-caste boys to the Marathi schools of the society. Dadaji candidly declared that this would destroy the monopoly of the higher castes over government jobs. The records of the Society show that many sons of artisans, cultivators, and fishermen read in the schools of the Society. In addition, private instruction, often imparted free, along with Christian missionary activity played its part.[7]

Our material occasionally reveals vivid instances of the urge of humbler persons to become literate. One of these is a very early petition, dated 1830. Gowria Dada Cooly, a fisherman who was in jail for debt, petitioned for protection, along with his son, Possia Gowria Cooly, who was a carpenter. Gowria inserted a mark that looks clearly like a fishing hook. His son wrote his name first in well-formed Devanagari and then wrote it again in English. His English handwriting appears somewhat ill formed, and he misspelt his name, spelling his middle name 'Powria' instead of 'Gowria'. As evocative as the marks and signatures on this petition are the details of the debts for which Gowria was in jail. The total debt was Rs 393. Most of this sum was owed to a number of Marwaris and to Gungather Mestry, who may have been a carpenter with whom Possia worked (Figure 3.3).[8]

In the following section we consider trends in incomes, especially in connection to commercial fluctuations.

Incomes

We have mentioned that net receipts are recorded on the debit side of each balance sheet and that for the purpose of our analysis, we take this figure as being equivalent to income, even though in many cases this figure may include items that may not have been income, such as amounts received on decrees of court, or amounts claimed as debt, or amounts drawn from a firm—perhaps out of its capital. Yet it is our impression that net receipts consist mainly of incomes. In assessing the authenticity of these figures, we should consider the possible existence of a built-in bias. It is arguable that insolvents may have been inclined to understate their incomes and overstate their essential expenditure. If so, we have no way of correcting this bias. Yet it is equally plausible that since petitions were scrutinized by the court before they were admitted and that false statements made them liable to be rejected, they may not have been far off the true figure. Traders and merchants may have been able to understate their incomes more easily. We have not worked out tables of the annual incomes of merchants and brokers with a debt amount of five digits and above. These incomes are included in the basic income file [Table 3A.18(i)]. For the years 1860–6, certain aspects of the debts of these insolvents are analysed (Tables 3A.19 and 3A.20). Here we consider types of debts and types of creditors. Table 3A.21 gives year-wise numbers of the petitions of these insolvents, the numbers of those who got an interim order for protection, and the numbers in jail. We have computed annual average incomes in the manner described next.

The petitions mention the income of the petitioner for the period over which the debt was contracted, generally giving the figures for each year or for a given period. Thus, in each balance sheet there are generally several income entries stretched over the entire debt period. First we calculate the number of months for each income entry. Then we divide the income amount of each entry by the number of months to get the monthly income for that year in the entry. If the starting date for a monthly entry is later than the 20th, we ignore that month. If the end date is earlier than the 10th, we ignore that month. Then we calculate the yearly or fractional year income, as the case may be, by multiplying the monthly income by the number of months for that entry. This is done for each entry of each petitioner. Finally, we add all income figures for each year to get the total income the petitioner received for that year. The merit of this procedure is that it uses individual incomes recorded for short periods, generally two to ten years, for building a continuous income series for the entire period of the study, based on all the income figures of all insolvents with the exception of those merchants and brokers whose debts ran into a minimum of five digits or more. An important item of information that eludes us is periods of unemployment. We have tabulated this information in the basic income file [Table 3A.18(i)]. Average annual incomes are tabulated for each year in blocks, starting with incomes of less than Rs 50, then proceeding upwards in blocks of Rs 100 to incomes of Rs 5,000 and above. The percentage of each block to the total number of incomes is also given. It should be noted that the grand total of petitioners drawing incomes for all the years and the total number of petitioners for the entire period do not coincide as the petitioners are counted for each of the years in which they drew an income. The former figure is higher. The method of calculating the income for each year and each fractional year of each petitioner has been devised to generate the basic income file [Table 3A.18(i)].

Two general features of the income files may be noticed. One is that there is a concentration of numbers at the lower end of the income scale, comprising yearly incomes between Rs 50 and Rs 600, and another concentration at the upper end, covering incomes above Rs 3,000. In other words, while insolvents of all income categories petitioned, it was in these groups that they were most numerous. We show elsewhere that a very large number of petitioners actually got protection. The high incidence of petitions at the two ends of the income spectrum emphasizes the active function of the law in protecting the poorest as well as the wealthiest debtors.

The second general feature concerns the temporal trend that pervades our data. An upswing in the number of income figures, which reflects the number of petitioners, occurred from about 1864, peaking in about 1870, and very gradually declining thereafter. These were the years of the crash of the cotton trade. The figures suggest that the crisis affected people from a wide range of incomes and was spread over many years. Of course, we must consider that those who petitioned may not have been led to do so simply because of hardship and indebtedness. The fact that so many petitioners got protection must have encouraged others to seek the benefit of the law.

From observing what levels of incomes are found among insolvent petitioners, we move on to consider whether we can use this data to study income trends. An initial objection to constructing trends from this data may be that they might not be representative. We have no way of determining the point conclusively, although we have argued earlier that the social and economic profiles of insolvents may not have been altogether different from those of other city dwellers. Another objection may be that the database is relatively small for the observation of trends. We endeavour to overcome this difficulty by looking at the more numerous groups.

Artisans

Our first analysis comprises all artisans (Occupation Codes 13, 15, 18, 19, and 20). This is a large group and the income data shows relatively greater flux.

There is perhaps only a fine line dividing artisans and skilled service people who comprise Occupation Code 19, or mechanics. We have included them among artisans (Table 3A.22). A notable feature of incomes in this analysis is that the sharp swing and dip associated with the commercial boom and depression are noticeable here as it is elsewhere in our study. With 1860 as the base, we notice that incomes went up sharply from 1864, dipped in 1874, rose again from 1884, and thereafter, with some fluctuations, remained moderately high except for the terminal year, 1898, when they were lower. As compared to 1860 and 1864, artisanal incomes increased and, but for a year or so—in 1881 they touched the 1860 level—they stayed steadily higher.

Next, we notice the incomes of a number of subsets of artisans, carpenters, mechanics, metal, brick, and stone workers, and textile workers.

Carpenters

Carpenters (Occupation Code 18) may have shared certain special characteristics. The extensive town-building activities in the city from the 1860s onwards may have provided particularly good employment to them. Nineteenth-century buildings involved much woodwork in stairways, doors and windows, and beams. Domestic furniture, often modelled on Western styles but also incorporating Indian motifs, filled the homes of the well-to-do. Their special skills may have brought carpenters into contact with contractors and entrepreneurs as well as with wealthy clients, giving them opportunities for upward mobility. Yet carpenters were also peculiarly vulnerable to indebtedness arising from fluctuations in the city's trade. They invariably used capital borrowed from clients, the source of which could suddenly dry up at times when trade was depressed. There were certainly more insolvent petitioners among carpenters than there were among mechanics, metal and stone workers, and textile workers.

The income profile of carpenters generally follows that of artisans as a whole, but at a lower level (Table 3A.23).

Mechanics

The incomes of mechanics (Occupation Code 19) may have been more varied than those of carpenters, considering the fact that they embraced a variety of skills. The conspicuously high figure for 1864, 1868, and 1869 is accounted for by the very high income of a single individual, a European plumber, William Patterson, whose total income for those years amounted to Rs 73,027.[9] Skilled modern-sector workmen such as plumbers could perhaps command higher incomes but, in general, the incomes of mechanics were not markedly different from those of carpenters (Table 3A.23).

Metal, Brick, and Stone Workers

The incomes of workers in metal, brick, and stone (Occupation Code 13) closely resembled those of carpenters and mechanics (Table 3A.25).

Textile Workers

By contrast, the incomes of textile workers seems to have been higher than those of the other artisans, while at the same time there were fewer insolvents among them (Table 3A.26).

The high income figures for 1892, 1893, 1894, and 1895 reflect mainly the high incomes of two dyers. Amen Jacob Bhujpur Khatri's incomes for the years 1893–4 and 1894–5 were Rs 29,739 and Rs 25,417 respectively.[10] The incomes of another dyer, Abdul Ali Halai, for 1891–2 and 1892–3 were Rs 16,705 and Rs 23,068 respectively.[11]

Thus dyers, all of whom were Muslims, were often considerably more affluent than many other artisans.[12]

Other Artisans

This group consists of all other types of artisans than those noted above. They are enumerated in Occupation Code 20. We have not classified each type separately as the total number in each is small and no meaningful study could be made. The incomes of these artisans appear to be higher than the incomes of those listed earlier. This suggests that individual members of this group may have had higher incomes (Table 3A.27).

Clerks and Writers

The incomes of clerks and writers signing in the Roman script (Occupation Code 6) appear to be conspicuously higher than those of writers and accountants using an Indian script, mainly Marathi or Gujarati (Occupation Code 7). The services of the latter were used mainly by numerous smaller Indian traders. They often wrote for several clients and earned a daily wage, whereas English writers were in demand as full-time employees in the offices of the larger mercantile firms of the city, both Indian and European. The income differential graphically illustrates the privileged position of English and the material advantage that the knowledge of the language conferred (Tables 3A.28 and 3A.29).

The incomes of Indian-language clerks peaked in 1864, that is, not at the beginning of the boom but close to its end. This may reflect a time lag in the multiplier effect of export trade on the indigenous market. Thereafter, they fell somewhat. For the rest of the period, they remained moderately high throughout, staying well over the 1860 level. The incomes of English clerks went up sharply earlier, namely in 1862, that is, nearer the beginning of the trade boom, and attained higher levels still in certain years, namely in 1865 and 1876. High levels of income among English clerks are noticeable for the period 1862 to 1877. In the following years they stayed moderately high, dropping to the pre-boom level and were lower in the last two years, namely 1897 and 1898.

There were many more English writers among insolvents than there were Indian-language writers. The reasons for this are, at best, a matter of conjecture. English writers, many of whom worked in the offices of firms connected with overseas trade, may themselves have traded and may have been more liable to get into debt in acute trade crises. They were probably more immediately affected by the adverse fortunes of their employers.

They were doubtless more aware of the legal system, which offered relief, and they readily availed of it. We are not able to say whether their absolute numbers may have been greater.

Managers

Managers (Occupation Code 8) include dubashes and mehtas who were generally literate and probably moved with ease in the world of business offices, as well as jobbers in mills and elsewhere in the labour market. The latter were not always literate and they functioned close to the ground level of the circuits of labour. Those we have grouped as managers were, therefore, somewhat heterogeneous. While many mehtas may have functioned as clerks and accountants, others we have grouped as managers were probably more closely integrated with labour.

The incomes of managers went up sharply in 1861, and in 1862 were almost three times the 1860 figure. After that, they gradually declined. There were sharp peaks and troughs and in several years they fell below the 1860 level. The incomes of managers were generally higher than those of both Indian and English writers, although in certain years they were lower than the latter. After 1872 there were many years in which the incomes of managers fell below the 1860 figure. The sharper peaks and troughs may have been a function of the more marked heterogeneity of this group (Table 3A.30). More English writers petitioned as insolvents than did managers.

Service People

The income levels of this group (Occupation Codes 10, 11, and 12) were, on the whole, lower than those of the groups we have so far considered (Table 3A.31). The conspicuously high figure for 1865 represents mainly the income of a single individual, Abu Ali, who was in jail when he petitioned. He is described in the petition as a 'servant'. His income for the period from 19 October 1864 to 15 May 1865 was Rs 253,006.[13]

Cases such as this raise significant issues concerning the position of servants and of others who were perhaps underprivileged in society, such as widows and other women. In many cases, these persons appear as co-petitioners although they did not have independent incomes. The question comes to mind whether they may have been induced to enter their names as parties to the debt and then made to go to jail if one of them was required to do so. Abu Ali may have himself earned the large income noted in his petition and may have got into debt. In the commercial climate of the 1860s, servants working for traders and others did trade on their own, often recklessly. On the other hand, it is also possible that Ali may have been used as a proxy for the liabilities of an influential master. It is noticeable that the incomes of the service group were higher in the base years, 1860 and 1861, than they were in the years following the end of the boom, and that thereafter the level remained almost constant for the rest of the period.

Food Dealers

The incomes of dealers of articles of food and drink (Occupation Code 16) went up steadily from the base year, 1860, and showed little signs of diminishing in the years when trade crashed (Table 3A.32). This fact should perhaps lead us to qualify the character of the crash itself. Unlike the incomes of artisans, clerical and managerial workers, and the service group, those of food dealers were almost uniformly high. Moreover, they showed a marked increase in the late 1860s and 1870s. Significantly, they peaked at the time of the famine, 1876 to 1878, and went up again from 1883 onwards. Food dealers may have benefitted from the scarcity of the famine. The year of highest income for food dealers, 1896, coincided with the year when plague struck the city. This, too, was a year of famine.

Other Dealers

The figures for the incomes of other dealers (Occupation Code 26) resemble those for food dealers but unlike the latter, they peaked in the three years immediately after the end of the American Civil War, a continuation perhaps of the trade boom (Table 3A.33). They did not go up in the famine years but, like the incomes of food dealers, were high in the 1880s and 1890s.

Landlords

A significant aspect of land use in a city is the way urban space generates rental income. Rental incomes are listed in the balance sheets of insolvents.

In all, 429 petitioners reported receiving income from rent. They belonged to various religious and occupational groups. The amounts too were quite varied. The existence of rental income opens up the question of how property was acquired and by whom. Doubtless there were times when there were rapid transfers of property. This happened in the late 1860s and early 1870s, at the time of the commercial crisis. But apart from distress sales, at least some property had been acquired by their owners in an earlier period of the city's history. It is well known that among the communities who had done so were the Parsis. To a remarkable extent, our data indicates the conspicuous place of Parsis among large rental earners. Admittedly, we are looking only at insolvents, but that very fact suggests that there were probably large landlords among other Parsis. This particular Parsi presence was probably related to close connections with the colonial ruling authorities in earlier times.

At the same time, our study identifies the large number of people with more meagre means who supplemented their incomes from rent. This must have been particularly important in times of unemployment and commercial distress. It was a specifically urban source of income.

Milk Vendors

The victualling trades occupied a significant place in city life. Among these was the sale of milk. Altogether 271 petitioners reported earnings from milk-vending. They included those who had earned a considerable amount thereby. In four years, from 1871 to 1875, the widow Suckoobaee earned Rs 32,850.[14] For others, milk-vending supplemented more substantial incomes from other sources. The *cusban* or dancing girl Rahimanbi and her co-petitioners, the 'fiddlers' (sarangi players) Hoosain Moideen and Ameer Moideen, reported an income of Rs 2,348 from their work as courtesan and accompanists for the years 1859 to 1860. They declared an additional income of Rs 360 from the sale of milk for 1860.[15] There were many who earned modest amounts from selling milk. Nurbheram Pitamber earned a mere Rs 42 from 1864 to 1866.[16] There are many names among milk vendors which suggest that their bearers were from the north, often with the appellation 'Pardesi'—foreigner—either at the beginning or at the end. Names such as Ramsarup Bhikh Pardesi[17] or Hanuman Sahaye Purdesi[18] have a clearly northern ring. In other names such as Kisson Hira Iyer Gowli or Maniram alias Laxuman Ayeer, Iyer and Ayeer may stand for Aheer, suggesting that their bearers belonged to a caste engaged in milk production. The demand for milk in the expanding city may have attracted such people to Bombay. The incentive may have been stronger during times of famine.

Milk consumers were very largely Indians, whereas meat was a prominent item in the diet of Europeans. The rules of the meat market ensured the supply of the freshest meat to Europeans.[19] By contrast, the authorities showed less concern for the supply of milk. When in 1856 the Water Supply Committee passed an order requiring cows and buffaloes to be removed to Mahim because of water scarcity in Bombay, there was a public outcry. Several Hindu and Muslim citizens petitioned the Committee in protest that the order did not affect Europeans who kept horses that consumed more water.[20]

Other than such measures, perhaps the biggest hazard milk vendors encountered was the loss of cattle. The milk vendors Babanbhoy Dadabhoy and Chandbee became insolvent when their buffaloes died.[21] Besides, with the growth of the city and the spread of buildings, there was a shrinkage of pastureland.

Real Incomes

The real incomes of all city dwellers were affected by prices, especially of articles of essential consumption. If we consider the incomes of the most numerous occupational category of insolvents—clerks signing in English—we will see that while money incomes went up in the boom years of the early 1860s, real incomes in terms of the prices both of wheat and common rice declined. Another decline took place in the famine years of the 1870s. In the last two years, 1897 and 1898, real incomes fell when prices, especially those of wheat, went up steeply as a consequence of poor harvests in the previous years.[22]

Except for these dips, the real incomes of the group, which formed a part of the potentially significant class of Western-educated intelligentsia, stayed above the 1861 level. But a sudden price rise, such as that of wheat in 1897, could place a substantial burden on their resources. It is possible that as people whose aspirations and life styles were more middle class, they consumed more wheat than they did jowar, bajra, and common rice. We do not have price figures for jowar and bajra, but the price of common rice did not escalate very sharply. The striking fact is that clerks and writers were sufficiently cohesive and confident to articulate their hardship, and that the government did not overlook their grievances. In 1897 the majority of clerks employed in Bombay city petitioned the government for a raise in salaries. A committee appointed to investigate prices reported that there had been a general rise in prices, that food stuffs had become 20 per cent more expensive, and that they were unlikely to drop to the levels of the 1870s and 1880s.[23]

As I have shown, the records of insolvents' petitions contain data that enable us to examine the use of marks and signatures, and these indicate that the number of petitioners signing in Indian languages was high and constant. In some occupations, the number of people signing in English increased and the use of marks decreased. The salient feature of incomes was that in many cases they fluctuated with the commercial fluctuations. In this period, there was a relatively large group of domestic servants who became insolvent and submitted petitions. The large number of people in these occupations shows that they were aware of the law and could refer to the law to protect themselves as they sought a way out of indebtedness.

Further, the high number of signatures in an Indian language and the rise in the number of signatures in English suggest that people in these occupations were able to learn how to sign. In the case of food dealers as well, the rising trend in the number of signatures in an Indian language and in English suggests that this group could access the means to learn how to sign.

Appendix

Occupation Codes and Tables

Occupation Codes

1 Medical practitioner: public vaccinator, apothecary, bone-setter, druggist, nurse, midwife, compounder, native doctor, assistant dentist, graduate of Grant Medical College

2 Teacher, priest: *mujawar*, caste inviter, *ramosee*, astrologer, 'fukeer or a priest or beggar', sexton of St Thomas's Cathedral (1880, 494),* 'worshipper' (1894, 326)

3 Other professional: architect, solicitor, pleader, engineer, chemist, assistant engineer, proprietor of printing press, surveyor, builder, timber measurer, law agent, reporter, journalist, editor, registered candidate at Bombay Court of Small Causes, engineer and iron founder, proprietor and publisher of *Sunday Comic* (1895, 123), candidate at Bombay Court of Small Causes (1892, 566)

4 Courtesan, dancing girl, brothel house keeper, 'singing girl' (1892, 70)

5 Other performing artists: actor, musician, magician, music teacher, proprietor of dramatic company, native band supplier, proprietor of circus, native drummer, tom-tom player, theatrical manager, musical instructor, conjurer (80), proprietors of Parsi Original Dramatic Co. (1887, 460)

6 Clerk, writer, accountant (English): 'Bharati proprietor of press' signing in Roman, compositor, proofreader, proof examiner, draughtsman,

* Figures within brackets refer to the number and year of a petition.

assistant reader, librarian, cotton examiner, examiner in press signing in Roman, plan maker, printer, sorter of railway mail service, ticket printer

7 Clerk, writer, accountant (Marathi, Gujarati, Persian, Hebrew): examiner in press, printer, petition writer, lithographer, compositor, loading inspector, weighing clerk, all signing SGO (Gujarati, Devanagari, Persian, Hebrew), Mooltanee writer, Hebrew clerk, Marwari writer, number-taker

8 Manager, jobber, contractor, mehta: *dubash*, *muccaddum*, assistant jobber, *gomastha*, *moonim*, house rent collector, money collector, bill collector, *karkoon*, recovery-man, receiver, overseer, wharfinger, loading inspector, delivery foreman, supervisor, godown keeper, store keeper, foreman, inspector, stevedore, supplier to ships, sub-inspector, superintendent, inspector, assistant, stock taker, business of *hamalage* (1887, 275)

9 Hotel and boarding house keeper: tavern keeper, refreshment room keeper, supplier of dinners, housekeeper, matron

10 Domestic servant, waiter: groom, butler, coachman

11 Miscellaneous service: *dhobi* (washerman), barber, sepoy, fireman, *chobdar*, butler, water carrier, messman, cook, salt *patra* cleaner, cloth stamper, sweeper, cloth-cutting assistant, constable, cloth bales packer, pressman, watchman, umbrella repairer, cotton sampler, time keeper, billiards marker, corn grinder, lighter, wool cleaner, *havildar*, glass cleaner, carriage cleaner, loading foreman, police havildar, corpse bearer, undertaker, measurer in Chamber of Commerce, number taker, loader, skin flayer, 'opium boiler', 'cot woman for khallasee' (1862, 2998), drum beater, operator at phone exchange, proof-sheet deliverer, pressman *of Bombay Samachar*, pressman of *Times of India*.

12 Labourer: job labourer, porter, *hamal*, coolie, 'workman'

13 Worker in metal, stone, brick: stonemason, stonecutter, tile maker, tile turner, brick maker, bricklayer, dealer and manufacturer of bricks, mason, potter, gilder, brazier, coppersmith, blacksmith, horse shoe maker, tin smith, tin pot maker, tin plate maker, electro plater, dammerman (1886, 340), lime pounder, gilder, 'dealer in electro plating and gilding', kettle maker, metal filer, glazier

14 Jeweller, goldsmith, silversmith: dealer in gold/silver, dealer in pearls, dealer in silver, petty dealer in false pearls, stamper in gold/silver, silver cutter, silver engraver, German silver ornaments maker

15 Textile worker: dyer, weaver, carpet maker, spinner, *choodri* binder (1879, 183), carding master, mill hand, sizer, 'mule jobber' in mill, 'silkman' (1898, 109), silk cleaner, lace weaver (1893, 329), spinning master (1898, 374), cotton spinner, apprentice in mill, labourer at Framji Petit Spinning and Weaving Co. Ltd (1892, 588)

16 Food and beverage processor, seller: butcher, milkman, country liquor seller, toddy drawer, baker, dealer in spices, dealer in asafoetida, soda water manufacturers, 'native cheroots' maker (1886, 434, widow,), snuff seller, native cheroot seller, sweetmeat maker, 'gowwala'

17 Opium seller, speculator, broker

18 Carpenter: *mistry*, cabinet maker, furniture maker

19 Mechanic: fitter, turner, plumber, riveter, joiner, hole borer, apprentice, moulder, 'armer', engine turner, shipwright, mechanical workshop keeper

20 Other artisans: saddle maker, saddler, harness maker, coach builder, workbox maker, frame maker, sawyer, woodcutter, boiler maker, watch maker, cobbler, shoemaker, tanner, carriage repairer, boiler repairer, musical instrument repairer, painter, polish-man, polisher, tailor, embroiderer, tassel maker (*patwagee*, 1862, 3176), carpet maker, sail maker, hemp rope maker, rope manufacturer, turban folder, turban binder, fireworks preparer, bookbinder, glass painter, ticket painter, picture painter, photographer, filer, fileman, metal filer, knife grinder, pearl borer, caulker of ships, cooper, sculptor/undertaker, gunnybag sewer, country soap maker, carder, cane worker, basket maker, cane-man, rattan worker (1895, 393), diamond setter, diamond filer, diamond polisher, mashal and kite maker, brass hinges manufacturer, bullock cart builder, engraver, cage maker, boat builder, leather dresser (1895, 339), surgical instruments maker ('European', 1898, 179), iron safe maker, metal filer, decorator, lapidary (1884, 16), county paper manufacturer, tools polisher, gun repairer, lock repairer, locksmith, hinges maker, key setter, nail maker, painter lithographer ('East Asian', 1895, 91), lithographer

21 Shipping, boat worker: *succanee* (pilot of ship or boat), fireman ship, boat supplier, ship chandler, renter country craft, shipping boats, lessee small boats, renter country boats, 'khulasi'

22 Beggar, begging Brahmin, mendicant, *bairagi*

23 Other transport: cart driver, buggy driver, coachman, farrier, horse breaker, livery stable keeper, steam roller driver, horse keeper, guard

of Great Indian Peninsula Railway (GIPR), station master, engine driver, foreman of GIPR, railway foreman, traffic inspector of Bombay Baroda and Central India Railway (BBCIR), number taker of GIPR, brakesman, time keeper of GIPR, 'starter', starter Bombay Tramway Co., conductor Tramway Co., inspector Bombay Tramway Co, weighing inspector of GIPR, time keeper of GIPR (1888, 282)

24 Government servant (126): preventive officer, constable, captain, telegraph master, signaler bailie, health inspector, inspector of police, assistant mail officer, sub-inspector Bombay Municipality water works, subedar marine battalion Bombay Infantry (1889, 208), public accountant, inspector Bombay Port Trust, sorter railway mail, inspector salt department, foreman fire brigade (1895, 85), police inspector, engine driver port trust, police havildar

25 Others, diver, veterinarian, sorcerer (1871, 8037 MU), student, 'proprietor', housewife, widow, varied numerous sources of income (1860, 3525), builder of houses, auctioneer, occupation not stated, soap manufacturer (EU 1886, 353), 'working partner' (1888, 548), 'captain' (1885, 132), 'horse racing businessman' (1892 621), 'apprentice' (1888, 282), engine driver Oriental Spinning and Weaving Co., furniture hirer, doctor of horse (1866, 4453), proprietor of hair cutting and dressing saloon, proprietor of American Steam Laundry (1883, 206), Secretary to H.E. Dewan of Maharaja of Kashmir, Dhanjibhai Kuverji Tasker (1887, 103), administrator of estate (1878, 105)

26 Other dealers, supplier: haberdasher, cutlery, cows, cotton, silk, and so on

27 Dealer in cloth, piece goods: shawls, clothes, gold lace

28 Broker, commission agent, speculator: dealer in shares, insurance agent, carriage and horse broker, charterer of steamers for passengers, shares merchant, petty agent, money broker, share speculator, government paper speculator, sub-carting agent, speculator, petty speculator, agent supplying telegraphic information, rain speculator, general speculator, hundi speculator, speculator gold/silver

29 Unemployed

30 Hawker, pedlar (including hawker in clothes)

31 Merchant, auctioneer firms, general merchant, 'petty merchant'

32 Pensioner, dependent

33 Landlord, person living mainly on unearned income

34 Cultivator

35 Fisherman, fisherwoman

36 Shroff: coin exchanger, moneylender, Mooltanee, gold and silver assayer, Marwari, hundi broker, dealer, money changer, bullion broker, dealer

Tables

Table 3A.1 Complete List of Insolvencies, Year-wise

Year	Total Petitions Filed	No. of Petitioners in Database	No. of Petitions in Database	Total Missing	Total IOB*	Total in Jail
1860	290	255	232	58	214	26
1861	331	320	297	34	296	39
1862	390	410	360	30	385	65
1863	279	313	272	7	285	33
1864	292	315	291	1	237	38
1865	340	301	281	59	177	33
1866	444	413	374	70	338	81
1867	248	461	437	111	262	76
1868	514	461	423	91	398	92
1869	580	525	498	82	475	109
1870	890	806	740	150	701	112
1871	796	748	712	84	656	117
1872	836	823	747	89	714	105
1873	799	770	720	79	625	82
1874	582	615	582	0	504	54
1875	632	628	588	44	498	71
1876	620	581	546	74	467	35
1877	470	464	425	45	365	37
1878	565	563	511	54	473	41
1879	606	547	503	103	427	41
1880	599	604	533	66	572	60
1881	489	506	446	43	448	38
1882	517	511	435	82	453	42
1883	509	561	497	12	510	31
1884	546	600	532	14	491	17
1885	590	636	535	55	587	57
1886	540	536	488	52	496	32
1887	698	689	611	87	619	31
1888	579	600	531	48	516	21

(Cont'd)

Table 3A.1 (*Cont'd*)

Year	Total Petitions Filed	No. of Petitioners in Database	No. of Petitions in Database	Total Missing	Total IOB*	Total in Jail
1889	680	533	488	192	467	33
1890	709	454	428	281	376	19
1891	681	519	487	194	479	25
1892	685	648	605	80	579	44
1893	689	535	504	185	485	41
1894	614	566	525	89	374	21
1895	648	624	584	64	580	36
1896	630	563	508	122	520	18
1897	484	462	431	53	422	16
1898	514	514	488	26	484	26
Total	**22,205**	**20,980**	**19,195**	**3,010**	**17,955**	**1,895**

Note: * Interim order for protection granted.

Table 3A.2 Complete List of Identifying Marks

Year	No. and % of SGO	No. and % of SGR	No. and % of MRK	No. and % of OTH	Total No. of Identifying Marks
1860	121	60	58	1	240
	50.42%	25.00%	24.17%	0.42%	
1861	171	67	69	2	309
	55.34%	21.68%	22.33%	0.65%	
1862	194	89	111	5	399
	48.62%	22.31%	27.82%	1.25%	
1863	144	49	106	0	299
	48.16%	16.39%	35.45%	0.00%	
1864	148	47	61	36	292
	50.68%	69.10%	20.89%	12.33%	
1865	129	55	56	0	240
	53.75%	22.92%	23.33%	0.00%	
1866	166	74	82	21	343
	48.40%	21.57%	23.91%	6.12%	
1867	213	91	114	3	421
	50.59%	21.62%	27.08%	0.71%	

(*Cont'd*)

Table 3A.2 (*Cont'd*)

Year	No. and % of SGO	No. and % of SGR	No. and % of MRK	No. and % of OTH	Total No. of Identifying Marks
1868	221	62	115	0	398
	55.53%	15.58%	28.89%	0.00%	
1869	293	92	103	2	490
	59.80%	18.78%	21.02%	0.41%	
1870	413	168	117	6	704
	58.66%	23.86%	16.62%	0.85%	
1871	405	154	108	3	670
	60.45%	22.99%	16.12%	0.45%	
1872	394	212	162	3	765
	51.50%	27.71%	20.39%	0.39%	
1873	392	171	122	8	693
	56.57%	24.68%	17.60%	1.15%	
1874	313	118	88	41	560
	55.89%	21.07%	15.71%	7.32%	
1875	327	154	94	3	578
	56.57%	26.64%	16.26%	0.52%	
1876	316	160	68	0	544
	58.09%	29.41%	12.50%	0.00%	
1877	244	121	74	4	443
	55.08%	27.31%	16.70%	0.90%	
1878	312	138	87	0	537
	58.10%	25.70%	16.20%	0.00%	
1879	273	154	75	1	503
	54.27%	30.62%	14.91%	0.20%	
1880	338	161	84	3	586
	57.68%	27.47%	14.33%	0.51%	
1881	250	145	85	2	482
	51.87%	30.08%	17.63%	0.41%	
1882	267	118	91	4	480
	55.63%	24.58%	18.96%	0.83%	
1883	296	159	63	1	519
	57.03%	30.64%	12.14%	0.19%	
1884	290	134	110	28	562
	51.60%	23.84%	19.57%	4.98%	
1885	341	162	101	0	604
	56.46%	26.82%	16.72%	0.00%	

(*Cont'd*)

Table 3A.2 (*Cont'd*)

Year	No. and % of SGO	No. and % of SGR	No. and % of MRK	No. and % of OTH	Total No. of Identifying Marks
1886	276	133	83	2	494
	55.87%	26.92%	16.80%	0.40%	
1887	374	177	100	1	652
	57.36%	27.15%	15.34%	0.15%	
1888	317	174	85	1	577
	54.94%	30.16%	14.73%	0.17%	
1889	266	147	61	0	474
	56.12%	31.01%	12.87%	0.00%	
1890	245	105	46	0	396
	61.87%	26.52%	11.62%	0.00%	
1891	275	147	48	1	471
	58.39%	31.21%	10.19%	0.21%	
1892	327	202	62	3	594
	55.05%	34.01%	10.44%	0.51%	
1893	265	166	51	1	483
	54.87%	34.37%	10.56%	0.21%	
1894	323	137	55	8	523
	61.76%	26.20%	10.52%	1.53%	
1895	361	189	41	1	592
	60.98%	31.93%	6.93%	0.17%	
1896	269	195	58	1	523
	51.43%	37.28%	11.09%	0.19%	
1897	235	139	29	3	406
	57.88%	34.24%	7.14%	0.74%	
1898	295	142	36	0	473
	62.37%	30.02%	7.61%	0.00%	
Total	**10,799**	**5,168**	**3,153**	**199**	**19,319**

Notes: Signatures of merchants not included.

SGO: Signatures in Script Other than Roman; SGR: Signatures in Roman; MRK: Mark; OTH: No Signature.

Table 3A.3 Signature List of Artisans (Occupation Codes 13, 15, 18, 19, and 20)

Year	No. and % SGO	No. and % SGR	No. and % MRK	OTH	**Total**
1860	121	60	58	1	**240**
	50.42%	25.00%	24.17%	0.42%	
1861	171	67	69	2	**309**
	55.34%	21.68%	22.33%	0.65%	
1862	194	89	111	5	**399**
	48.62%	22.31%	27.82%	1.25%	
1863	144	49	106	0	**299**
	48.16%	16.39%	35.45%	0.00%	
1864	148	47	61	36	**292**
	50.68%	16.10%	20.89%	12.33%	
1865	129	55	56	0	**240**
	53.75%	22.92%	23.33%	0.00%	
1866	166	74	82	21	**343**
	48.40%	21.57%	23.91%	6.12%	
1867	213	91	114	3	**421**
	50.59%	21.62%	27.08%	0.71%	
1868	221	62	115	0	**398**
	55.53%	15.58%	28.89%	0.00%	
1869	293	92	103	2	**490**
	59.80%	18.78%	21.02%	0.41%	
1870	413	168	117	60.85%	**704**
	58.66%	23.86%	16.62%		
1871	405	154	108	3	**670**
	60.45%	22.99%	16.12%	0.45%	
1872	394	212	156	3	**765**
	51.50%	27.71%	20.39%	0.39%	
1873	392	171	122	8	**693**
	56.57%	24.68%	17.60%	1.15%	
1874	313	118	88	41	**560**
	55.89%	21.07%	15.71%	7.32%	
1875	327	154	94	3	**578**
	56.57%	26.64%	16.26%	0.52%	
1876	316	160	68	0	**544**
	58.09%	29.41%	12.50%	0.00%	
1877	244	121	74	4	**443**
	55.08%	27.31%	16.70%	0.90%	

(Cont'd)

Table 3A.3 (*Cont'd*)

Year	No. and % SGO	No. and % SGR	No. and % MRK	OTH	Total
1878	312	138	87	0	**537**
	58.10%	25.70%	16.20%	0.00%	
1879	273	154	75	1	**503**
	54.27%	30.62%	14.91%	0.20%	
1880	338	161	84	3	**586**
	57.68%	27.47%	14.33%	0.51%	
1881	250	145	85	2	**482**
	51.87%	30.08%	17.63%	0.41%	
1882	267	118	91	4	**480**
	55.63%	24.58%	18.96%	0.83%	
1883	296	159	63	1	**519**
	57.03%	30.64%	12.14%	0.19%	
1884	290	134	110	28	**562**
	51.60%	23.84%	19.57%	4.98%	
1885	341	162	101	0	**604**
	56.46%	26.82%	16.72%	0.00%	
1886	276	133	83	2	**494**
	55.87%	26.92%	16.80%	0.40%	
1887	374	177	100	1	**652**
	57.36%	27.15%	15.34%	0.15%	
1888	317	174	85	1	**577**
	54.94%	30.16%	14.73%	0.17%	
1889	266	147	61	0	**474**
	56.12%	31.01%	12.87%	0.00%	
1890	245	105	46	0	**396**
	61.87%	26.52%	11.62%	0.00%	
1891	275	147	48	1	**471**
	58.39%	31.21%	10.19%	0.21%	
1892	327	202	62	3	**594**
	55.05%	34.01%	10.44%	0.51%	
1893	265	166	51	1	**483**
	54.87%	34.37%	10.56%	0.21%	
1894	323	137	55	8	**523**
	61.76%	26.20%	10.52%	1.53%	
1895	361	189	41	1	**592**
	60.98%	31.93%	6.93%	0.17%	

(*Cont'd*)

Table 3A.3 (*Cont'd*)

Year	No. and % SGO	No. and % SGR	No. and % MRK	OTH	**Total**
1896	269	195	58	1	**523**
	51.43%	37.28%	11.09%	0.19%	
1897	235	139	29	3	**406**
	57.88%	34.24%	7.14%	0.74%	
1898	295	142	36	0	**473**
	62.37%	30.02%	7.61%	0.00%	
Total	**10,799**	**5,168**	**3,153**	**199**	

Notes: SGO: Signatures in Script Other than Roman; SGR: Signatures in Roman; MRK: Mark; OTH: No Signature.

Table 3A.4 Signature List of Carpenters (Occupation Code 18)

Year	No. and % SGO	No. and % SGR	No. and % MRK	No. and % OTH	**Total**
1860	8	0	0	1	**9**
	88.89%	0.00%	0.00%	11.11%	
1861	10	0	1	0	**11**
	90.91%	0.00%	9.09%	0.00%	
1862	13	2	5	1	**21**
	61.90%	9.52%	23.81%	4.76%	
1863	10	0	5	0	**15**
	66.67%	0.00%	33.33%	0.00%	
1864	11	1	7	4	**23**
	47.83%	4.35%	30.43%	17.39%	
1865	16	2	0	0	**18**
	88.89%	11.11%	0.00%	0.00%	
1866	16	0	6	0	**22**
	72.73%	0.00%	27.27%	0.00%	
1867	17	1	3	0	**21**
	80.95%	4.76%	14.29%	0.00%	
1868	14	0	8	0	**22**
	63.64%	0.00%	36.36%	0.00%	
1869	19	4	7	1	**31**
	16.29%	12.90%	22.58%	3.23%	
1870	23	1	6	0	**30**
	76.67%	3.33%	20.00%	0.00%	

(*Cont'd*)

Table 3A.4 (*Cont'd*)

Year	No. and % SGO	No. and % SGR	No. and % MRK	No. and % OTH	**Total**
1871	31	1	7	0	**39**
	79.49%	2.56%	17.95%	0.00%	
1872	19	3	11	0	**33**
	57.58%	9.09%	33.33%	0.00%	
1873	21	2	9	0	**32**
	65.63%	6.25%	28.13%	0.00%	
1874	26	0	3	1	**30**
	86.67%	0.00%	10.00%	3.33%	
1875	23	2	7	0	**32**
	71.88%	6.25%	21.88%	0.00%	
1876	13	1	2	0	**16**
	81.25%	6.25%	12.50%	0.00%	
1877	11	2	5	0	**18**
	61.11%	11.11%	27.78%	0.00%	
1878	18	3	2	0	**23**
	78.26%	13.04%	8.70%	0.00%	
1879	16	2	1	0	**19**
	84.21%	10.53%	5.26%	0.00%	
1880	22	1	5	0	**28**
	78.57%	3.57%	17.86%	0.00%	
1881	22	2	3	0	**27**
	18.48%	7.41%	11.11%	0.00%	
1882	19	3	1	3	**26**
	73.08%	11.54%	3.85%	11.54%	
1883	27	2	3	0	**32**
	84.38%	6.25%	9.38%	0.00%	
1884	29	1	7	0	**37**
	78.38%	2.70%	18.92%	0.00%	
1885	42	1	8	0	**51**
	82.35%	1.96%	15.69%	0.00%	
1886	12	2	2	0	**16**
	75.00%	12.50%	12.50%	0.00%	
1887	27	1	9	0	**37**
	72.97%	2.70%	24.32%	0.00%	
1888	20	0	4	0	**24**
	83.33%	0.00%	16.67%	0.00%	

(*Cont'd*)

Table 3A.4 (*Cont'd*)

Year	No. and % SGO	No. and % SGR	No. and % MRK	No. and % OTH	Total
1889	17	1	5	0	**23**
	73.91%	4.35%	21.74%	0.00%	
1890	10	1	4	0	**15**
	66.67%	6.67%	26.67%	0.00%	
1891	23	0	2	0	**25**
	92.00%	0.00%	8.00%	0.00%	
1892	18	2	2	0	**22**
	81.82%	9.09%	9.09%	0.00%	
1893	18	0	2	0	**20**
	90.00%	0.00%	10.00%	0.00%	
1894	32	1	5	0	**38**
	84.21%	2.63%	13.16%	0.00%	
1895	29	0	2	0	**31**
	93.55%	0.00%	6.45%	0.00%	
1896	14	2	1	0	**17**
	82.35%	11.76%	5.88%	0.00%	
1897	6	1	2	0	**9**
	66.67%	11.11%	22.22%	0.00%	
1898	20	2	4	0	**26**
	76.92%	7.69%	15.38%	0.00%	
Total	**742**	**50**	**166**	**11**	

Notes: SGO: Signatures in Script other than Roman; SGR: Signatures in Roman; MRK: Mark; OTH: No Signature.

Table 3A.5 Signature List of Mechanics (Occupation Code 19)

Year	No. and % SGO	No. and % SGR	No. and % MRK	No. and % OTH	Total
1860	0	1	0	0	**1**
	0.00%	100.0%	0.00%	0.00%	
1861	0	0	0	0	**0**
	0.00%	0.00%	0.00%	0.00%	
1862	0	1	1	0	**2**
	0.00%	50.00%	50.00%	0.00%	
1863	0	0	0	0	**0**
	0.00%	0.00%	0.00%	0.00%	

(*Cont'd*)

Table 3A.5 (*Cont'd*)

Year	No. and % SGO	No. and % SGR	No. and % MRK	No. and % OTH	**Total**
1864	0	0	0	0	**0**
	0.00%	0.00%	0.00%	0.00%	
1865	2	2	0	0	**4**
	50.00%	50.00%	0.00%	0.00%	
1866	1	2	0	0	**3**
	33.33%	66.67%	0.00%	0.00%	
1867	0	0	2	1	**3**
	0.00%	0.00%	66.67%	33.33%	
1868	2	2	0	0	**4**
	50.00%	50.00%	0.00%	0.00%	
1869	3	2	1	0	**6**
	50.00%	33.33%	16.67%	0.00%	
1870	3	11	1	0	**15**
	20.00%	73.33%	6.67%	0.00%	
1871	7	6	0	0	**13**
	53.85%	46.15%	0.00%	0.00%	
1872	6	9	1	0	**16**
	37.50%	56.25%	6.25%	0.00%	
1873	8	5	0	1	**14**
	57.14%	35.71%	0.00%	7.14%	
1874	6	4	0	1	**11**
	54.55%	36.36%	0.00%	9.06%	
1875	7	7	3	0	**17**
	41.18%	41.18%	17.65%	0.00%	
1876	5	10	2	0	**17**
	29.41%	58.82%	11.76%	0.00%	
1877	4	2	1	0	**7**
	57.14%	28.57%	14.29%	0.00%	
1878	7	2	1	0	**10**
	70.00%	20.00%	10.00%	0.00%	
1879	9	4	1	0	**14**
	64.29%	28.57%	7.14%	0.00%	
1880	9	8	5	0	**22**
	40.91%	36.36%	22.73%	0.00%	
1881	6	8	3	0	**17**
	35.29%	47.06%	17.65%	0.00%	

(*Cont'd*)

Table 3A.5 (*Cont'd*)

Year	No. and % SGO	No. and % SGR	No. and % MRK	No. and % OTH	**Total**
1882	6	4	2	1	**13**
	46.15%	30.77%	15.38%	7.69%	
1883	15	10	1	0	**26**
	57.69%	38.46%	3.85%	0.00%	
1884	9	1	3	1	**14**
	64.29%	7.14%	21.43%	7.14%	
1885	17	6	3	0	**26**
	65.38%	23.08%	11.54%	0.00%	
1886	13	6	2	0	**21**
	61.90%	28.57%	9.52%	0.00%	
1887	9	7	7	0	**23**
	39.13%	30.43%	30.43%	0.00%	
1888	13	1	3	0	**17**
	76.47%	5.88%	17.65%	0.00%	
1889	9	8	4	0	**21**
	42.86%	38.10%	19.05%	0.00%	
1890	8	3	2	0	**13**
	61.54%	23.08%	15.38%	0.00%	
1891	6	4	1	0	**11**
	54.55%	36.36%	9.09%	0.00%	
1892	15	4	0	1	**20**
	75.00%	20.00%	0.00%	5.00%	
1893	10	2	4	0	**16**
	62.50%	12.50%	25.00%	0.00%	
1894	17	5	7	0	**29**
	58.62%	17.24%	24.14%	0.00%	
1895	16	8	0	0	**24**
	66.67%	33.33%	0.00%	0.00%	
1896	12	13	6	0	**31**
	38.71%	41.91%	19.35%	0.00%	
1897	15	5	1	0	**21**
	71.43%	23.81%	4.76%	0.00%	
1898	22	4	1	0	**27**
	81.48%	14.81%	3.70%	0.00%	
Total	**297**	**177**	**69**	**6**	

Notes: SGO: Signatures in Script other than Roman; SGR: Signatures in Roman; MRK: Mark; OTH: No Signature.

Table 3A.6 Signature List of Metal, Stone, and Brick Workers (Occupation Code 13)

Year	No. and % SGO	No. and % SGR	No. and % MRK	No. and % OTH	**Total**
1860	6	0	7	0	**13**
	46.15%	0.00%	53.85%	0.00%	
1861	3	0	7	0	**10**
	30.00%	0.00%	17.00%	0.00%	
1862	2	0	6	0	**8**
	25.00%	0.00%	75.00%	0.00%	
1863	7	0	6	0	**13**
	53.85%	0.00%	46.15%	0.00%	
1864	15	0	7	2	**24**
	62.50%	0.00%	29.17%	8.33%	
1865	1	0	4	0	**5**
	20.00%	0.00%	80.00%	0.00%	
1866	8	0	10	0	**18**
	44.44%	0.00%	55.56%	0.00%	
1867	6	0	14	0	**20**
	30.00%	0.00%	70.00%	0.00%	
1868	8	0	7	0	**15**
	53.33%	0.00%	46.67%	0.00%	
1869	14	0	12	0	**26**
	53.85%	0.00%	46.15%	0.00%	
1870	11	0	7	0	**18**
	61.11%	0.00%	38.89%	0.00%	
1871	20	0	8	2	**30**
	66.67%	0.00%	26.67%	6.67%	
1872	17	3	9	0	**29**
	58.62%	10.34%	31.03%	0.00%	
1873	15	1	8	0	**24**
	62.50%	4.17%	33.33%	0.00%	
1874	17	1	5	0	**23**
	73.91%	4.35%	21.74%	0.00%	
1875	11	0	9	0	**20**
	55.00%	0.00%	45.00%	0.00%	
1876	20	1	3	0	**24**
	83.33%	4.17%	12.50%	0.00%	
1877	3	0	2	0	**5**
	60.00%	0.00%	40.00%	0.00%	

(*Cont'd*)

Table 3A.6 (*Cont'd*)

Year	No. and % SGO	No. and % SGR	No. and % MRK	No. and % OTH	**Total**
1878	15	2	1	0	**18**
	83.33%	11.11%	5.56%	0.00%	
1879	11	1	1	0	**13**
	84.62%	7.69%	7.69%	0.00%	
1880	13	0	3	2	**18**
	17.22%	0.00%	16.67%	11.11%	
1881	2	0	1	1	**4**
	50.00%	0.00%	25.00%	25.00%	
1882	6	0	2	0	**8**
	75.00%	0.00%	25.00%	0.00%	
1883	3	0	4	0	**7**
	42.86%	0.00%	57.14%	0.00%	
1884	11	0	2	0	**13**
	84.62%	0.00%	15.38%	0.00%	
1885	9	0	6	0	**15**
	60.00%	0.00%	40.00%	0.00%	
1886	9	0	6	0	**15**
	60.00%	0.00%	40.00%	0.00%	
1887	13	1	6	0	**20**
	65.00%	5.00%	30.00%	0.00%	
1888	17	0	5	0	**22**
	77.27%	0.00%	22.73%	0.00%	
1889	4	0	5	0	**9**
	44.44%	0.00%	55.56%	0.00%	
1890	9	0	1	0	**10**
	19.00%	0.00%	10.00%	0.00%	
1891	7	0	4	0	**11**
	63.64%	0.00%	36.36%	0.00%	
1892	9	0	1	0	**10**
	19.00%	0.00%	10.00%	0.00%	
1893	19	1	3	0	**23**
	82.61%	4.35%	13.04%	0.00%	
1894	12	0	3	1	**16**
	75.00%	0.00%	18.75%	6.25%	
1895	8	1	2	0	**11**
	72.73%	9.09%	18.88%	0.00%	

(*Cont'd*)

Table 3A.6 (*Cont'd*)

Year	No. and % SGO	No. and % SGR	No. and % MRK	No. and % OTH	**Total**
1896	7	0	1	0	**8**
	87.50%	0.00%	12.50%	0.00%	
1897	11	0	1	0	**12**
	91.67%	0.00%	8.33%	0.00%	
1898	5	0	1	0	**6**
	83.33%	0.00%	16.67%	0.00%	
Total	**384**	**12**	**190**	**8**	

Notes: SGO: Signatures in Script other than Roman; SGR: Signatures in Roman; MRK: Mark; OTH: No Signature.

Table 3A.7 Signature List of Textile Workers (Occupation Code 15)

Year	No. and % SGO	No. and % SGR	No. and % MRK	No. and % OTH	**Total**
1860	1	0	0	0	**1**
	100.0%	0.00%	0.00%	0.00%	
1861	5	0	0	0	**5**
	100.0%	0.00%	0.00%	0.00%	
1862	6	0	3	0	**9**
	66.67%	0.00%	33.33%	0.00%	
1863	1	0	3	0	**4**
	25.00%	0.00%	75.00%	0.00%	
1864	4	1	0	0	**5**
	80.00%	20.00%	0.00%	0.00%	
1865	3	0	5	0	**8**
	37.50%	0.00%	62.50%	0.00%	
1866	4	0	4	0	**8**
	50.00%	0.00%	50.00%	0.00%	
1867	1	0	2	0	**3**
	33.33%	0.00%	66.67%	0.00%	
1868	9	0	2	0	**11**
	81.82%	0.00%	18.18%	0.00%	
1869	2	0	1	0	**3**
	66.67%	0.00%	33.33%	0.00%	
1870	6	1	2	0	**9**
	66.67%	11.11%	22.22%	0.00%	

(*Cont'd*)

Table 3A.7 (*Cont'd*)

Year	No. and % SGO	No. and % SGR	No. and % MRK	No. and % OTH	**Total**
1871	10	1	1	1	**13**
	76.92%	7.69%	7.69%	7.69%	
1872	5	0	5	0	**10**
	50.00%	0.00%	50.00%	0.00%	
1873	4	1	1	0	**6**
	66.67%	16.67%	16.67%	0.00%	
1874	5	0	6	0	**11**
	45.45%	0.00%	54.55%	0.00%	
1875	8	0	0	1	**9**
	88.89%	0.00%	0.00%	11.11%	
1876	2	0	1	0	**3**
	66.67%	0.00%	33.33%	0.00%	
1877	8	1	4	0	**13**
	61.54%	7.69%	30.77%	0.00%	
1878	9	0	1	0	**10**
	90.00%	0.00%	10.00%	0.00%	
1879	5	0	2	0	**7**
	71.43%	0.00%	28.57%	0.00%	
1880	10	0	3	0	**13**
	76.92%	0.00%	23.08%	0.00%	
1881	11	0	1	0	**12**
	91.67%	0.00%	8.33%	0.00%	
1882	10	0	5	0	**15**
	66.67%	0.00%	33.33%	0.00%	
1883	13	0	2	1	**16**
	81.25%	0.00%	12.50%	6.25%	
1884	8	0	4	1	**13**
	61.54%	0.00%	30.77%	7.69%	
1885	11	0	2	0	**13**
	84.62%	0.00%	15.38%	0.00%	
1886	2	0	4	0	**6**
	33.33%	0.00%	66.67%	0.00%	
1887	20	0	4	0	**24**
	83.33%	0.00%	16.67%	0.00%	
1888	8	0	2	0	**10**
	80.00%	0.00%	20.00%	0.00%	

(*Cont'd*)

Table 3A.7 (*Cont'd*)

Year	No. and % SGO	No. and % SGR	No. and % MRK	No. and % OTH	**Total**
1889	5	0	6	0	**11**
	45.45%	0.00%	54.55%	0.00%	
1890	1	0	1	0	**2**
	50.00%	0.00%	50.00%	0.00%	
1891	3	0	2	0	**5**
	60.00%	0.00%	40.00%	0.00%	
1892	4	1	4	0	**9**
	44.44%	11.11%	44.44%	0.00%	
1893	3	0	2	0	**5**
	60.00%	0.00%	40.00%	0.00%	
1894	7	0	1	0	**8**
	87.50%	0.00%	12.50%	0.00%	
1895	7	1	7	0	**15**
	46.67%	6.67%	46.67%	0.00%	
1896	3	2	4	0	**9**
	33.33%	22.22%	44.44%	0.00%	
1897	2	0	4	0	**6**
	33.33%	0.00%	66.67%	0.00%	
1898	9	2	2	0	**13**
	69.23%	15.38%	15.38%	0.00%	
Total	**235**	**11**	**103**	**4**	

Notes: SGO: Signatures in Script other than Roman; SGR: Signatures in Roman; MRK: Mark; OTH: No Signature.

Table 3A.8 Signature List of Service People (Occupation Codes 10, 11, and 12)

Year	SGO	SGR	MRK	OTH	**TOT**
1860	121	60	58	1	**240**
	50.42%	25.00%	24.17%	0.42%	
1861	171	67	69	2	**309**
	55.34%	21.68%	22.33%	0.65%	
1862	194	89	111	5	**399**
	48.62%	22.31%	27.82%	1.25%	
1863	144	49	106	0	**299**
	48.16%	16.39%	35.45%	0.00%	
1864	148	47	61	36	**292**
	50.68%	16.10%	20.89%	12.33%	

(*Cont'd*)

Table 3A.8 (*Cont'd*)

Year	SGO	SGR	MRK	OTH	TOT
1865	129	55	56	0	**240**
	53.75%	22.92%	23.33%	0.00%	
1866	166	74	82	21	**343**
	48.40%	21.57%	23.91%	6.12%	
1867	213	91	114	3	**421**
	50.59%	21.62%	21.08%	0.71%	
1868	221	62	115	0	**398**
	55.53%	15.58%	28.89%	0.00%	
1869	293	92	103	2	**490**
	59.80%	18.78%	21.02%	0.41%	
1870	413	168	117	6	**704**
	58.66%	23.86%	16.62%	0.85%	
1871	405	154	108	3	**670**
	60.45%	22.99%	16.12%	0.45%	
1872	394	212	156	3	**765**
	51.50%	27.71%	20.39%	0.39%	
1873	392	171	122	8	**693**
	56.57%	24.68%	17.60%	1.15%	
1874	313	118	88	41	**560**
	55.89%	21.07%	15.71%	7.32%	
1875	327	154	94	3	**578**
	56.57%	26.64%	16.26%	0.52%	
1876	316	160	68	0	**544**
	58.09%	29.41%	12.50%	0.00%	
1877	244	121	74	4	**443**
	55.08%	27.31%	16.70%	0.90%	
1878	312	138	87	0	**537**
	58.10%	25.70%	16.20%	0.00%	
1879	273	154	75	1	**503**
	54.27%	30.62%	14.91%	0.20%	
1880	338	161	84	3	**586**
	57.68%	27.47%	14.33%	0.51%	
1881	250	145	85	2	**482**
	51.87%	30.08%	17.63%	0.41%	
1882	267	118	91	4	**480**
	55.63%	24.58%	18.96%	0.83%	

(*Cont'd*)

Table 3A.8 (*Cont'd*)

Year	SGO	SGR	MRK	OTH	TOT
1883	296	159	63	1	**519**
	57.03%	30.64%	12.14%	0.19%	
1884	290	134	110	28	**562**
	51.60%	23.84%	19.57%	4.98%	
1885	341	162	101	0	**604**
	56.46%	26.82%	16.72%	0.00%	
1886	276	133	83	2	**494**
	55.87%	26.92%	16.80%	0.40%	
1887	374	177	100	1	**652**
	57.36%	27.15%	15.34%	0.15%	
1888	317	174	85	1	**577**
	54.94%	30.16%	14.73%	0.17%	
1889	266	147	61	0	**474**
	56.12%	31.01%	12.87%	0.00%	
1889	245	105	46	0	**396**
	61.87%	26.52%	11.62%	0.00%	
1890	245	105	46	0	**396**
	61.87%	26.52%	11.62%	0.00%	
1891	275	147	48	1	**471**
	58.39%	31.21%	10.19%	0.21%	
1892	327	202	62	3	**594**
	55.05%	34.01%	10.44%	0.51%	
1893	265	166	51	1	**483**
	54.87%	34.37%	10.56%	0.21%	
1894	323	137	55	8	**523**
	61.76%	26.20%	10.52%	1.53%	
1895	361	189	41	1	**592**
	60.98%	31.93%	6.93%	0.17%	
1896	269	195	58	1	**523**
	51.43%	37.28%	11.09%	0.19%	
1897	235	139	29	3	**406**
	57.88%	34.24%	7.14%	0.74%	
1898	295	142	36	0	**473**
	62.37%	30.02%	7.61%	0.00%	
Total	**10799**	**5168**	**3153**	**199**	

Notes: SGO: Signatures in Script other than Roman; SGR: Signatures in Roman; MRK: Mark; OTH: No Signature; TOT: Total.

Table 3A.9 Signature List of Food Dealers (Occupation Code 16)

Year	No. and % SGO	No. and % SGR	No. and % MRK	No. and % OTH	Total
1860	10	0	15	0	**25**
	40.00%	0.00%	60.00%	0.00%	
1861	21	0	9	0	**30**
	70.00%	0.00%	30.00%	0.00%	
1862	20	0	18	1	**39**
	51.28%	0.00%	46.15%	2.56%	
1863	21	1	12	0	**34**
	61.76%	2.94%	35.29%	0.00%	
1864	17	0	9	0	**26**
	65.38%	0.00%	34.62%	0.00%	
1865	7	0	17	0	**24**
	29.17%	0.00%	70.83%	0.00%	
1866	21	0	8	5	**34**
	61.76%	0.00%	23.53%	14.71%	
1867	31	1	27	0	**59**
	52.54%	1.69%	45.76%	0.00%	
1868	21	0	16	0	**37**
	56.76%	0.00%	43.24%	0.00%	
1869	31	2	27	0	**60**
	51.67%	3.33%	45.00%	0.00%	
1870	60	2	32	0	**94**
	63.83%	2.13%	34.04%	0.00%	
1871	61	0	29	0	**90**
	67.78%	0.00%	32.22%	0.00%	
1872	53	3	40	0	**96**
	55.21%	3.13%	41.67%	0.00%	
1873	59	1	34	2	**96**
	61.46%	1.04%	35.42%	2.08%	
1874	46	1	23	3	**73**
	63.01%	1.37%	31.51%	4.11%	
1875	42	3	29	1	**75**
	56.00%	4.00%	38.67%	1.33%	
1876	48	4	14	0	**66**
	72.73%	6.06%	21.21%	0.00%	
1877	36	1	17	1	**55**
	65.45%	1.82%	30.91%	1.82%	

(Cont'd)

Table 3A.9 (*Cont'd*)

Year	No. and % SGO	No. and % SGR	No. and % MRK	No. and % OTH	**Total**
1878	52	2	29	0	**83**
	62.65%	2.41%	34.94%	0.00%	
1879	38	1	18	0	**57**
	66.67%	1.75%	31.58%	0.00%	
1880	55	1	20	0	**76**
	72.37%	1.32%	26.32%	0.00%	
1881	41	2	24	0	**67**
	61.19%	2.99%	35.82%	0.00%	
1882	38	4	22	0	**64**
	59.38%	6.25%	34.38%	0.00%	
1883	37	0	20	0	**57**
	64.91%	0.00%	35.09%	0.00%	
1884	36	1	31	1	**69**
	52.17%	1.45%	44.93%	1.45%	
1885	39	3	15	0	**57**
	68.42%	5.26%	26.32%	0.00%	
1886	39	2	21	1	**63**
	61.90%	3.17%	33.33%	1.59%	
1887	36	2	20	0	**58**
	62.07%	3.45%	34.48%	0.00%	
1888	32	0	19	1	**52**
	61.54%	0.00%	36.54%	1.92%	
1889	35	1	5	0	**41**
	85.37%	2.44%	12.20%	0.00%	
1890	26	0	10	0	**36**
	72.22%	0.00%	27.78%	0.00%	
1891	44	1	15	0	**60**
	73.33%	1.67%	25.00%	0.00%	
1892	52	5	15	0	**72**
	72.22%	6.94%	20.83%	0.00%	
1893	31	2	14	0	**47**
	65.96%	4.26%	29.79%	0.00%	
1894	41	7	10	0	**58**
	70.69%	12.07%	17.24%	0.00%	
1895	39	3	11	0	**53**
	73.58%	5.66%	20.75%	0.00%	

(*Cont'd*)

Table 3A.9 (*Cont'd*)

Year	No. and % SGO	No. and % SGR	No. and % MRK	No. and % OTH	**Total**
1896	33	3	11	0	**47**
	70.21%	6.38%	23.40%	0.00%	
1897	33	4	4	0	**41**
	80.49%	9.76%	9.76%	0.00%	
1898	45	4	8	0	**57**
	78.95%	7.02%	14.04%	0.00%	
Total	**1,427**	**67**	**718**	**16**	

Notes: SGO: Signatures in Script other than Roman; SGR: Signatures in Roman; MRK: Mark; OTH: No Signature

Table 3A.10 Signature List of Other Dealers (Occupation Code 26)

Year	No. and % SGO	No. and % SGR	No. and % MRK	No. and % OTH	**Total**
1860	19	0	4	0	**23**
	82.61%	0.00%	17.39%	0.00%	
1861	31	1	9	0	**41**
	75.61%	2.44%	21.95%	0.00%	
1862	29	1	8	0	**38**
	76.32%	2.63%	21.05%	0.00%	
1863	16	0	6	0	**22**
	72.73%	0.00%	27.27%	0.00%	
1864	10	2	2	4	**18**
	55.56%	11.11%	11.11%	22.22%	
1865	8	0	4	0	**12**
	66.67%	0.00%	33.33%	0.00%	
1866	19	2	6	0	**27**
	70.37%	7.41%	22.22%	0.00%	
1867	23	2	5	0	**30**
	76.67%	6.67%	16.67%	0.00%	
1868	17	3	15	0	**35**
	48.57%	8.57%	42.86%	0.00%	
1869	37	1	12	1	**51**
	72.55%	1.96%	23.53%	1.96%	
1870	52	3	12	0	**67**
	77.61%	4.48%	17.91%	0.00%	

(*Cont'd*)

Table 3A.10 (*Cont'd*)

Year	No. and % SGO	No. and % SGR	No. and % MRK	No. and % OTH	**Total**
1871	43	1	12	0	**56**
	76.79%	1.79%	21.43%	0.00%	
1872	35	2	11	0	**48**
	72.92%	4.17%	22.92%	0.00%	
1873	56	5	9	0	**70**
	80.00%	7.14%	12.86%	0.00%	
1874	32	1	9	3	**45**
	71.11%	2.22%	20.00%	6.67%	
1875	30	4	6	0	**40**
	75.00%	10.00%	15.00%	0.00%	
1876	35	0	10	0	**45**
	77.78%	0.00%	22.22%	0.00%	
1877	34	0	4	0	**38**
	89.47%	0.00%	10.53%	0.00%	
1878	32	1	6	0	**39**
	82.05%	2.56%	15.38%	0.00%	
1879	37	2	5	0	**44**
	84.09%	4.55%	11.36%	0.00%	
1880	24	4	5	0	**33**
	72.73%	12.12%	15.15%	0.00%	
1881	15	4	6	0	**24**
	60.00%	46.00%	24.00%	0.00%	
1882	18	2	2	0	**22**
	81.82%	9.09%	9.09%	0.00%	
1883	22	2	4	0	**28**
	78.57%	7.14%	14.29%	0.00%	
1884	23	1	8	1	**33**
	69.70%	3.03%	24.24%	3.03%	
1885	25	3	5	0	**33**
	75.76%	9.09%	15.15%	0.00%	
1886	23	2	4	0	**29**
	79.31%	6.90%	13.79%	0.00%	
1887	35	3	5	0	**43**
	81.40%	6.98%	11.63%	0.00%	
1888	30	4	13	0	**47**
	63.83%	8.51%	27.66%	0.00%	

(*Cont'd*)

Table 3A.10 (*Cont'd*)

Year	No. and % SGO	No. and % SGR	No. and % MRK	No. and % OTH	**Total**
1889	37	6	7	0	**50**
	74.00%	12.00%	14.00%	0.00%	
1890	27	1	4	0	**32**
	84.38%	3.13%	12.50%	0.00%	
1891	22	1	5	0	**28**
	78.57%	3.57%	17.86%	0.00%	
1892	35	4	5	0	**44**
	79.55%	9.09%	11.36%	0.00%	
1893	28	4	2	0	**34**
	82.35%	11.76%	5.88%	0.00%	
1894	29	2	1	0	**32**
	90.63%	6.25%	3.13%	0.00%	
1895	25	1	3	0	**29**
	86.21%	3.45%	10.34%	0.00%	
1896	18	2	8	1	**29**
	62.07%	6.90%	27.59%	3.45%	
1897	28	4	0	0	**32**
	87.50%	12.50%	0.00%	0.00%	
1898	31	3	3	0	**37**
	83.78%	8.11%	8.11%	0.00%	
Total	**1,090**	**84**	**245**	**10**	

Notes: SGO: Signatures in Script other than Roman; SGR: Signatures in Roman; MRK: Mark; OTH: No Signature.

Table 3A.11 Signature List of Managers (Occupation Code 8)

Year	No. and % SGO	No. and % SGR	No. and % MRK	No. and % OTH	**Total**
1860	5	0	0	0	**5**
	100.0%	0.00%	0.00%	0.00%	
1861	11	4	1	0	**16**
	68.75%	25.00%	6.25%	0.00%	
1862	7	5	0	0	**12**
	58.33%	41.61%	0.00%	0.00%	
1863	10	0	2	0	**12**
	83.33%	0.00%	16.67%	0.00%	

(*Cont'd*)

Table 3A.11 (*Cont'd*)

Year	No. and % SGO	No. and % SGR	No. and % MRK	No. and % OTH	**Total**
1864	7	5	1	0	**13**
	53.85%	38.46%	7.69%	0.00%	
1865	10	7	1	0	**18**
	55.56%	38.89%	5.56%	0.00%	
1866	19	6	0	1	**26**
	73.08%	23.08%	0.00%	3.85%	
1867	22	10	2	0	**34**
	64.71%	29.41%	5.88%	0.00%	
1868	32	5	7	0	**44**
	72.73%	11.36%	15.91%	0.00%	
1869	30	6	1	0	**37**
	81.08%	16.22%	2.70%	0.00%	
1870	57	12	3	0	**72**
	79.17%	16.67%	4.17%	0.00%	
1871	45	9	1	0	**55**
	81.82%	16.36%	1.82%	0.00%	
1872	33	12	4	0	**49**
	67.35%	24.49%	8.16%	0.00%	
1873	42	13	6	0	**61**
	68.85%	21.31%	9.84%	0.00%	
1874	40	6	6	1	**53**
	75.47%	11.32%	11.32%	1.89%	
1875	24	17	0	0	**41**
	58.54%	41.46%	0.00%	0.00%	
1876	22	8	1	0	**31**
	70.97%	25.81%	3.23%	0.00%	
1877	17	7	4	2	**30**
	56.67%	23.33%	13.33%	6.67%	
1878	20	12	1	0	**33**
	60.61%	36.36%	3.03%	0.00%	
1879	25	9	1	0	**35**
	71.43%	25.71%	2.86%	0.00%	
1880	39	8	7	0	**54**
	72.22%	14.81%	12.96%	0.00%	
1881	28	8	2	0	**38**
	73.68%	21.05%	5.26%	0.00%	

(*Cont'd*)

Table 3A.11 (*Cont'd*)

Year	No. and % SGO	No. and % SGR	No. and % MRK	No. and % OTH	**Total**
1882	37	7	4	0	**48**
	77.08%	14.58%	8.33%	0.00%	
1883	25	10	2	0	**37**
	67.57%	27.03%	5.41%	0.00%	
1884	24	8	5	1	**38**
	63.16%	21.05%	13.16%	2.63%	
1885	30	11	1	0	**42**
	71.43%	26.19%	2.38%	0.00%	
1886	29	5	6	0	**40**
	72.50%	12.50%	15.00%	0.00%	
1887	42	15	3	0	**60**
	70.00%	25.00%	5.00%	0.00%	
1888	36	8	3	0	**47**
	76.60%	17.02%	6.38%	0.00%	
1889	26	9	3	0	**38**
	68.42%	26.68%	7.89%	0.00%	
1890	30	7	2	0	**39**
	76.92%	17.95%	5.13%	0.00%	
1891	27	9	2	0	**38**
	71.05%	23.68%	5.26%	0.00%	
1892	31	16	4	0	**51**
	60.78%	31.37%	7.84%	0.00%	
1893	22	9	5	0	**36**
	61.11%	25.00%	13.89%	0.00%	
1894	28	8	4	0	**40**
	70.00%	20.00%	10.00%	0.00%	
1895	44	6	2	0	**52**
	84.62%	11.54%	3.85%	0.00%	
1896	21	12	2	0	**35**
	60.00%	34.29%	5.71%	0.00%	
1897	15	4	1	0	**20**
	75.00%	20.00%	5.00%	0.00%	
1898	26	11	3	0	**40**
	65.00%	27.50%	7.50%	0.00%	
Total	**1,038**	**324**	**103**	**5**	

Notes: SGO: Signatures in Script other than Roman; SGR: Signatures in Roman; MRK: Mark; OTH: No Signature.

Table 3A.12 Income: All Artisans (Occupation Codes 13, 15, 18, 19, and 20)

Year	Average Yearly Income	No. of Artisans
1860	326.58	196
1861	338.95	220
1862	338.72	238
1863	389.39	230
1864	512.37	237
1865	604.97	293
1866	575.41	312
1867	631.49	310
1868	659.52	365
1869	576.78	369
1870	490.16	385
1871	467.74	369
1872	452.78	327
1873	406.04	304
1874	352.72	290
1875	402.70	271
1876	407.86	302
1877	412.16	344
1878	438.12	352
1879	380.22	361
1880	341.64	325
1881	325.85	352
1882	363.86	340
1883	412.73	377
1884	477.10	367
1885	444.75	362
1886	445.96	351
1887	483.14	311
1888	521.52	288
1889	561.55	273
1890	547.27	292
1891	496.03	289
1892	461.29	304
1893	468.11	316
1894	493.34	308
1895	478.06	279
1896	521.57	222
1897	431.20	158
1898	368.44	55

Table 3A.13 Income: All Artisans except Mechanics (Occupation Codes 13, 15, 18, and 20)

Year	Average Yearly Income	No. of Artisans
1860	324.56	195
1861	338.42	219
1862	337.63	236
1863	389.12	225
1864	519.20	226
1865	623.33	280
1866	592.75	294
1867	577.18	289
1868	590.90	337
1869	515.13	326
1870	477.44	348
1871	460.85	324
1872	452.92	285
1873	412.49	269
1874	328.79	257
1875	411.84	225
1876	436.78	254
1877	436.77	293
1878	452.78	298
1879	380.15	303
1880	333.94	270
1881	326.04	290
1882	381.29	275
1883	435.40	310
1884	510.89	293
1885	461.14	284
1886	465.09	280
1887	506.80	240
1888	553.09	227
1889	598.11	214
1890	557.68	235
1891	520.08	227
1892	497.86	233
1893	496.70	238
1894	545.70	220
1895	519.51	192
1896	586.09	159
1897	462.53	115
1898	377.58	40

Table 3A.14 Women's Year-wise Income 1860–98, in Blocks of 500 and 100

YR/IN	1–100	100–500	500–1000	1000–2000	2000–3000	3000–5000	5000–10000	>10000	Total
1860	7	32	6	2	0	1	1	0	**49**
	14.29	65.31	12.24	4.08	0.00	2.04	2.04	0.00	
1861	5	26	8	3	0	1	1	0	**44**
	11.36	59.09	18.18	6.82	0.00	2.27	2.27	0.00	
1862	6	19	5	2	0	1	0	0	**33**
	18.18	57.58	15.15	6.06	0.00	3.03	0.00	0.00	
1863	8	14	4	1	1	1	0	0	**29**
	27.59	48.28	13.79	3.45	3.45	3.45	0.00	0.00	
1864	9	16	6	5	1	1	2	0	**40**
	22.50	40.00	15.00	12.50	2.50	2.50	5.00	0.00	
1865	12	20	5	5	1	1	2	0	**46**
	26.09	43.48	10.87	10.87	2.17	2.17	4.35	0.00	
1866	10	27	8	5	1	2	1	0	**54**
	18.52	50.00	14.81	9.26	1.85	3.70	1.850	0.00	
1867	11	26	5	5	0	1	1	0	**49**
	22.45	53.06	10.20	10.20	0.00	2.04	2.04	0.00	
1868	11	30	10	5	1	3	2	0	**62**
	17.74	48.39	16.13	8.06	1.61	4.84	3.23	0.00	
1869	11	34	9	5	1	2	1	1	**64**
	17.19	53.13	14.06	7.81	1.56	3.13	1.56	1.56	

(Cont'd)

Table 3A.14 *(Cont'd)*

YR/IN	1–100	100–500	500–1000	1000–2000	2000–3000	3000–5000	5000–10000	>10000	Total
1870	14	32	9	4	1	1	1	0	**62**
	22.58	51.61	14.52	6.45	1.61	1.61	1.61	0.00	
1871	12	34	11	6	0	1	1	0	**65**
	18.46	52.31	16.92	9.23	0.00	1.54	1.54	0.00	
1872	10	22	5	6	0	0	1	0	**44**
	22.73	50.00	11.36	13.64	0.00	0.00	2.27	0.00	
1873	12	26	6	7	1	0	1	0	**53**
	22.64	49.06	11.32	13.21	1.89	0.00	1.89	0.00	
1874	14	24	7	6	2	0	1	0	**54**
	25.93	44.44	12.96	11.11	3.70	0.00	1.85	0.00	
1875	10	19	9	2	2	0	0	0	**42**
	23.81	45.24	21.43	4.76	4.76	0.00	0.00	0.00	
1876	11	22	9	5	2	2	0	0	**51**
	21.57	43.14	17.65	9.80	3.92	3.92	0.00	0.00	
1877	6	27	11	5	1	1	0	0	**51**
	11.76	52.94	21.57	9.80	1.96	.96	0.00	0.00	
1878	7	23	9	3	3	2	0	0	**47**
	14.89	48.94	19.15	6.38	6.38	4.26	0.00	0.00	

1879	11	23	4	4	0	1	0	0	**43**
	25.58	53.49	9.30	9.30	0.00	2.33	0.00	0.00	
1880	18	17	1	3	0	2	0	0	**41**
	43.90	41.46	2.44	7.32	0.00	4.88	0.00	0.00	
1881	16	32	7	4	0	2	0	0	**61**
	26.23	52.46	11.48	6.56	0.00	3.28	0.00	0.00	
1882	17	28	8	3	0	1	0	0	**57**
	29.82	49.12	14.04	5.26	0.00	1.75	0.00	0.00	
1883	12	31	9	4	0	1	0	1	**58**
	20.69	53.45	15.52	6.90	0.00	1.72	0.00	1.72	
1884	16	31	8	3	0	1	0	0	**59**
	27.12	52.54	13.56	5.08	0.00	1.69	0.00	0.00	
1885	10	27	5	4	0	1	0	1	**48**
	20.83	56.25	10.42	8.33	0.00	2.08	0.00	2.08	
1886	9	27	4	1	1	0	0	1	**43**
	20.93	62.79	9.30	2.33	2.33	0.00	0.00	2.33	
1887	3	22	3	0	0	1	0	0	**29**
	10.34	75.86	10.34	0.00	0.00	3.45	0.00	0.00	
1888	1	10	6	2	0	0	0	0	**19**
	5.26	52.63	31.58	10.53	0.00	0.00	0.00	0.00	
1889	2	12	2	2	0	0	0	0	**18**
	11.11	66.67	11.11	11.11	0.00	0.00	0.00	0.00	

(*Cont'd*)

Table 3A.14 (*Cont'd*)

YR/IN	1–100	100–500	500–1000	1000–2000	2000–3000	3000–5000	5000–10000	>10000	Total
1890	2	6	2	3	0	0	0	0	**13**
	15.38	46.15	15.38	23.08	0.00	0.00	0.00	0.00	
1891	3	10	1	0	0	1	0	0	**15**
	20.00	66.67	6.67	0.00	0.00	6.67	0.00	0.00	
1892	4	7	2	2	0	1	0	0	**16**
	25.00	43.75	12.50	12.50	0.00	6.25	0.00	0.00	
1893	2	7	3	3	0	2	0	0	**17**
	11.76	41.18	17.65	17.65	0.00	11.76	0.00	0.00	
1894	1	6	6	1	0	1	1	1	**17**
	5.88	35.29	35.29	5.88	0.00	5.88	5.88	5.88	
1895	1	8	4	0	0	1	1	1	**16**
	6.25	50.00	25.00	0.00	0.00	6.25	6.25	6.25	
1896	0	9	0	0	0	2	1	0	**12**
	0.00	75.00	0.00	0.00	0.00	16.67	8.33	0.00	
1897	0	41	0	0	0	0	0	0	**4**
	0.00	00.00	0.00	0.00	0.00	0.00	0.00	0.00	
1898	0	11	0	0	0	0	0	0	**1**
	0.00	00.00	0.00	0.00	0.00	0.00	0.00	0.00	
Total	**314**	**791**	**217**	**12**	**19**	**39**	**19**	**6**	**1526**
	20.58	**51.83**	**14.22**	**17.93**	**1.25**	**2.56**	**1.25**	**0.39**	

Table 3A.15 Women with No Income, Year-wise

Year	No.
1860	2
1861	0
1862	0
1863	1
1864	1
1865	0
1866	0
1867	2
1868	1
1869	2
1870	2
1871	3
1872	2
1873	3
1874	3
1875	2
1876	3
1877	1
1878	0
1879	1
1880	0
1881	0
1882	2
1883	0
1884	2
1885	1
1886	2
1887	2
1888	2
1889	2
1890	2
1891	3
1892	0
1893	2
1894	3
1895	0
1896	2
1897	1
1898	0
Total	**55**

Table 3A.16 Signatures of Women

Year	No. and % SGO	No. and % SGR	No. and % MRK	No. and % OTH	**Total**
1860	1	2	16	0	**19**
	5.26	10.53	84.21	0.00	
1861	2	0	17	0	**19**
	10.53	0.00	89.47	0.00	
1862	2	0	24	0	**26**
	7.69	0.00	92.31	0.00	
1863	1	2	14	0	**17**
	5.88	11.76	82.35	0.00	
1864	1	1	10	0	**12**
	8.33	8.33	83.33	0.00	
1865	0	0	81	0	**8**
	0.00	0.00	00.0	0.00	
1866	2	0	6	0	**8**
	25.00	0.00	75.00	0.00	
1867	4	0	19	0	**23**
	17.39	0.00	82.61	0.00	
1868	3	1	13	0	**17**
	17.65	5.88	76.47	0.00	
1869	4	0	13	0	**17**
	23.53	0.00	76.47	0.00	
1870	8	3	18	2	**31**
	25.81	9.68	58.06	6.45	
1871	6	1	16	0	**23**
	26.09	4.35	69.57	0.00	
1872	10	1	29	0	**40**
	25.00	2.50	72.50	0.00	
1873	3	0	12	0	**15**
	20.00	0.00	80.00	0.00	
1874	2	3	11	0	**16**
	12.50	18.75	68.75	0.00	
1875	7	1	17	0	**25**
	28.00	4.00	68.00	0.00	
1876	4	0	13	0	**17**
	23.53	0.00	76.47	0.00	
1877	2	2	13	0	**17**
	11.76	11.76	76.47	0.00	

(Cont'd)

Table 3A.16 (*Cont'd*)

Year	No. and % SGO	No. and % SGR	No. and % MRK	No. and % OTH	**Total**
1878	8	0	12	0	**20**
	40.00	0.00	60.00	0.00	
1879	7	4	12	0	**23**
	30.43	17.39	52.17	0.00	
1880	6	3	11	0	**20**
	30.00	15.00	55.00	0.00	
1881	1	1	7	0	**9**
	11.11	11.11	77.78	0.00	
1882	9	1	15	0	**25**
	26.00	4.00	60.00	0.00	
1883	4	3	8	0	**15**
	26.67	20.00	53.33	0.00	
1884	9	6	18	0	**33**
	27.27	18.18	54.55	0.00	
1885	5	2	14	0	**21**
	23.81	9.52	66.67	0.00	
1886	5	2	11	0	**18**
	27.78	11.11	61.11	0.00	
1887	5	0	21	0	**26**
	19.23	0.00	80.77	0.00	
1888	4	2	10	0	**16**
	25.00	12.50	62.50	0.00	
1889	3	0	6	0	**9**
	33.33	0.00	66.67	0.00	
1890	3	2	4	0	**9**
	33.33	22.22	44.44	0.00	
1891	2	2	3	0	**7**
	28.57	28.57	42.86	0.00	
1892	0	1	5	0	**6**
	0.00	16.67	83.33	0.00	
1893	4	3	1	1	**9**
	44.44	33.33	11.11	11.11	
1894	3	1	6	0	**10**
	30.00	10.00	60.00	0.00	
1895	3	3	0	0	**6**
	50.00	50.00	0.00	0.00	

(*Cont'd*)

Table 3A.16 (*Cont'd*)

Year	No. and % SGO	No. and % SGR	No. and % MRK	No. and % OTH	**Total**
1896	2	2	6	0	**10**
	20.00	20.00	60.00	0.00	
1897	2	1	3	0	**6**
	33.33	16.67	50.00	0.00	
1898	0	2	2	0	**4**
	0.00	50.00	50.00	0.00	
Total	**147**	**58**	**444**	**3**	**652**

Notes: SGO: Signatures in Script other than Roman; SGR: Signatures in Roman; MRK: Mark; OTH: No Signature.

Table 3A.17 Occupation by Religion, Total Numbers, and Percentages

Occupation Code	No. and % Hindu	No. and % Parsi	No. and % Jewish	No. and % Muslim	No. and % Christian	No. and % Other	**Total**
1	38	17	0	18	28	0	**101**
	37.62%	16.83%	0.00%	17.82%	27.72%	0.00%	
2	120	78	5	33	29	0	**265**
	45.28%	29.43%	1.89%	12.45%	10.94%	0.00%	
3	24	17	1	9	56	0	**107**
	22.43%	15.89%	0.93%	8.41%	52.34%	0.00%	
4	159	0	0	91	1	0	**251**
	63.35%	0.00%	0.00%	36.25%	0.40%	0.00%	
5	21	18	0	22	13	0	**74**
	28.38%	24.32%	0.00%	29.73%	17.57%	0.00%	
6	1380	460	33	44	577	6	**2500**
	55.20%	18.40%	1.32%	1.76%	23.08%	0.24%	
7	345	63	4	51	11	0	**474**
	72.78%	13.29%	0.84%	10.76%	2.32%	0.00%	
8	922	217	16	187	12	1	**1471**
	62.68%	14.75%	1.09%	12.71%	88.70%	0.07%	
9	25	24	0	13	49	0	**111**
	22.52%	21.62%	0.00%	11.71%	44.14%	0.00%	
10	391	74	2	193	7	1	**668**
	58.53%	11.08%	0.30%	28.89%	1.05%	0.15%	

(*Cont'd*)

Table 3A.17 (*Cont'd*)

Occupation Code	No. and % Hindu	No. and % Parsi	No. and % Jewish	No. and % Muslim	No. and % Christian	No. and % Other	Total
11	406	59	5	157	51	2	**680**
	59.71%	8.68%	0.74%	23.09%	7.50%	0.29%	
12	344	5	2	93	7	1	**452**
	76.11%	1.11%	0.44%	20.58%	1.55%	0.22%	
13	457	1	0	129	7	0	**594**
	76.94%	0.17%	0.00%	21.72%	1.18%	0.00%	
14	306	8	1	11	0	0	**326**
	93.87%	2.45%	0.31%	3.37%	0.00%	0.00%	
15	134	8	2	207	3	0	**354**
	37.85%	2.26%	0.56%	58.47%	0.85%	0.00%	
16	1231	180	10	767	37	3	**2228**
	55.25%	8.08%	0.45%	34.43%	1.66%	0.13%	
17	117	9	0	20	10	1	**157**
	74.52%	5.73%	0.00%	12.74%	6.37%	0.64%	
18	614	165	27	83	53	0	**969**
	66.15%	17.03%	2.79%	8.57%	5.47%	0.00%	
19	163	96	7	119	163	1	**549**
	29.69%	17.49%	1.28%	21.68%	29.69%	0.18%	
20	324	99	7	208	133	0	**771**
	42.02%	12.84%	0.91%	26.98%	17.25%	0.00%	
21	24	4	0	181	34	0	**243**
	9.88%	1.65%	0.00%	74.49%	13.99%	0.00%	
22	27	0	0	1	0	0	**28**
	96.43%	0.00%	0.00%	3.57%	0.00%	0.00%	
23	210	112	8	218	418	3	**969**
	21.67%	11.56%	0.83%	22.50%	43.14%	0.31%	
24	22	5	3	12	100	0	**142**
	15.49%	3.52%	2.11%	8.45%	70.42%	0.00%	
25	41	25	2	20	27	0	**115**
	35.65%	21.74%	1.74%	17.39%	23.48%	0.00%	
26	561	107	2	859	22	1	**1552**
	36.15%	6.89%	0.13%	55.35%	1.42%	0.06%	
27	201	19	1	87	2	0	**310**
	64.84%	6.13%	0.32%	28.06%	0.65%	0.00%	

(*Cont'd*)

Table 3A.17 (*Cont'd*)

Occupation Code	No. and % Hindu	No. and % Parsi	No. and % Jewish	No. and % Muslim	No. and % Christian	No. and % Other	Total
28	815	222	7	162	66	0	**1272**
	64.07%	17.45%	0.55%	12.74%	5.19%	0.00%	
29	65	67	0	38	21	1	**192**
	33.85%	34.90%	0.00%	19.79%	10.94%	0.52%	
30	128	1	2	196	1	1	**329**
	38.91%	0.30%	0.61%	59.57%	0.30%	0.30%	
31	144	21	3	48	1	1	**218**
	66.06%	9.63%	1.38%	22.02%	0.46%	0.46%	
32	155	54	6	51	73	2	**341**
	45.45%	15.84%	1.76%	14.96%	21.41%	0.59%	
33	28	31	1	20	3	0	**83**
	33.73%	37.35%	1.20%	24.10%	3.61%	0.00%	
34	44	3	0	2	24	0	**73**
	60.27%	4.11%	0.00%	2.74%	32.88%	0.00%	
35	31	0	0	0	3	0	**34**
	91.18%	0.00%	0.00%	0.00%	8.82%	0.00%	
36	46	10	0	5	1	0	**62**
	74.19%	16.13%	0.00%	8.06%	1.61%	0.00%	
37	133	25	6	69	20	1	**254**
	52.36%	9.84%	2.36%	27.17%	7.87%	0.39%	

Table 3A.18(i) Basic Income File

Year	Income Bracket: No. and %	Income Bracket: No. and %	Income Bracket: No. and %	Income Bracket: No. and %	Income Bracket: No. and %	Income Bracket: No. and %	Income Bracket: No. and %	Income Bracket: No. and %	**Total**
	1–100	100–500	500–1000	1000–2000	2000–3000	3000–5000	5000–10000	>10000	
1860	122	572	132	56	12	11	11	9	**925**
	13.19	61.84	14.27	6.05	1.30	1.19	1.19	0.97	
1861	123	544	126	60	19	12	14	11	**909**
	13.53	59.85	13.86	6.60	2.09	1.32	1.54	1.21	
1862	106	489	118	66	15	16	13	15	**838**
	12.65	58.35	14.08	7.88	1.79	1.91	1.55	1.79	
1863	80	505	129	71	24	28	19	20	**876**
	9.13	57.65	14.73	8.11	2.74	3.20	2.17	2.28	
1864	85	510	191	115	34	45	29	29	**1038**
	8.19	49.13	1 8.40	11.08	3.28	4.34	2.79	2.79	
1865	94	631	252	169	60	50	40	47	**1343**
	7.00	46.98	18.76	12.58	4.47	3.72	2.98	3.50	
1866	98	714	312	210	66	51	45	41	**1537**
	6.38	46.45	20.30	13.66	4.29	3.32	2.93	2.67	
1867	105	741	312	219	53	41	42	32	**1545**
	6.80	47.96	20.19	14.17	3.43	2.65	2.72	2.07	
1868	113	822	369	218	66	50	45	27	**1710**
	6.61	48.07	21.53	12.75	3.86	2.92	2.63	1.58	

(Cont'd)

Table 3A.18(i) *(Cont'd)*

Year	Income Bracket: No. and % 1–100	Income Bracket: No. and % 100–500	Income Bracket: No. and % 500–1000	Income Bracket: No. and % 1000–2000	Income Bracket: No. and % 2000–3000	Income Bracket: No. and % 3000–5000	Income Bracket: No. and % 5000–10000	Income Bracket: No. and % >10000	Total
1869	125	916	401	241	68	53	45	27	**1876**
	6.66	48.83	21 .38	12.85	3.62	2.83	2.40	1.44	
1870	135	978	417	246	72	54	44	26	**1972**
	6.85	49.59	21.15	12.47	3.65	2.74	2.23	1.32	
1871	136	1040	405	234	65	52	41	26	**1999**
	6.80	52.03	20.26	11.71	3.25	2.60	2.05	1.30	
1872	128	956	340	202	60	42	27	24	**1779**
	7.20	53.74	19.11	11.35	3.37	2.36	1.52	1.35	
1873	124	861	306	177	55	44	16	21	**1604**
	7.73	53.68	19.03	11.03	3.43	2.74	1.00	1.31	
1874	127	815	300	160	57	42	20	15	**1536**
	8.27	53.06	19.53	10.42	3.71	2.73	1.30	0.98	
1875	114	783	242	164	46	33	21	18	**1421**
	8.02	55.10	17.03	11.54	3.24	2.32	1.48	1.27	
1876	142	768	242	141	30	32	26	14	**1395**
	10.18	55.05	17.35	10.11	2.15	2.29	1.86	1.00	
1877	100	832	266	141	45	28	25	16	**1453**
	6.88	57.26	18.31	9.70	3.10	1.93	1.72	1.10	

1878	134	841	262	146	39	30	28	12	**1492**
	8.98	56.37	17.56	9.79	2.61	2.01	1.88	0.80	
1879	145	835	241	154	28	38	26	14	**1481**
	9.79	56.38	16.27	10.40	1.89	2.57	1.76	0.95	
1880	155	784	243	127	34	26	30	17	**1416**
	10.95	55.37	17.16	8.97	2.40	1.84	2.12	1.20	
1881	116	886	233	136	25	34	31	14	**1475**
	7.86	60.07	15.80	9.22	1.69	2.31	2.10	0.95	
1882	117	905	234	131	36	33	27	17	**1500**
	7.80	60.33	15.60	8.73	2.40	2.20	1.80	1.13	
1883	138	893	227	161	47	34	20	19	**1539**
	8.97	58.02	14.75	10.46	3.05	2.21	1.30	1.23	
1884	158	907	268	151	46	28	20	15	**1593**
	9.92	56.94	16.82	9.48	2.89	1.76	1.26	0.94	
1885	116	915	256	159	39	25	15	23	**1548**
	7.49	59.11	16.54	10.27	2.52	1.61	0.97	1.49	
1886	111	893	263	137	32	26	16	245	**1502**
	7.39	59.45	17.51	9.12	2.13	1.73	1.07	1.60	
1887	118	82656.97	24116.62	1419.72	473.24	402.76	161.10	211.45	**1450**
	8.14								

(Cont'd)

Table 3A.18(i) (*Cont'd*)

Year	Income Bracket: No. and %	Income Bracket: No. and %	Income Bracket: No. and %	Income Bracket: No. and %	Income Bracket: No. and %	Income Bracket: No. and %	Income Bracket: No. and %	Income Bracket: No. and %	Total
	1–100	100–500	500–1000	1000–2000	2000–3000	3000–5000	5000–10000	>10000	
1888	110	759	244	140	42	34	22	26	**1377**
	7.99	55.12	17.72	10.17	3.05	2.47	1.60	1.89	
1889	90	721	229	162	49	33	21	24	**1329**
	6.77	54.25	17.23	12.19	3.69	2.48	1.58	1.81	
1890	102	758	233	165	55	28	34	22	**1397**
	7.30	54.26	16.68	11.81	3.94	2.00	2.43	1.57	
1891	92	756	260	167	45	37	28	16	**1401**
	6.57	53.96	18.56	11.92	3.21	2.64	2.00	1.14	
1892	97	793	235	141	39	30	17	12	**1364**
	7.11	58.14	17.23	10.34	2.86	2.20	1.25	0.88	
1893	86	762	245	122	32	31	14	11	**1303**
	6.60	58.81	18.80	9.36	2.46	2.38	1.07	0.84	
1894	86	751	246	122	23	22	16	11	**1277**
	6.73	58.81	19.26	9.55	1.80	1.72	1.25	0.86	
1895	87	673	216	101	19	22	17	12	**1147**
	7.59	58.67	18.83	8.81	1.66	1.92	1.48	1.05	
1896	71	526	161	83	22	28	15	16	**922**
	7.70	57.05	17.46	9.00	2.39	3.04	1.63	1.74	

1897	50	341	101	50	18	11	9	7	**587**
	8.52	58.09	17.21	8.52	3.07	1.87	1.53	1.19	
1898	42	155	33	17	4	5	2	3	**261**
	16.09	59.39	12.64	6.51	1.53	1.92	0.77	1.15	
Total	**4278**	**29157**	**9531**	**5603**	**1568**	**1279**	**947**	**754**	**53117**
	8.05	**54.89**	**17.94**	**10.55**	**2.95**	**2.41**	**1.78**	**1.42**	

Table 3A.18(ii) Number of Zero Income in Each Year

Year	Number
1860	8
1861	11
1862	9
1863	6
1864	7
1865	8
1866	7
1867	16
1868	13
1869	16
1870	29
1871	26
1872	35
1873	25
1874	25
1875	32
1876	22
1877	13
1878	24
1879	26
1880	25
1881	13
1882	18
1883	16
1884	14
1885	12
1886	17
1887	13
1888	13
1889	16
1890	13
1891	12
1892	20
1893	27
1894	29
1895	14
1896	15
1897	17
1898	7
Total	669

Table 3A.19 Bigger Merchants: Number of Insolvencies, Year-wise, and by Type of Debt (1860–6)

Year	RAC	RDC	LOR	SSS	IPP	DSI	MSC
1860	21	4	2	0	25	1	2
1861	26	0	1	0	14	0	0
1862	15	0	6	0	11	4	0
1863	18	0	5	0	17	5	1
1864	6	0	39	0	42	1	0
1865	13	5	16	42	153	6	0
1866	54	20	7	38	147	9	3

Notes: Bigger merchants include all those with total debts of Rs 10,000 and above.
(*a*) Table covers merchants with total debts of Rs 10,000 and above.
(*b*) Credit analysis is based on the five largest debt items of each merchant. The total number of debts, the range of debt amounts, and the total amount of debt have been entered in the database, but not used in this analysis.
Types of debts: RAC: Goods purchased, running account, goods supplied; RDC: Redrafts and amounts due on shipment of goods; LOR: Losses in trade/business other than redrafts; SSS: Share speculation and share transaction; IPP: Amounts due for interest/premium, money borrowed, promissory notes, balance of account; DSI: Amounts due as a result of decree of suit against insolvent, judgment obtained by creditor; MSC: Others.

Table 3A.20 Types of Creditors of Bigger Merchants, Year-wise (1860–6)

Year	KNB	ITC	ETC	MRW	IND	SOL
1860	4	1	7	4	39	0
1861	0	7	6	1	27	0
1862	1	1	6	6	21	1
1863	0	6	1	0	39	0
1864	2	6	9	1	70	0
1865	59	28	28	1	118	0
1866	69	27	43	6	130	3

Notes: Bigger merchants include all those with total debts of Rs 10,000 and above.
(*a*) Table covers merchants with total debts of Rs 10,000 and above.
(*b*) Credit analysis is based on the five largest debt items of each merchant. The total number of debts, the range of debt amounts, and the total amount of debt have been entered in the database, but not used in this analysis.
Types of creditors: KNB: Bank; ITC: Indian trading company; ETC: European trading company; MRW: Marwari; IND: Individual; SOL: Solicitor, lawyer.

Table 3A.21 Bigger Merchants and Number of Insolvencies, Year-wise

Year	Total Petitions	Total IOB*	Total in Jail
1860	15	12	1
1861	11	9	1
1862	11	8	3
1863	14	7	2
1864	23	17	3
1865	56	27	2
1866	70	52	18
1867	40	24	3
1868	63	51	13
1869	35	31	9
1870	102	85	9
1871	78	59	16
1872	58	47	10
1873	77	60	9
1874	55	42	4
1875	50	39	6
1876	37	26	1
1877	21	15	2
1878	26	15	3
1879	44	16	1
1880	18	11	0
1881	24	14	1
1882	31	16	2
1883	42	31	3
1884	38	25	3
1885	32	24	2
1886	42	32	1
1887	37	27	6
1888	23	12	0
1889	59	35	3
1890	58	41	5
1891	48	35	3
1892	54	37	4
1893	52	44	7
1894	43	19	2
1895	32	27	3
1896	40	33	2

(*Cont'd*)

Table 3A.21 (*Cont'd*)

Year	Total Petitions	Total IOB*	Total in Jail
1897	56	45	3
1898	41	32	3
Total	**1656**	**1182**	**169**

Note: Bigger merchants include all those with total debts of Rs 10,000 and above.
* Interim order for protection granted.

Table 3A.22 Income: All Artisans (Occupation Codes 13, 15, 18, 19, and 20)

Year	Ave.	No.
1860	326.58	196
1861	338.95	220
1862	338.72	238
1863	389.39	230
1864	512.37	237
1865	604.97	293
1866	575.41	312
1867	631.49	310
1868	659.52	365
1869	576.78	369
1870	490.16	385
1871	467.74	369
1872	452.78	327
1873	406.04	304
1874	352.72	290
1875	402.70	271
1876	407.86	302
1877	412.16	344
1878	438.12	352
1879	380.22	361
1880	341.64	325
1881	325.85	352
1882	363.86	340
1883	412.73	377
1884	477.10	367
1885	444.75	362
1886	445.96	351

(*Cont'd*)

Table 3A.22 (*Cont'd*)

Year	Ave.	No.
1887	483.14	311
1888	521.52	288
1889	561.55	273
1890	547.27	292
1891	496.03	289
1892	461.29	304
1893	468.11	316
1894	493.34	308
1895	478.06	279
1896	521.57	222
1897	431.20	158
1898	368.44	55

Table 3A.23 Carpenters (Occupation Code 18)

Year	Ave.	No.
1860	225.81	52
1861	223.95	76
1862	246.63	91
1863	220.78	90
1864	324.54	98
1865	370.02	105
1866	357.36	112
1867	352.71	101
1868	392.58	129
1869	420.17	122
1870	340.43	124
1871	358.39	121
1872	333.30	110
1873	323.55	107
1874	297.36	92
1875	326.14	80
1876	302.18	89
1877	335.58	116
1878	330.83	99
1879	339.74	105
1880	351.48	101

(*Cont'd*)

Table 3A.23 (*Cont'd*)

Year	Ave.	No.
1881	304.67	118
1882	281.95	116
1883	288.49	131
1884	294.75	113
1885	306.52	97
1886	355.19	95
1887	465.24	84
1888	404.48	80
1889	442.66	85
1890	450.98	94
1891	394.86	90
1892	327.68	85
1893	290.86	88
1894	264.35	82
1895	332.63	60
1896	430.43	46
1897	367.94	36
1898	269.50	12

Table 3A.24 Mechanics (Occupation Code 19)

Year	Ave.	No.
1860	720.00	1
1861	453.00	1
1862	467.50	2
1863	401.40	5
1864	372.00	11
1865	209.62	13
1866	292.22	18
1867	1378.95	21
1868	1485.36	28
1869	1044.14	43
1870	609.84	37
1871	517.38	45
1872	451.83	42
1873	356.46	35
1874	539.06	33

(*Cont'd*)

Table 3A.24 *(Cont'd)*

Year	Ave.	No.
1875	357.96	46
1876	254.83	48
1877	270.76	51
1878	357.24	54
1879	380.59	58
1880	379.42	55
1881	324.95	62
1882	290.12	65
1883	307.82	67
1884	343.32	74
1885	385.06	78
1886	370.55	71
1887	403.15	71
1888	404.07	61
1889	428.95	59
1890	504.37	57
1891	407.97	62
1892	341.30	71
1893	383.01	78
1894	362.47	88
1895	386.61	87
1896	358.75	63
1897	347.42	43
1898	344.07	15

Table 3A.25 Income: Workers in Metal, Brick, and Stone (Occupation Code 3)

Year	Ave.	No.
1860	302.12	49
1861	353.26	50
1862	291.82	61
1863	277.16	61
1864	427.86	59
1865	387.99	92
1866	340.20	99
1867	287.36	96

(Cont'd)

Table 3A.25 (*Cont'd*)

Year	Ave.	No.
1868	368.99	110
1869	401.02	96
1870	407.68	114
1871	381.33	102
1872	389.52	86
1873	433.20	81
1874	340.47	70
1875	326.25	48
1876	424.51	51
1877	334.83	52
1878	324.85	48
1879	303.02	45
1880	249.28	32
1881	336.00	33
1882	354.53	34
1883	316.02	48
1884	358.83	52
1885	399.71	58
1886	323.11	53
1887	303.89	45
1888	313.00	46
1889	470.36	45
1890	504.64	42
1891	429.05	39
1892	494.93	46
1893	393.08	37
1894	358.87	30
1895	313.75	24
1896	446.21	24
1897	256.93	14
1898	218.33	3

Table 3A.26 Income: Textile Workers (Occupation Code 15)

Year	Ave.	No.
1860	463.59	22
1861	403.88	24

(*Cont'd*)

Table 3A.26 (*Cont'd*)

Year	Ave.	No.
1862	458.18	28
1863	851.66	29
1864	753.97	31
1865	569.66	32
1866	460.14	28
1867	524.13	30
1868	709.45	31
1869	785.82	33
1870	802.33	33
1871	640.71	31
1872	632.53	30
1873	704.30	27
1874	398.75	28
1875	303.29	31
1876	313.24	34
1877	409.20	35
1878	492.47	47
1879	513.73	51
1880	406.77	53
1881	354.46	56
1882	312.48	46
1883	314.44	39
1884	649.49	39
1885	552.14	43
1886	424.67	48
1887	395.09	35
1888	345.50	30
1889	636.62	21
1890	656.82	28
1891	714.10	29
1892	1036.21	28
1893	1246.45	31
1894	1304.21	34
1895	1075.41	29
1896	856.42	26
1897	658.00	21
1898	409.08	12

Table 3A.27 Income: Other Artisans (Occupation Code 20)

Year	Ave.	No.
1860	368.67	72
1861	431.00	69
1862	475.13	56
1863	579.51	45
1864	971.50	38
1865	1603.06	51
1866	1594.20	55
1867	1417.26	62
1868	1282.22	67
1869	696.57	75
1870	662.12	77
1871	674.16	70
1872	677.02	59
1873	411.78	54
1874	330.52	67
1875	628.97	66
1876	646.84	80
1877	636.83	90
1878	609.96	104
1879	388.97	102
1880	299.17	84
1881	333.30	83
1882	578.75	79
1883	758.15	92
1884	813.42	89
1885	631.48	86
1886	702.05	84
1887	724.32	76
1888	963.80	71
1889	886.27	63
1890	691.21	71
1891	653.33	69
1892	491.45	74
1893	478.89	82
1894	584.69	74
1895	519.87	79
1896	641.46	63
1897	512.05	44
1898	485.00	13

Table 3A.28 Income: Clerks (Occupation Code 6)

Year	Ave.	No.
1860	371.66	161
1861	390.98	161
1862	655.84	148
1863	646.43	148
1864	688.82	195
1865	787.13	231
1866	640.51	253
1867	649.56	247
1868	677.07	288
1869	701.07	331
1870	723.32	365
1871	693.27	370
1872	569.23	285
1873	652.57	233
1874	681.97	221
1875	705.12	237
1876	791.76	224
1877	667.08	244
1878	602.04	241
1879	531.28	229
1880	532.53	243
1881	526.87	230
1882	591.63	242
1883	647.64	228
1884	575.88	246
1885	545.77	245
1886	539.42	212
1887	596.42	221
1888	660.22	192
1889	591.71	207
1890	583.32	212
1891	586.06	234
1892	540.69	217
1893	506.05	221
1894	475.88	218
1895	550.75	196
1896	544.19	136
1897	376.78	79
1898	262.00	20

Table 3A.29 Income: Clerks (Occupation Code 7)

Year	Ave.	No.
1860	171.50	20
1861	116.75	20
1862	150.09	22
1863	157.97	36
1864	334.32	38
1865	414.32	53
1866	325.10	70
1867	321.75	61
1868	251.22	67
1869	247.24	70
1870	340.39	84
1871	361.65	83
1872	297.11	76
1873	304.62	77
1874	326.37	82
1875	263.46	68
1876	273.36	61
1877	283.92	48
1878	222.46	35
1879	262.88	34
1880	282.17	36
1881	244.88	24
1882	225.88	26
1883	285.33	27
1884	327.68	34
1885	298.07	41
1886	339.68	41
1887	331.29	38
1888	296.00	48
1889	331.56	36
1890	295.29	35
1891	309.42	40
1892	324.02	41
1893	275.59	39
1894	323.85	40
1895	355.81	27
1896	324.21	29
1897	339.12	26
1898	258.53	15

Table 3A.30 Income: Managers (Occupation Code 8)

Year	Ave.	No.
1860	682.46	70
1861	1038.14	83
1862	1997.96	91
1863	1532.72	122
1864	1220.99	194
1865	1060.40	278
1866	993.38	313
1867	774.35	321
1868	752.99	296
1869	733.47	305
1870	1164.66	267
1871	815.17	274
1872	793.18	249
1873	543.02	205
1874	513.40	184
1875	628.93	152
1876	788.44	123
1877	719.32	155
1878	529.90	154
1879	499.43	162
1880	681.30	140
1881	570.10	139
1882	447.09	136
1883	705.55	155
1884	772.74	156
1885	619.43	170
1886	480.24	175
1887	1778.70	152
1888	1880.68	138
1889	995.82	147
1890	798.54	141
1891	671.29	143
1892	585.57	120
1893	399.50	113
1894	389.71	112
1895	954.27	105
1896	1068.10	78
1897	819.17	54
1898	1087.46	26

Table 3A.31 Income: Service People (Occupation Codes 10, 11, and 12)

Year	Ave.	No.
1860	424.60	106
1861	472.53	98
1862	201.66	87
1863	295.24	87
1864	331.36	116
1865	1029.86	140
1866	914.73	165
1867	256.37	168
1868	289.67	197
1869	325.77	213
1870	301.93	214
1871	295.19	208
1872	254.80	187
1873	248.60	175
1874	274.44	174
1875	309.73	175
1876	274.47	174
1877	264.98	167
1878	242.80	155
1879	202.11	141
1880	189.53	145
1881	199.12	164
1882	199.01	186
1883	220.39	171
1884	207.00	167
1885	229.89	164
1886	241.30	153
1887	235.19	142
1888	249.55	141
1889	252.23	118
1890	315.93	163
1891	328.62	178
1892	237.94	178
1893	235.76	155
1894	242.71	144
1895	266.31	123
1896	293.42	91
1897	274.11	61
1898	218.27	22

Table 3A.32 Income: Food Dealers (Occupation Code 16)

Year	Ave.	No.
1860	493.93	136
1861	596.46	135
1862	531.60	121
1863	704.13	120
1864	827.07	150
1865	744.21	230
1866	947.01	283
1867	863.42	296
1868	897.50	320
1869	918.37	366
1870	890.00	362
1871	846.97	357
1872	867.71	333
1873	1126.55	297
1874	1230.94	281
1875	1041.60	263
1876	1177.32	265
1877	1059.21	272
1878	935.98	258
1879	992.66	252
1880	863.98	245
1881	897.25	244
1882	976.00	216
1883	1371.97	235
1884	1045.92	221
1885	1131.53	196
1886	1108.70	175
1887	1130.11	160
1888	1298.33	166
1889	1543.43	182
1890	1400.11	193
1891	1375.07	188
1892	1329.92	180
1893	1597.54	160
1894	1723.16	146
1895	1943.57	136
1896	2448.10	124
1897	1506.85	78
1898	1190.14	29

Table 3A.33 Income: Other Dealers (Occupation Code 26)

Year	Ave.	No.
1860	486.61	120
1861	534.83	103
1862	521.14	92
1863	752.90	105
1864	868.96	133
1865	1012.50	197
1866	1161.57	247
1867	1038.38	240
1868	909.56	264
1869	917.62	277
1870	923.10	259
1871	823.90	250
1872	824.29	222
1873	722.45	183
1874	861.54	177
1875	900.67	178
1876	690.39	168
1877	620.97	155
1878	426.06	139
1879	744.68	123
1880	757.31	90
1881	1420.19	88
1882	1014.51	107
1883	889.42	118
1884	868.97	133
1885	1366.36	131
1886	1328.93	145
1887	1513.71	150
1888	1399.68	176
1889	1401.55	152
1890	1304.54	145
1891	1240.46	151
1892	1278.25	122
1893	1210.79	105
1894	1150.97	108
1895	1156.25	109
1896	1167.95	92
1897	835.78	65
1898	632.69	29

Notes and References

1. See deposition of Hoolbajee Tindal of the Cooda Buccus; examination of Gowrojee Tindal of the Hanoventgalivat. Marks of Hoolbajee, Gowrojee and others. Public Department Diary, 1762, no. 39, part 1, pp. 287, 289, Maharashtra State Archives. Also, marks of Nusseir Nacqua, Amed Patel, and Ally Mahimcur. Public Department Diary, 1781, no. 78, pp. 446–8, Maharashtra State Archives.
2. See Charles Sisson, 'Marks as Signatures', *The Library, Fourth Series* 9, no. 1 (June 1928): 1–37.
3. Insolvency schedule 8743, 1872, minutes of evidence. All insolvency schedules refer to the records of the Bombay High Court and are cited by number and date.
4. See Lawrence Stone, 'Literacy and Education in England 1640–1900', *Past and Present* 42, no. 1 (1969): 69–139. David Cressy, *Literacy and the Social Order: Reading and Writing in Tudor and Stuart England* (Cambridge: Cambridge University Press, 1980).
5. Keith Thomas, 'Literacy in Early Modern England', in *The Written Word: Literacy in Transition*, edited by Gerd Baumann (Oxford: Clarendon Press 1986), p. 103.
6. Lawrence Stone, 'Literacy and Education in England 1640–1900'.
7. *Gazetteer of Bombay City and Island* [hereafter *Bombay Gaz*] III (1910): 99ff. Mridula Ramanna, 'Social Background of the Educated in Bombay City: 1824–58', *Economic and Political Weekly* 24, no. 4 (1989): 203–11.
8. Insolvency schedule 80, 1830.
9. Insolvency schedule 6448, 1870.
10. Insolvency schedule 612, 1895.
11. Insolvency schedule 401/402, 1894.
12. For upward mobility among dyers, see 'Musalman Classes: The Khatris or Rangaris', vol. 25, General Department, Maharashtra State Archives, 1896.
13. Insolvency schedule 6125, 1865.
14. Insolvency schedule 10563, 1875.
15. Insolvency schedule 60, 1860.
16. Insolvency schedule 4424, 1866.
17. Insolvency schedule 85508, 1885.
18. Insolvency schedule 86213, 1886.
19. See Chapter 6 of this book, p. 164.
20. Water Supply Committee to Government, 23 May 1856, General Department, vol. 102, Maharashtra State Archives.

21. Insolvency schedule 4786, 1867.
22. *Bombay Gaz* 1: 318.
23. *Bombay Gaz* 1: 318–20.

4 *Religion and Occupation*

In our analysis, we have noticed that certain occupations were connected to particular religions. For instance, dyers and printers of cloth were almost always Muslims. Muslims were also prominent among sailors. In this chapter we try and understand the reasons for connections between religion and certain occupations. Earlier, we have examined the relative numbers of insolvents in various occupations and tried to observe correlations between religion and occupation (Table 3A.17).

It is not surprising that the largest cluster of insolvents should occur among clerical workers signing in Roman script (2,500). As persons who worked in close contact with commercial dealings and perhaps themselves engaged in trade, they were likely to borrow capital and to be in debt, especially at times of commercial distress. At the same time, their command of English and proximity to the bureaucratic and legal apparatus of the city enabled them, perhaps more readily than it did many others, to turn to the court for relief. In short, the fact that so many of them did so is an indication not simply of their financial vulnerability, but also of their adaptation to the city's commercial and legal resources.

Yet the striking fact about Bombay's culture was that while being conversant in English undoubtedly conferred certain advantages, these advantages were not always exclusive. For example, the next most numerous group among insolvents consists of dealers of food (2,228, Occupation Code 16), the majority of whom signed their names in an Indian script, while many used marks and only a few used the Roman script. The next largest group, that of 'other dealers' (1,552, Occupation Code 26), is similar, although in this case there were fewer insolvents who used marks and a somewhat larger number who used the Roman script. Most of these persons were able to take advantage of the law of insolvency. So too were the numerous 'managers', a heterogeneous group, some of whom used a mark.

The occupational concentrations among insolvents reflect, on the one hand, access to work and the risks involved in borrowing and trading, and on the other hand, access to legal resources. Occupational clusters reflect, at the same time, links between religion and certain occupations. These groupings have to be seen in relation to the religious distribution of the city's population.

The census of 1872 recorded a total population of 644,405. Of this 63 per cent were Hindus, 21.3 per cent Muslims, 6.8 per cent Parsis, 5.3 per cent Christians, and 2.35 per cent Buddhists and Jains. As Buddhists and Jains are not recorded separately in our data, we may add Hindus, Buddhists, and Jains to give a figure of 65 per cent. This includes Brahmins (4 per cent), Lingayats (0.19 per cent), Bhattias (1.47 per cent), Hindus of other castes (52.9 per cent), and Hindu outcastes (4.86 per cent).[1]

Religious affiliation and occupational grouping, we may suppose, together influenced inter-communal as well as collective consciousness. Our analysis enables us to identify the relative prominence of particular groups in certain occupations among the insolvent petitioners of Bombay (Table 3A.17).

Almost all (96 per cent) of the small number of twenty-eight beggars were Hindus. Hindus figure high in proportion to their numbers in the total population—among jewellers (93 per cent), workers in metal, stone, and brick (76 per cent), labourers (76 per cent), opium dealers (74 per cent), writers using an Indian script (72 per cent), and carpenters (66 per cent). Their proportions are only a little less among brokers (64 per cent), dancing girls (63 per cent), managers (62 per cent), miscellaneous service people (59 per cent), domestic servants (58 per cent), clerks using English (55 per cent), and dealers in food stuffs (55 per cent). A conspicuously high percentage of shipping workers (74 per cent) were Muslim, far in excess of the proportion of Muslims in the city's population. An ancient connection with Arab mariners who first settled along the western coast of the country probably explains this preponderance.[2] By the end of the century, sailing ships, the special domain of these sailors, were on the decline. It is likely that displaced sailors were taking to other occupations. Chand bin Goolam, a labourer, used as his mark an anchor commonly used by sailors.[3] This was true also of Fuckeera Moheedeen, a dealer in hides, who petitioned from jail.[4] They both may have at one time been sailors.

Another specialized profession in which Muslims were concentrated was textiles (58 per cent). While many of them were weavers, they were particularly conspicuous among dyers: almost all the dyers in our sample were Muslims. The services of dyers engaged in indigo dyeing of mill and handloom cloth were vital to the city's textile industry. Many dyers earned good incomes. For instance, Noor Mahomed Salla Mahomed earned an average of over Rs 200 per month.[5] Their professional skills, considerable incomes, and social cohesiveness—dyers were organized in a *jamat* (group) and functioned in closely disciplined workplaces—fostered their sense of group identity.[6] A non-specialized occupation in which Muslims were numerous was that of hawkers (59 per cent). Here we often notice the existence of sect-based connections. Many Muslim hawkers of 'Europe articles', for instance, had been advanced goods for sale by persons who appear in their lists of creditors. The facts that many of them resided in Khoja Mohalla and that their names indicate that both the insolvents and creditors were often Khojas suggest that sectarian links played a part in market networks: bigger merchants and traders advanced goods on credit to be hawked by members of their sect.

Hawkers' incomes could be considerable. Kirparam Parbhuram Vanker Khatri, a hawker of cloth, had a debt of Rs 35,322 and a monthly income of Rs 700.[7]

In proportion to their numbers, Muslims figure high among dealers (55 per cent), dancing girls (36 per cent), dealers of food stuffs (34 per cent), performing artists (29 per cent), domestic servants (28 per cent), 'other artisans' (26 per cent), and landlords (24 per cent).

Parsis, who numbered somewhat over 6 per cent of the population, comprised 37 per cent of the landlords among insolvents. We shall return to this feature when we look more closely at the distribution of rental incomes among insolvents.

Parsis are numerous also among the 'unemployed' (34 per cent). This is a somewhat ambiguous category as many of those who may have had support but not an occupation sometimes identified themselves as 'unemployed'. Parsis figure prominently high among teachers and priests (29 per cent). Not a single Parsi dancing girl is found, but there are many Parsis among 'other performing artists' (24 per cent). They are numerous also among hotel and boarding-house keepers (21 per cent), clerks using English (18 per cent), as well as carpenters (17 per cent), mechanics (17 per cent), brokers (17 per cent), medical persons (16 per cent), and 'other professionals' (15 per cent). Strikingly, only a very small fraction of Parsi insolvents were government servants (3 per cent).[8]

Europeans, Eurasians, and Indian Christians could not be coded separately. The heterogeneity of the group coded as Christians, which numbered a little less than the Parsis, is reflected in its heavy concentration, on the one hand, in government service (70 per cent), the literate professions—'other professionals' (52 per cent), medical persons (27 per cent), and clerks signing in English (23 per cent)—and on the other hand, among cultivators. Of the seventy-three cultivators 32 per cent were Christians, descendants in all probability of older settlers converted under Portuguese rule. Christians were numerous also among hoteliers and boarding-house keepers (44 per cent), transport workers (43 per cent)—large numbers were employed in the railways—mechanics (29 per cent) and 'other artisans' (17 per cent), but were comparatively few among carpenters (8 per cent). A considerable number (21 per cent) were pensioners, a fact perhaps explained by their high representation among government servants.[9]

Rental Incomes

Milk Vending

The victualing trades, again, were particularly important to city life. Among these was milk vending. Our analysis shows that as many as 552 insolvents were engaged in selling milk. They included those for whom it was the principal source of livelihood, and others who made only a small income through the trade. Their ethnic identities, too, differed considerably. Many names among milk vendors were typically north Indian. They often had the suffix 'pardesi'. But milk vendors were by no means predominantly 'bhaiyas'.[10]

Group identity, we have indicated, was, in certain cases, defined by religion-based occupation. A conspicuous example, as mentioned earlier, is that of dyers, who were largely Muslim. Again, bullion dealers seem to have been predominantly Hindus. But in much of the world of trade and retailing, there were often few exclusive preserves. This is noticeable, for instance, among food dealers and dealers of cloth. Borrowing and lending in many cases took place across the boundaries of caste and community. Yet there must have also been competition. Borah and Parsi traders of European articles, for instance, vied with each other to obtain stocks as the ships arrived in the harbour.[11]

The experience of urban living appears, if at all, to have sharpened rather than dissolved sectarian identities. Our evidence vividly illuminates this in a conspicuous change noticeable in the names of petitioners towards the end of the period. From about the year 1887 occupational, regional, or sectarian features are often included in names, something that was rarely the case earlier. We find, for instance, names such as 'Mahomed Usaman Cutchi Sutar'[12] or 'Bhoodabhai Kandass Kathiawadi Sonar'. A moulder in the Great Indian Peninsula Railway notes his name as 'Sayana bin Sayana Telangi Dhobi',[13] while a weaver calls himself 'Pirbux Hooseinbux soonuthjamath'.[14]

The sense of belonging to a region and to a religion or occupation must, of course, have been present all along. A specific explanation of why it began to be expressed more pointedly might have been a heightened awareness as a result of the censuses which required people to give personal information. On the other hand, this may simply have been a consequence of close encounters between people of different backgrounds that took place in city life.

Separate identities might also have been sharpened by the occurrence of clashes between communities. The earlier inter-communal riots, those of 1851 and 1874, were between Muslims and Parsis. The first serious Hindu–Muslim riot took place in 1893.

The way ordinary persons' lives were affected by these events is brought home by the petitions of two insolvents. Goolam Nubee Lalla Meeya, a dealer in silk cloth, became insolvent when his goods were destroyed in the riot of 1874. He was reduced to being a servant and was in jail when he petitioned.[15] Nathu Raja Marakia, dealer in oil, suffered losses in the Hindu–Muslim riots of 1893 and became a hawker.[16]

Notes and References

1. *Gazetteer of Bombay City and Island* [hereafter, *Bombay Gaz*] I (1909): 164.
2. See *Bombay Gaz* I: 255.
3. Insolvency schedule 6599, 1872. All insolvency schedules refer to the records of the Bombay High Court and are cited by number and date.
4. Insolvency schedule 8991, 1873.
5. Insolvency schedule 8608, 1870.
6. *Bombay Gaz* I: 180, 463. See also 'Musalman Classes: The Khatris or Rangaris', vol. 25, General Department, Maharashtra State Archives, 1896.
7. Insolvency schedule 615, 1893.
8. See Asiya Siddiqi, 'The Business World of Jamsetjee Jejeebhoy', in *Trade and Finance in Colonial India*, edited by Asiya Siddiqi (New Delhi: Oxford University Press, 1995), pp. 186–217.
9. Siddiqi, 'The Business World of Jamsetjee Jejeebhoy'.
10. 'Pardesi' refers to someone who is not from Bombay itself but from somewhere outside Bombay. 'Bhaiya' also refers to someone from the north and not from Bombay.
11. See A.A.A. Fyzee, 'The Autobiography of Tyabjee Bhoymeeah, Merchant Prince of Bombay 1803–1863', *Journal of the Asiatic Society of Bombay* 36–7, supplement 1961–2, new series 12 (1964).
12. Insolvency schedule 289, 1892.
13. Insolvency schedule 326, 1892.
14. Insolvency schedule 475, 1895.
15. Insolvency schedule 10732, 1875.
16. Insolvency schedule 447, 1894.

5 *Insolvent Women*

We have noted that the law made it possible for insolvent married women to petition for protection. However, it allowed them a lesser status as compared to men in the matter of the articles they were allowed to keep. While men were allowed to retain articles worth Rs 300, women were allowed only personal possessions worth Rs 200 that they could hold back.

Of the 651 women petitioners in our data, 251, constituting the largest occupational group, are described as dancing girls, courtesans, and prostitutes. This perhaps reflects the fact that they were among the very few categories of women who earned an independent income. According to the Act XXVIII of 1865, only married women could seek protection from the court, but these women were not necessarily married. Yet the court overlooked the letter of the law and allowed them to seek protection. Their petitions for insolvency yield clues about their lives and concerns.

Dancing girls were known by a variety of names: *naikins*, *bhavins*, *murlis*, and *kasbins* or *cusbans*. Some of these names, such as *kalavatin*, denoted their acknowledged position as practitioners of an art, generally dancing and singing.[1] The words kasbin or cusban perhaps identified them as residents of *kasbas*—small townships—distinguishing them from humble village prostitutes. The appellation 'woman', probably a translation of the word *randi*, was often used to mean 'prostitute'. It frequently appears as a suffix with the name of a prostitute.

A matrilineal bias was conspicuous in the inheritance customs of dancing girls. While a son was heir to the property of a dancing girl in preference to an adopted daughter, a natural daughter normally inherited the property rather than a son.[2] This was perhaps an acknowledgement of the fact that a daughter was the professional heir as well, and it was her profession that defined her place in society.

The incomes of courtesans and dancing girls could vary considerably. In our material they ranged from less than Rs 10 to Rs 2,348 a year, which was the income of Rahimanbi.[3] Those at the upper end of this range were probably singers and dancers, while those with smaller incomes were perhaps humble prostitutes. Many dancing girls earned a good deal more than our sample indicates. On festive occasions and during ceremonies, a dancing girl could earn from Rs 30 to Rs 60 in a single night. Out of this, she paid each of her two fiddlers, that is, sarangi players, two annas out of every rupee, and the drummer three annas. She kept the balance herself.[4]

It was a measure of the independence a dancing girl enjoyed that she could be the mistress of a client and, at the same time, practice her profession. For instance, Huseni Jan earned a substantial income as 'dancing girl' and, at the same time, as 'mistress'. She noted each item separately. As dancing girl she earned from 1880 to1881 Rs 1,800 at the rate of Rs 75 per month; from 1882 to 1883 she earned Rs 2,400 at the rate of Rs 100 per month; and from 1 January to 31 August 1884 her earning was Rs 400 at the rate of Rs 50 per month.[5] The same was true of Gunga Naikin Dhargurker, who between December 1887 and December 1890 earned Rs 900 a year as 'salary as kept woman' and for the same years had an income of Rs 200 a year as 'singing and dancing girl'.[6] On the other hand, Bhicoo Woman Nandodkarin earned more as a dancing girl than she did as a mistress. As dancing girl she earned from 1882 to 1886 Rs 1,200 a year and received from her 'master' Rs 900 a year between 1882 and 1887, and Rs 675 from 1 January to 1 September 1888.[7] Sagunabai, described as 'kept mistress' of Bhicoo Gunaji Ayar Maratha, a mill hand in the Union Mill, earned a modest income of Rs 120 a year. [8]

A matriarchal connection is perhaps evident where younger dancing girls were under the protection of older women who may have belonged to the same profession. For instance, Sajoo was 'protected by her grandmother.'[9] In contrast, Kashi Naikin Kamburlikarin was protected by her daughter.[10]

Despite their independent status, dancing girls may have felt the need for male protection. Each dancing girl, we are told, supported three or four fiddlers (sarangi players) and drummers.[11] Perhaps informal relationships were involved in the instances of co-petitioning: fiddlers and dancing girls often appear as co-petitioners. For instance, the dancing girl Bhowani petitioned with a fiddler.[12] So too did Rahimanbi, cited earlier, who was in jail for debt. Suckeena, another dancing girl, petitioned with the fiddler Dawood Khan Dildar Khan.[13] A fiddler, Hyat bin Husain Khan, petitioned with the courtesan Jumilabeebee.[14] Umrao, a dancing girl, petitioned together with the fiddler Ahmed Miya Mahomed Maruf.[15] Their joint income was entered. Were these working arrangements or did they involve personal relationships? We do not know. It is equally difficult to tell whether there was a personal connection between Durga, Raju, and Esu, all courtesans with the surname of Serodker, and an English writer, Atmaram Tulsidas Serodker, with whom they petitioned.[16] Three courtesans petitioned together with a seller of spice and a Hindu priest.[17] Salim bin Ibrahim Munshi, who earned Rs 15 a month, had as a co-petitioner Habiba, a prosititute whose average monthly income was Rs 30.[18] A hack buggy keeper, Mohammad Ali, petitioned with Jani Woman, a Hindu brothel-house keeper.[19] There were many such cases.

Courtesans seemed to acknowledge their profession quite frankly in their petitions. Thus, Mariam candidly declared her earnings from 'prostitution.'[20] Their confidence may have stemmed from the considerable incomes they often earned as well as from the existence of distinct family structures. Duthoo Naikin Pednekereen had a family of five.[21] Patrons often took good care of their favourites. For instance, Hussein Beebee, mistress of the late Dr N.C. Veigas, received, in accordance with his will, Rs 8 as monthly rental from a *chal* (a modest tenement, also spelled 'chawl'). This sum supported her and her co-petitioner, the widow Pessoo Beebee.[22] Dancing girls bore children who were often brought up to follow the customs of the religious community to which they themselves belonged. The dancing girl Ameena listed in her expenditure the sum she had spent on the circumcision of her son.[23]

High medical expenses are often noticeable in the balance sheets of courtesans—the result of illnesses that may have been a professional hazard. For instance, Yamoona, who had earlier earned an average of Rs 27 a month, was so sick at the time of petitioning that she was unable to work.[24]

Muslim dancing girls were especially remarkable for their pleasing manners and singing skills.[25] Conversion to Islam may have been a way of achieving social respectability. One reason may have been that being Muslim ensured, among other things, that a person would get a decent burial after death. To this end, we are told, Hindu and Bene-Israeli dancing girls often called themselves Muslim and some even converted.[26] Luisa 'alias Fatima Ajai', who worked as a dancing girl in Bombay and Karachi, declared herself to be a Muslim.[27] Yet her name and the fact that she signed in English suggest a Christian affiliation. We cannot tell if she had converted.

The education of an accomplished dancing girl was often costly. The teachers who taught the young women to sing, we are told, were paid Rs 50 to Rs 500.[28] We find an insolvent courtesan, Durga, whose main source of income was her daughter's earnings, and she had paid Rs 500 to her daughter's singing teacher.[29] It seems they belonged to the class of skilled performers. The articles they had pawned included the fine clothes customarily used in dance—a 'peshvaz' and an 'odhani'. For such insolvents, whose costly clothes were professional necessities, being allowed to keep belongings worth no more than Rs 200 may have been a handicap.

In keeping with the considerable cultural range of courtesans was the difference in their lifestyles. While many lived in chals, others lived in 'banglas' (bungalows) furnished in the European fashion.[30] 'The trained Naikins, the Marwadi, Bene Israel and Musalman dancing girls,' we are told, 'live in some style in the neighbourhood of Kalbadevi road and Grant road'.[31] The vogue for domestic display, so conspicuous in nineteenth-century Bombay, was, evidently, shared by the upper crust of courtesans. In this respect they were a part of bourgeois society. Very different was the situation of the humbler prostitutes. 'Perhaps the most pitiful sight of all is the streets where the women cluster like caged birds behind the bars, awaiting the meager wage of shame.'[32]

A different sort of relationship from that of dancing girls and their clients and associates is noticeable in the petition of Mullaee Ahmed Dolla, a *tendal* (head sailor), and his two co-petitioners, both women,

Haleemabaee and Mullaeen Subilbaee, who declared themselves to be cooks. Included in the balance sheet of Mullaeen Subilbaee are sums on account of the income of her first and second husbands as *khullasees* (sailors), while Haleemabaee earned an income 'as cot woman for khullasee'. The Muslim institution of temporary marriages, known as *muta*, was not uncommon among sailors, who were often away from home for long periods. The question arises if these were instances of muta.

Over the entire period, fifty-five women reported not having any income at all. Most of them got protection. We have tabulated women's incomes in a basic income file (Table 3A.14) along the same lines as the basic income file presented in Table 3A.18(i). Our table of the range of women's incomes shows women to have been among low earners. They are concentrated in the Rs 100 to Rs 500 a year group. The same concentration is found in the basic income file. Dancing girls, who were most numerous among women insolvents, were probably to be found mainly in this group, although some may have been poorer and a few may have earned considerably more. However, there is a significant difference between the basic income file and the file of women's incomes in that while in the former the next densest cluster is in the higher income group of Rs 500 to Rs 1,000, in the latter the next more numerous is the lower group of less than Rs 100. If we look at the number of petitioners in the group of less than Rs 50 a year, the difference is quite sharp, proportionately more women insolvents being in this group. At the same time in the higher group of Rs 1,000 and above, the proportion of women is lower. Women insolvents, therefore, appear to have been poorer earners.

Among the more well-off women was the dancing girl Bhicoo Woman Nandodkarin, to whom we have referred earlier, who in certain years earned Rs 2,100. There were other more prosperous and better-endowed women such as the Parsi widow Aeme, who drew Rs 100 a month as interest from her mother's estate.[33]

Many poor women, of whom several were widows, made a living selling milk. This could be quite lucrative. For instance, one such widow had an average monthly income of Rs 60 between 1860 and 1862.[34] Somewhat poorer were those who made a meagre sum making *bidis* or grinding corn. Rajabaee Kamateen earned Rs 6 a month making bidis.[35] Another bidi seller earned Rs 15 to Rs 20 a month.[36] Bhagambai, a maker of bidis, had an income of Rs 30 a month.[37] Keserbai, a widow, earned Rs 9.35 a month sewing clothes.[38] Persons like the widow Golabbai, who between

1879 and 1882 earned Rs 4.48 a month grinding corn and begging, earned only slightly more than the mendicant Gunga, who made about Rs 3 a month.[39] The striking fact about the social and legal culture of the city was that such persons could earn a livelihood, though on the margin of existence, and that they could turn to the insolvency law for relief.

A gender disparity shows up not only in incomes but also in literacy. Out of our sample of 16,345 petitioners, in which clerks are excluded, 17 per cent had signed in the Roman script, 63 per cent had signed in other, mainly Indian, scripts, and 19 per cent had used marks (Table 3A.2). This works out to 80 per cent signatures against 19 per cent marks. Women are included in this sample. If we look at women separately, we find that 9 per cent had signed in the Roman script, 22 per cent in other scripts, while 68 per cent had used marks (Table 3A.16). In other words, the proportion is 32 per cent signatures to 68 per cent marks. This suggests that literacy levels among women were considerably lower.

The lives of dancing girls, courtesans, and prostitutes were both similar and different in the context of literacy, incomes, and social status. Literary levels for all of these women insolvents were low. Incomes were also mostly low. Some dancing girls had higher incomes. This reflects the fact that some dancing girls were more accomplished as performers and that they were supported by clients who paid more. The social status of courtesans, dancing girls, and prostitutes often varied according to the status of their clients. Women who converted to Islam received a proper burial at death, which they would not be otherwise assured of.

Notes and References

1. K. Raghunathji, 'Bombay Dancing Girls', *Indian Antiquary* (June 1884): 165–78, 166.
2. Raghunathji, 'Bombay Dancing Girls': 165–178.
3. Insolvency schedule 2455, 1860. All insolvency schedules refer to the records of the Bombay High Court and are cited by number and date.
4. Raghunathji, 'Bombay Dancing Girls': 170.
5. Insolvency schedule 419, 1884.
6. Insolvency schedule 662, 1890.
7. Insolvency schedule 464, 1888.
8. Insolvency schedule 342, 1892.
9. Insolvency schedule 4043, 1865.
10. Insolvency schedule 549, 1878.

11. *Gazetteer of Bombay City and Island* [hereafter *Bombay Gaz*] I (1909): 191.
12. Insolvency schedule 14, 1880.
13. Insolvency schedule 2503,1860.
14. Insolvency schedule 2453, 1860.
15. Insolvency schedule 301, 1881.
16. Insolvency schedule 389, 1883.
17. Insolvency schedule 453, 1884.
18. Insolvency schedule 170, 1881.
19. Insolvency schedule 109, 1891.
20. Insolvency schedule 328, 1881.
21. Insolvency schedule 9958, 1874.
22. Insolvency schedule 3626, 1864.
23. Insolvency schedule 6472, 1870.
24. Insolvency schedule 3678, 1864.
25. See Raghunathji, 'Bombay Dancing Girls.'
26. *Bombay Gaz* I: 191.
27. Insolvency schedule 3552, 1863.
28. The period of the payment is not mentioned. Raghunathji, 'Bombay Dancing Girls,' p. 166.
29. Insolvency schedule 6707, 1870.
30. Raghunathji, 'Bombay Dancing Girls,' p. 170.
31. *Bombay Gaz* I: 190.
32. *Bombay* Gaz I: 170.
33. Insolvency schedule 100, 1882.
34. Insolvency schedule 3260, 1862.
35. Insolvency schedule 58, 1894.
36. Insolvency schedule 428, 1883.
37. Insolvency schedule 111, 1888.
38. Insolvency schedule 180, 1881.
39. Insolvency schedule 186, 1882; Insolvency schedule 7700, 1871.

6 *Ayesha's World*

*A Butcher's Family in Nineteenth-Century Bombay**

Little is known of the private worlds of working people in the growing cities of nineteenth-century India, still less of the space women occupied in them. Historical documentation is almost silent on information about their everyday lives. Exceptions perhaps are certain legal records, such as the proceedings on petitions of insolvents. From the early nineteenth century onwards, many humble citizens of metropolitan cities were able to petition the courts for protection from their creditors. As we saw in the last chapter, many of those who petitioned for insolvency were women, and from an analysis of the data in the petitions we have gleaned information about their income, professions, literary levels, and social status. This chapter draws mainly upon documentation generated by the hearings on Ismail Sobhan's petition to the High Court of

* Published in *Comparative Studies in Society and History*, 43, no. 1 (Cambridge University Press, January 2001), pp. 101–29.

Bombay for protection: (*a*) insolvency schedule of Ismail Sobhan and his wife, Hamidabai, no. 8743, 1872 and (*b*) minutes of evidence of the hearings on Ismail's petition, July to December 1873, recorded in notebook entitled 'Notes by Justice Pinhey, Insolvent Court, Bombay, 1873'. From this material, I have constructed a narrative of the life and connections of Ayesha, the mother of this insolvent butcher. As a witness in the hearing of her son's petition, Ayesha provided details of her own life.

Ayesha and Her 'Bungalow'

Ayesha, giving evidence in the High Court of Bombay, belied the stereotype of the cloistered, veiled woman who would leave her affairs in the hands of the men. In a court conspicuous for its bewildering procedure, its ceremony, its aura of English judges, and its use of English (a language she did not understand), Ayesha spoke with impressive self-assurance in support of her son's petition and in defence of her own property. The house in which she lived, Ayesha declared, was her own. Her husband had gifted it to her in 1854. From then on, she claimed, she herself had managed the property. She had paid the municipal tax to the tax collector herself. Her husband and her son had not been involved. The bill collector would bring the bills, and she would show them to 'some person' to check the amount before she paid them. The bill collector would write a receipt on the bill, which she would put away in a box, the key of which she kept herself. 'I never let my husband or Ismail have the key of that box,' Ayesha said.

Ayesha gave a vivid account of the first time she had paid the tax after the house had been transferred to her. Her husband was not at home. Her son, Ismail, too had gone to the bazaar. The bill collector brought the bill while she was upstairs. He called out her name, 'Ayeshabai'. She knew him, as he had been there before. She came down, he gave her the bill, she showed it 'to a few', and then paid it, standing on the verandah of the house. When she learnt the bill was in her husband's name, she told the bill collector the house had passed to her and asked him in future to have the bill made out in her name.

A few years after the house had been gifted to her, Ayesha said, 'I being a woman, asked my husband to take [my] money and build me a house like a bungalow.' Her husband applied to the municipal commissioner and the executive engineer for permission to rebuild the house. Sometime before Sobhan (Ayesh's husband) died, the 'bungalow' had come up in the form of an upper storey over the house. This upper storey, occupied solely by the family, included a *diwan khana*, or reception room, situated at the back, where the members of the family sat and kept their jewels and books. It was in this room that visitors were received and where Ismail was given his Quran lessons. On the ground floor were the family hearth and rooms rented out to tenants.[1] Ayesha herself would go around to collect the rents. Occasionally she would send Ismail, who would give her the rents he had collected.[2] In what way the 'bungalow' was distinct from other houses is not quite clear. As noted earlier, it did have a verandah, where Ayesha would come out to pay the tax collector. It was the only house on Dontad Street to be rebuilt, and it must have marked out its owners as being more affluent than their neighbours.[3] It contained furniture worth Rs 400 or Rs 500, a considerable sum.[4]

According to one of the witnesses, Jamnadas Nagardas, who had been the municipal tax receiver for five or six years for Umarkhadi, the district in which Dontad Street was situated, there were at the time more than four hundred houses in the area. Before a tax bill was paid at these small houses, he said, he would have to visit them many times. The number of bills had gone up in recent years.[5] Umarkhadi seems to have been a modest but reasonably secure and growing neighbourhood. It appears to have had a mixed population, a fact to which its old buildings and the names of its streets still bear witness. The presence of Jewish people is indicated by street names such as Samuel Street and Israel Mohalla.[6] A 200-year-old synagogue still stands on Samuel Street. Here, too, resided Khojas such as the brothers Abdullabhai Lalljee and Jumabhai Lalljee, migrants from Mandvi in Kutch.[7] The Lalljees became prominent in trade and politics, and at a later date, Abdullabhai moved his residence to a more fashionable area, Breach Candy.[8]

The names, too, of insolvents who resided in Umarkhadi in the last quarter of the century indicate that the locality was a heterogeneous one, in some ways a microcosm of the city in terms of religion, ethnicity, and occupation. Among its Jewish residents were the Kooroolkers, Reuben Benjamin, and Moses Benjamin, compositors, and Abraham Daniel, an English-language clerk.[9] Other Jewish residents were Samuel Ballajee and Arun (Aaron) Banaji Chinchonker, carpenters; Samuel Salamjee, an 'engineer'; and Aaron Daniel Tulker, a pensioner.[10] Of the Europeans, Theophilus Dismer was an 'extra writer', Christopher Fell a tanner and currier, and Charles Doneaud a 'guard'.[11] The 'East Asians' Patrick Vernon and James Lord declared themselves to be a 'guard' and a 'government guard' respectively.[12] The Hindus included Visram Esu Katchraker, a bookbinder; Vithu Jothiba Kadam, a public vaccinator; Namdeo Bakaji Saly Vaday, a compositor; and his brother Laxumon Bakaji Saly Vaday, a 'weighing' foreman.[13] The lone 'Portuguese', Alexander Texeira, was a clerk.[14]

The small houses of Umarkhadi and Ayesha's bungalow were perhaps distinct from the *havelis*—residences characteristic of the central parts of the Indian town.[15] The havelis, situated in the precincts of *pols*, or smaller private lanes leading off from the main streets, were designed to provide both physical security and exclusivity. By contrast, the mushrooming of small independent houses in Umarkhadi suggests that their occupants may have been socially less exclusive. It also perhaps indicates the existence of a reasonable degree of security, as well as a measure of civic control, even at the outer reaches of the Indian town. Sobhan, for example, had to apply for permission to the municipal authorities before the house could be rebuilt. We shall note the ways in which security was a consideration for the organization of space in these humbler neighbourhoods.

Ayesha asserted that she herself had paid the Rs 3,000 or Rs 4,000 it cost to rebuild the house. For this purpose she had sold her jewels, worth Rs 2,000 or Rs 2,500, and, in addition, used her savings from the rents she had received. Her income from rents had been Rs 15 or Rs 20 per month before the house was rebuilt. Afterwards it was Rs 25 or Rs 27.[16] During her husband's lifetime, she had participated in the business in a small way: she used to sell the feet and entrails of animals. We learn this from Ismail's former accountant, Govindrao Ramchunder Deshpande, not from Ayesha herself. As one aspiring to higher social status, she may have been reluctant to disclose her involvement in this lowly activity. At home, her position was enhanced by the fact that the valuable jewels and important papers were kept in her custody. On occasion, such as when a creditor had to be reassured, she was asked to bring out the jewels. This happened when Dorabji, who had lent money to Sobhan, visited him for the last time.[17]

Among the tasks Ayesha accomplished after her husband's death was that of arranging her youngest daughter's marriage. For the expenses of the wedding, she sold jewels worth Rs 4,000 or Rs 5,000 and borrowed money from her brother-in-law. She spent Rs 500 to Rs 600 altogether, besides jewels worth Rs 400 to Rs 500 that she gave to her daughter. The bride also received Rs 500 or Rs 600 worth of jewels from her father-in-law. 'When my three elder daughters married,' reported Ayesha, 'each of them got ornaments worth Rs 500 or 600. This is the usual amount of ornaments given to girls in our station in life. Their father-in-law gave them about the same amount.' In other words they received equal amounts from their own parents and those of their husbands. The jewels given to these women were their own property. In value they amounted to the considerable sum of about Rs 1,000—a half to a third of the value of a house. The house in which Ayesha's family lived was worth about Rs 2,500 before it was rebuilt.[18] These gifts conferred both prestige and security. The owners could, as Hamida—Ismail's wife—did, pawn them for a loan, or they could be used as security for money borrowed by a family. As we have noticed, when creditors with whom there were long-standing relations were involved, the owners could secure loans by simply allowing the creditors to see their jewels, without having to actually hand them over.[19] In families such as this one, the marriage of a daughter was probably no costlier than that of a son. To that extent, daughters may not have been considered a liability.

Ayesha declared that she was in no way dependent on her son. She paid for her own food and had an adequate income, Rs 25–30 from the rents of a portion of her house, over which she had full control. One of her tenants testified that she had on one occasion threatened to lock up his room. When he complained, Sobhan told him that the house belonged to his wife. She was free to manage it as she wished.[20] In fact, she claimed, her son was dependent on her, as he occupied a room in her house. 'I have given him one room in the name of God,' she declared, implying that this was like an act of charity. They shared the hearth but cooked their food separately. However, against Ayesha's evidence is that of Sena Wakhta, the family's creditor and adversary. He asserted that they cooked and ate together. Ayesha must of course have been anxious to proclaim her independence so that the house would not be deemed to belong to Ismail and encumbered for his debts. What is impressive is the boldness with which she made her claim and the manner in which she presented evidence to support it. Her painstaking description of the procedure of tax payment suggests that she was aware of the importance of recounting the details in order to carry conviction that she herself had paid the tax, and that, therefore, the house belonged to her. The fact that her account was apparently free of overstatement may have made it more convincing. She was not sure that her request to have her name entered in the tax records had been attended to. 'I don't know how such transfers are made in the government books,' she declared.

Ayesha's competence was evident both in the way she managed her property and the manner in which she carried out her responsibility to her family. With all that, it is evident that she was aware of the limits of her own situation. There were certain things a woman could not do. She was less competent than a man was to handle matters at the outer boundaries of her immediate environment. Although she provided the money to have her house rebuilt, she had to turn to her husband to organize the project. Again, as a woman she could not have her own name entered in the government records and, indeed, was ignorant about how this was done. She had the presence to admit her disability as a woman in such a manner as to make a plea in her own favour. Although she was not literate, Ayesha nevertheless respected the written word that secured her. She had preserved the deed of gift and the tax records of the house. While she was conscious that she enjoyed a certain 'station in life', she also knew that, as one unable to read, she had to get help from her neighbours in such matters as, for instance, checking the amount on the tax bill.

In a society in which many children died young, the fact that she had mothered six children to adulthood must have been an affirmative experience for Ayesha. One of her sons was no longer living. His son lived with Ismail. But her robust self-confidence probably also had a good deal to do with the successful career of her late husband, Sobhan Balaji, in a rapidly expanding city.

Borrowing and Lending

People in the city often incurred debts in the course of their daily existence. They bought groceries on credit from the neighbourhood *bania* (moneylender, grocer). When money was required for a personal purpose, such as a marriage, they invariably turned to the local Marwari.[21] Besides, credit arrangements were involved in many business dealings. Hawkers and retailers would be advanced goods on credit by the bigger merchants and wholesalers, who often belonged to their own caste. Thus caste links, in many cases, enmeshed with trading arrangements, although, as we shall note, such arrangements were also made across the boundaries of caste and community. There were instances in which traders would borrow money in order to buy trade goods from persons to whom they later sold a part of their goods. These persons were advantageously placed to make a profit on both transactions. They could then use the accumulated gain for further moneylending.

Structures of borrowing and lending were precarious partly because borrowers were often indigent. Physical force was one of the means that creditors used to enforce repayment.[22] Persuasion and pressure from communities, a vivid instance of which we shall recount, was a less obtrusive method that must have played its part in closely peopled neighbourhoods. In addition, the English law of debt had made its appearance in Bombay in the early nineteenth century. It enabled creditors to sue their debtors in the Court of Small Causes and, if the debt were established, to have them jailed. Creditors had to pay for the prisoners' food, a sum which was generally piteously meagre. This and the fact that the prisoners and their families suffered from their not being able to earn their livelihood acted as a strong deterrent to nonpayment of debt. State machinery was designed, above all, to preserve order and allow 'normal' life to be lived. This would be disrupted if countless debtors were locked in jail and prevented from earning a living. The state, it would seem, played the Hobbesian role of holding the ring that at once shut out chaos and allowed day-to-day activity, rather than closely controlling individual lives. The law that allowed debtors to petition the High Court for protection from their creditors, discussed earlier, smoothed the course of financial dealings in the city..

The witnesses in the hearing of Ismail's petition included members of his community, his teacher, his principal creditors, his accountants, and a number of municipal officials. The only woman to appear in court was Ayesha, his mother. Her evidence is particularly rich in the information it provides about the lifestyle of the family. We assume that most of the evidence was given in an Indian language, and then translated and recorded in English. Although we cannot capture the original spoken word, the records convey a vivid picture of the life of the community. We are given a glimpse of interlocking worlds that involved credit and patron–client relationships, as well as links of language, occupation, kinship, caste, and religion. The contours of these worlds may have been common to other small business families in the city.

A Butcher's Business

In an expanding city, the victualling trades occupied a vital niche. One of these trades was the selling of mutton. While most Gujaratis and Brahmins were vegetarians, then, as now, there was a sizeable, often wealthy, population of meat-eaters that included Muslims, Indian Christians, Europeans, Parsis (Zoroastrians), Jews, and Marathas (members of several middle-level, originally agricultural castes of Maharashtra). Europeans constituted an elite clientele, being provided with the freshest meat. For them, and for consumption at wedding feasts, animals were slaughtered at five in the evening, while for others they were killed in the night and the meat sold the next day.[23] Mutton for sale to Europeans cost more; as a successful butcher, Sobhan Balaji may have had a share of this market.

When he died in 1868, Sobhan left a large business to his son, Ismail. Sena Wakhta, a Marwari to whom Ismail was indebted, described him as 'a great merchant. There are not any larger butchers than he'. A well-managed butcher's business was a specialized trade which rested on dependable credit resources and access to livestock. The business had been built by Sobhan. It thrived on the sale of mutton, and of goat and sheep skins.

Three people figured prominently in Sobhan's business dealings. Each belonged to a different community. With two of them the connection had extended over most of Sobhan's active life. This signified mutual trust, vital to the smooth running of a business. An important implication of trust was that credit was granted and goods were advanced without a break. Accounts were squared only periodically and balances paid. Trust rested, of course, on a perception of mutual creditability. It was often affirmed by personal friendship.

Sobhan seems to have had cordial relations with Dorabji, a Parsi who sold him goats. 'Subhan and I were on friendly terms,' declared Dorabji. He had done business with Sobhan and his son, Ismail, for twenty-five to thirty years. He visited Sobhan two or three days before Sobhan died. Sobhan asked him if he had come to ask for money. Dorabji replied that he had come to inquire after his health, not to ask for money. Sobhan then went on to disclose his debts and assets. He owed various people in the bazaar Rs 3,000–4,000, while the amount owed to him was Rs 8,000–10,000. Dorabji did not doubt these figures, as he knew Sobhan had a very large business. Besides this amount, Sobhan's assets included two houses: one in his own name, the other in Ismail's. There were also family jewels worth Rs 4,000–5,000, which his wife brought out for

Dorabji to see. Sobhan told Dorabji that he wished to appoint him and another creditor, Allarakhya, trustees of his estate, so that the property might be protected and his son helped to carry on the business. But a few days later he died.

Sobhan owed Dorabji Rs 1,000, which the latter asked Ismail to pay. Although Dorabji was not able to recover the debt, he did not stop his dealings with Ismail for two or three years. Rather than sue Ismail in the Court of Small Causes, Dorabji then sued another butcher, Ismail Sahu, as Ismail Sobhan had given him an order for payment due from Ismail Sahu. Dorabji failed to recover the money. He declared bitterly that Ismail Sobhan had concealed his wealth and withheld some of his account books from the court, but he did not oppose Ismail's petition for protection.[24]

The most active opponent of Ismail's petition was Allarakhya, along with his partner, Ismail Sahu. Allarakhya was the only one of Sobhan and Ismail's business associates who was a Muslim. Allarakhya was described variously as an 'Arab', a 'Memon' (that is, a member of one of several Muslim sects of western India), a 'banker', and a 'merchant', who advanced money to butchers in exchange for skins. A year and a half before Ismail filed his insolvency petition, he wished to borrow Rs 500 from Allarakhya to buy sheep and goats. Unlike Ismail, who was scarcely literate, Allarakhaya could write, though he employed a mehta to add up his accounts. He asked Ismail what his 'outstandings' were: namely the sums owed to him by other people. He noted the figures that Ismail disclosed from memory, and told Ismail he could not lend him any more money, as Ismail already owed him a considerable amount, while his outstandings were small. Earlier, when Ismail's dealings amounted to Rs 5,000–6,000, he used to pay Allarakhya regularly, but lately he had accumulated a large unsettled balance.[25] The disagreement between the two men hinged mainly on the price which Allarakhya was prepared to pay for goat and sheep skins. Some time before he died, Sobhan had borrowed Rs 5,000 from Allarakhya, and entered into a contract to sell sheep and goat skins to him. Ismail calculated the price of the skins that had been sold to Allarakhya at the market rate: Rs 9–10 per score for sheep skins, and Rs 20–8 per score for goat skins, whereas Allarakhya, alleged Ismail, reckoned the price at Rs 2.25 per score for sheep skins and Rs 4.50 per score for goat skins. The supposed debt of Rs 12,000 to Allarakhya, Ismail claimed, arose from the difference in these rates. If true, Ismail's statement indicated the highly usurious credit on which the business operated.

A third person to whom Sobhan and Ismail were indebted was the Marwari Sena Wakhta, about whom we shall have more to say later in the chapter. The association with him and his brother, Rakhina Hata, was more than fifteen years old.

Ismail Sobhan

Ismail lived in the house which supposedly belonged to his mother, as head of an extended family that consisted of himself, his wife and two sons, a servant, his brother-in-law, and his nephew. The latter were both orphans and minors. His sons were schoolboys. As the only surviving son of a successful butcher, Ismail had been well provided for. Unlike boys of other business communities, such as Marwaris, Ismail did not actively participate in the family business. As a young boy, he would leave the house early, go to the bazaar, and sit at the shop until nine or ten o'clock. Having earned two or three annas selling entrails, he would spend some more time in the bazar, then go home, eat his breakfast, and go to school. He would return from school at four o'clock. But this routine lasted only two or three years; he must have been eleven or twelve when he stopped going to school. From then on he would simply spend the afternoon at home. It was at this early age, or perhaps a year or two later, that his father gave him a house, the rents from which amounted to about Rs 30 a month. Ismail spent the money on a horse and carriage. 'I kept a horse and carriage to drive and please myself,' he said. At first, being very young, he had a horse-keeper to drive the carriage which was a 'mail phaeton' that accommodated three in front and two at the back. It cost Rs 300. He used it for eighteen years and then sold it for Rs 40. Not as expensive or as elegant as the fancy carriages that the wealthy citizens vied with each other to own, his phaeton must yet have marked Ismail out as a person of means in the modest community of butchers.[26]

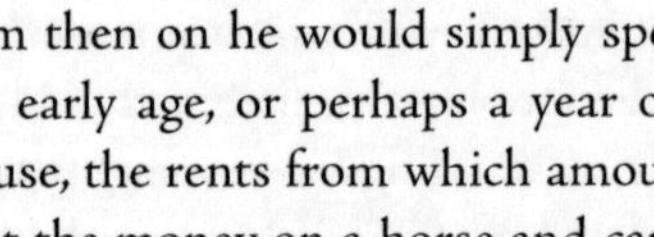

Figure 6.1 Signature of Ismail Sobhan

Ismail was almost illiterate. 'I can write badly in Balbodh, but only my name and the names of other persons,' he declared.[27] During his all-too-brief schooling, Ismail probably acquired rudimentary writing skills. We do not know whether, while in school, he may also have imbibed the ideas of the Balbodh primers, designed to teach elementary wisdom to a child. Nor do we know why he stopped going to school. The only other education Ismail received consisted of lessons in reading the Quran. His teacher was Sheikh Ali Sheikh Mohammad, a contractor for road metal, who knew a little Persian and taught boys to read the Quran and other books, but not to write.[28]

Ismail was wholly dependent on accountants for keeping his accounts. Soon after his father died, he engaged a Brahmin writer, Govindrao Ramchundar Deshpande, who wrote his accounts for two years. Ismail would give him verbal instructions together with the memoranda he kept.[29] He did not pay Govindrao a monthly salary, but only a daily wage. When Govindrao did not come, Ismail would employ casual writers who would come to write every two or three days and be paid two or four annas on each occasion.[30] Among these were young Brahmin boys such as Ganpat, Govindrao's nephew. Ganpat's brother, Trimbak, may have been a writer. These boys had entered the profession of bookkeeping at a young age under the guidance of older relatives. One of the writers Ismail employed was a Prabhu by the name of Dadaji. Others who wrote for him included Gopal Sakharam and Balwant, a young Brahmin.

The evidence of the Marathi writers who worked for Ismail gives us a glimpse of the culture of bookkeeping among traders, and suggests what the incomes of the writers may have been. Men such as Govindrao Ramchunder Deshpande and Raghunath Vishnu each wrote the accounts of three or four butchers, and earned two to four annas at each place on each occasion. They would first write the *rozmal*, or daily accounts, from memoranda supplied by their employers and use these to compile the fair account books. Young boys who worked with them would at first be allowed to handle only the rozmal.[31] The monthly earnings of a writer would thus be up to Rs 30, an adequate though not too sumptuous sum. If there was more than one earner in a family, the family's income would be that much more. Bouyant trade was as vital to the well-being of writers as were their services to the largely unlettered butchers they served.

Several languages were employed in bookkeeping, a reflection of the cultural heterogeneity of the city. Marwaris, as we shall notice, used Marwari.

At the slaughterhouse, the accounts of butchers were noted in Persian. The clerk to the superintendent of markets could not read Persian. He relied on an inspector to tell him what the accounts of individual butchers were.[32] The butchers' own accounts may have been written either in Marathi or Modi by the accountants they employed.[33] Ismail, who could not read, could not check what had been written. 'I can't read or write and can't explain my books except what I have written with my own hand,' he told the court. So helpless was he that he used to get the Marwari, who later turned hostile, to enter a loan in his books. Ismail proved to be equally inept at the difficult task of realizing his 'outstandings', the money owed by customers for goods sold on credit. His father, he declared, 'left outstandings amounting to Rs 16,000. I recovered none of these.'[34]

Neither Ismail nor his family seem to have valued the importance of literacy as a means of exercising control over their business. At a crucial age, Ismail dropped out of school and was endowed with the means to adopt a life of ease, including leisured afternoons spent at home and a carriage in which to be driven. Ismail evidently derived his sense of security from his wealth. He declared that his father did not ask Dorabji to continue his custom to him (that is, Ismail) 'because he had two houses and many ornaments'. On his deathbed, Sobhan seems to have had misgivings about his son's ability to carry on the business. But during his son's youth the father appears to have made little effort to involve him in the trade. A clue to this family's attitude toward learning was the importance it gave to reading the Quran. The emphasis seems to have been on being able to recite the holy word, not on reading as a skill and not on writing. Badruddin Tyabji, Ismail's counsel, declared that Ismail's actions were 'transparently honest altho' [his] accounts [were] not very accurately kept.... What more,' he asked, '[could] be expected from an ignorant butcher?'[35] A very different personality and business culture are revealed in the activities of the Marwari, Sena Wakhta.

Sena Wakhta

The candour with which Sena Wakhta narrated his dealings reveals a well-honed culture of moneylending, in which abstract notions of fair play and truthfulness had little place. His evidence brings to light features that may have been shared by other Marwari firms engaged in moneylending in the city. Prominent among these features was the existence of strong family ties among the partners, buttressed by a continuing link with their homeland, Marwar. Equally striking was an abundant pragmatism that enabled them to manoeuvre their way deftly in the law courts, especially the Court of Small Causes and the police court, as well as to come to terms with their adversaries out of court if the occasion so demanded. Frugality was another important trait. Sena Wakhta wrote all his accounts himself and did not require a mehta. He wrote in Marwari, and, in fact, could not read either Modi or Gujarati. His use of Marwari was an added safeguard of the privacy of his books. With an eye to saving, and in order to keep a close watch on the affairs of an important client, he and his brother would live in the client's house, adjusting the rent against their loan. As to policy, their principle seems to have been to ensure ample coverage for the money lent in the value of the jewels they demanded as security.

Sena Wakhta came to Bombay from Marwar in 1859 or 1860 to join his older brother, Rakhina Hata, who had set up a moneylending concern some years earlier. Sena was then about thirteen years old. They lived and had their shop in a house on Khadak Road, 'also known as Dontad Road', which Sobhan had purchased in the name of Ismail. The rent was Rs 5 a month. However, as Sobhan had borrowed money from him, having pledged ornaments as security, the rent was adjusted in the accounts against the loan. Sena's dealings with Sobhan, claimed the Marwari, amounted to Rs 5,000–10,000. Within three years of Sena's coming to Bombay, when he must have been sixteen, Sena Wakhta said he had acquired full control of the business. His brother then began to travel back and forth between Marwar and Bombay. He 'went to his native place and after that he returned to Bombay and again returned to his native place. He used to go backwards and forwards'. His brother, declared Sena Wakhta, 'had full confidence in me that I would manage business properly. Our business is about Rs 25,000. That is, this [is] the capital of the firm. I had full charge of this business when my brother left. I did not require a metha. I could do all the business myself'. Sena Wakhta prided himself on his good memory and could recall the exact date on which, in 1865, he vacated the house. On that date he made a new arrangement with another party and moved into a house in a neighbouring street, Chintz Bandar. From Sena Wakhta's account we get a vivid picture of his boldness in handling court proceedings and his prowess in attaching the property of debtors. Clearly, here was a world of hundreds of impecunious borrowers and of moneylenders who were none too scrupulous in the methods they employed. But here too, as we shall note, group pressure from a person's community was often an effective determinant of conduct.

Sena Wakhta actively opposed Ismail's petition. He had sued Ismail's wife in the Court of Small Causes for a loan of Rs 100 given on personal security, and had got a decree against her for Rs 173. Apart from this loan, and another for Rs 700 that had been cleared, Sena Wakhta declared he had no dealings with Ismail and his wife. He did not mention a loan which Ismail said his wife had taken and for which ornaments had been pledged. According to Ismail, Sena Wakhta had appropriated jewels worth Rs 275 for a loan of Rs 150. Ismail had sued Sena Wakhta in his wife's name and lost the suit because, he said, the Brahmin who used to write for him had given false evidence.[36] Pressed about the jewels he had kept back, Sena Wakhta admitted he had indeed retained jewels worth about Rs 300. These, he alleged, had been pledged not by Ismail but by his mother for a loan to her.

It is difficult to pick out the true facts in this labyrinth of conflicting evidence. What does emerge is the image of an exacting moneylender. Sena Wakhta declared that Ismail had offered to pay him Rs 150 if he, Ismail, won his case, this being the amount of the debt, and had asked Sena Wakhta not to give evidence against him. But Sena Wakhta had refused; he expected to recover the entire amount of the decree, Rs 173, if Ismail's petition were rejected. To this end he bent his efforts to convince the court that Ismail had not disclosed all his wealth in his petition. The house in which Ismail lived, said Sena Wakhta, was his own, not his mother's; he had jewels besides those he had disclosed to the court. If he could secure a decree against Ismail in the Court of Small Causes, Sena Wakhta might have reckoned, he could have him arrested and imprisoned. The fear of going to jail, he perhaps calculated, would be strong enough to induce Ismail to pay the full amount of the decree.

Marwaris such as Sena Wakhta probably preferred to keep a low profile, rather than resorting to overt force in dealing with debtors, and were adept in working their way through the web of the lower courts. On the very day when he gave evidence at the hearing on Ismail's petition, Sena Wakhta declared that he had come to the court directly after having attached a debtor's property. Moreover, he did not function as an isolated individual. We noted the presence of a family base in his business. Besides, there was also a link with the Marwari community, which helped to furnish a code of conduct. This is brought out vividly in Sena Wakhta's description of another dealing. His adversary, in this instance, belonged to a community with a code as pragmatic as that of the Marwaris.

When pressed by Tyabji, Sena Wakhta admitted he was not a stranger to the police court. He had been prosecuted there for forgery and perjury by Hilan Musaji, who was Jewish. Sena had Musaji arrested in execution of a decree he had obtained against him. Musaji made an application to the Court of Small Causes, in which he declared he had already paid the amount of the decree. The judge asked Musaji if he had a receipt for the payment, and when he said he had no receipt, he was advised to go to the police court. Accordingly, Hilan Musaji brought a suit of forgery and perjury against Sena Wakhta in the police court: forgery for having presented the same decree twice, and perjury for having sworn in court that he had not been paid the amount of the decree.[37] Recounting the incident, Sena Wakhta stoutly denied the charge. 'I had not committed forgery,' he said. At this point, pressure from their respective communities came into play. 'Three or four Jews and three or four Marwadis [Marwaris]', related Sena Wakhta, 'said we were businessmen and should not spend money, but should settle the case. Upon this the case was settled. They said that I should repay the money that I had received under the Small Causes Court decree. I refused at first, but afterwards consented.' The case was withdrawn and there the matter ended. We have in Sena Wakhta's story a remarkably transparent statement of his own dealings, as well as a clear instance of the restraining power of unofficial sanction, namely community opinion, to contain fraud and dispute within certain bounds.

For every large Marwari firm which operated in the world of big business, there were numerous smaller concerns, such as that of the brothers Rakhina Hata and Sena Wakhta, which did not move on from money-lending to large-scale trade and industrial and financial enterprise. These smaller concerns thrived in the vast zone of the city where neediness was bounded by extreme poverty on the one hand, and considerable wealth on the other. But while Rakhina Hata and Sena Wakhta did not, it would seem, aspire to more ambitious business, they helped fuel the capital of traders and small entrepreneurs. The firm of 'Sena Vakta & Co.' is listed for a loan of Rs 4,500 among the creditors of the Jewish building contractor Haskel Babaji Penker, who lived in the neighbouring street, Masjid Bunder Road.[38] Another debtor was Mohanaji Januji Londay who lived in Chinch Bunder, sold fruit, and operated country craft and, in addition, had a small income from rent. He owed Sena Wakhta Rs 2,000.[39]

While for thirty years or so of the record Sena Wakhta appears to have functioned mainly as a neighbourhood moneylender, his brother Rakhina Hata's trips back and forth between Bombay and Marwar are perhaps significant in suggesting the flow of money between Marwar and the metropolis. Although Sena Wakhta did not state the purpose of his brother's travel, the fact that he gave this information in the course of a description of his business suggests that there may have been a financial purpose. In other words, Rakhina Hata, like the bigger Marwaris, may have been engaged in moving resources back and forth.[40]

Caste, Occupation, Religion

The picture we form of the private world of Ismail and his family contains clues about the many-layered identities that sustained them. According to Ayesha, the family spoke Hindustani. This would suggest a Deccani origin. Maharashtrian Muslims from the Konkan generally speak Marathi, whereas the spoken language of Muslims from the Deccan, whether Karnataka or Hyderabad or the Marathwada region, is generally Urdu or Hindustani. There are other indications of a possible connection with the northern Karnataka or southern Maharashtra region. Ayesha described a close associate of Sobhan's, Bhau Ranoji Chogule, as being 'of our caste, but not a relation'. The prefix 'bhau', meaning 'brother', is a form of address common in Maharashtra. The word *chogule* does not occur in Kannada. It is a Marathi word found in northern Karnataka, southern Maharashtra, and Goa, to denote a village official under a *patil*, who performed minor law and order functions.[41] It is nowhere explicitly stated whether or not Bhau Ranoji Chogule was a Muslim. If he was not, it is remarkable that he should have testified as a witness in the transfer deed of Ayesha's house—a document that had a pronounced Islamic ambience. In referring to Bhau Ranoji Chogule, it was his caste identity that seems to have been uppermost in Ayesha's mind. Another suggestive name in the list of the family's close associates was that of Ismail's partner, Husain Chandaji Dhangar. While the first name, Husain, is distinctly Islamic, the middle and last names are not. Like the name Chogule, the name Dhangar denotes an origin in rural, pastoral society.

The classical description of *dhangar*s in the Bombay Presidency, published in 1920, identifies them as pastoralists, some of whom, such as the *gavali dhangar*s, were cattle breeders, while others kept goats and sheep. Still others specialized in weaving blankets. They were among the oldest tribes of the region and were spread over central India and the Deccan, including parts of Maharashtra and Karnataka. Of the twenty-three endogamous subdivisions of dhangars, one was that of Musalmans. While many dhangars at this date were still nomads who moved with their animals over a considerable area in the course of the seasons, many others had become settled agriculturalists. Still others had taken up a variety of occupations, whether in the countryside or in the cities.[42] Of the numerous service people and traders who formed a part of the growing population of Bombay in the first half of the nineteenth century, some may have been dhangars. Among the dhangars we encounter in the insolvency records are the Muslim butcher Chandbabani Dhungar and the Hindu day-labourer Laduji Ramji Dhangar.[43]

Might we suppose that the community of butchers with which we are concerned belonged to a group that, at some unknown date in the past, had converted to Islam, while retaining its pastoral identity expressed through caste? Among the castes from which butchers are said to have been drawn were dhangars, who took to slaughtering their animals when Muslim penetration of the Deccan created a demand for meat.[44] Those dhangars who opted for this market opportunity—namely the supply of meat to Muslims—would, we presume, have had to convert in order to meet the canonical requirement for slaughter (*zabiha*). The earliest conversions, therefore, may have taken place about the thirteenth century. It is remarkable that butchers continued to identify themselves as dhangars for several centuries.

At the point in time when they come into our view, the butchers in our story were ordering their lives simultaneously in terms of at least three distinct cultural schemes, in addition to kinship ties. These schemes denoted occupation, caste, and religion, respectively. In the first place, butchers were practicing their trade in the business environment of a growing metropolis—an environment that held out great opportunities for success, but was also fraught with risk. We have noticed the way Sobhan was able to expand his business through his ability to establish working relations with his caste brethren as well as with other persons.

Being butchers, at the same time, defined their caste. In some ways, the cultural category of caste provided the family with the most unchanging structure of relationships, in stability next only to the still more abiding category of kinship. Kinship ties were intimate, but because they were so, they were also liable to be stressful. There are hints that Sobhan had had a quarrel with his brother, Wali.[45] He may have gifted a house to Wali in order to resolve the differences. But caste identities were enacted in a specific urban setting and, in the process, were often reordered and redefined.

The third cultural scheme that influenced the family was its religion, Islam. This scheme functioned not in contradiction to caste but along with it, as a lifeline that formed links beyond the boundaries of caste, while it drew upon a tradition of supra-cultural identity. Here again, the urban environment provided an important backdrop. In the actions of Sobhan, Ayesha, and Ismail, we notice ways in which caste and religion were articulated. In the event, unbeknown to the subjects, both caste and religion took on some new meanings.

The word 'caste' occurs in translation in the record. We are, therefore, left to guess that the original word may have been *jat* or *zat*. But whatever the word, it is its context, its perceived status and actualization in social praxis that hold the key to its meaning. It has been argued that the act of definition as it occurred in official documentation imperceptibly altered social categories by appropriating meanings other than those present in the historical context. But in order to identify transformation in the cultural category of caste, we must first observe how it was perceived and practised by the subjects themselves. To Ayesha, Ismail, and their friends, caste implied a very real, tangible relationship. We have noticed Ayesha's affirmative statement, 'Bhau Ranoji was of our caste, but not a relation.' Another witness, Balaji Bhikaji, also a mutton butcher, declared, 'I am the same caste as [the] insolvent.' A focal institution of the caste of butchers was the butchers' *jamatkhana*, or communal club, in which one of the witnesses, Mohammad Amin, earlier Ayesha's tenant, lived.[46] In common with the clubs of other communities in the city, the jamatkhana may have provided a range of services, especially accommodation to those in need.[47]

Butchers also shared a symbol in the mark they used in place of a signature, if they could not write. 'My father,' declared Ismail, 'was an uneducated man and could not write. He used to make a mark of a pair of scales, when he wanted to sign a paper. He never signed his name as he could not write. He used to draw scales like those used by butchers.' Ayesha's nephew, Kasam Ahmed Lamtari, also used scales as his mark. 'I have attested other writings ... and executed deeds with my mark, scales,' he said.[48] In this record we find corroborative evidence of a usage, namely, the use of occupational symbols as substitutes for signatures. The fact that the symbol occurred in more than one context, was used, as we shall notice, in a private deed, and was explicitly acknowledged by those who used it suggests that it was an established convention. However remotely, the symbol served to link members of the caste.

Caste was enacted in a particularly tangible way in the family's ordering of its private space. As if to replicate the model of a village, in which the leading families of a dominant caste occupied the central, most protected, areas of a village site, neighboured by their caste brethren, Ayesha, Ismail, and his family occupied the first floor of the house. The ground floor was let to tenants. This physical position was attained as a result of the growing prosperity of the family, which enabled it to enlarge the house. Affluence thus led in a visible way to social elevation, enabling Ayesha to function as a matriarch in relation to her tenants, two of whom were, and others who may have been, of the caste of butchers. The two, Balaji Bhikaji and Mohammad Amin, had been Ayesha's tenants for fourteen to fifteen years, and were in fact living in the house when the upper storey was built. They appeared as witnesses and were at pains to assert that the house belonged to Ayesha. She had admitted them as tenants, they said, she had received the rents, and she had paid the workmen who rebuilt the house. It was Balaji Bhikaji whose room, as we have noted earlier, that Ayesha had threatened to lock up. Recalling the incident, he emphasized her claim to the house and acknowledged her dominance over him as his landlady.[49] The dominance may not have been consolidated: the family's affluence was transient. But perhaps we have here an aspect of the caste linkages of class, one that was peculiar to urban life with its greater possibility of differential wealth and its spatial compulsions. It made for security and cultural sharing for those who could afford to live in proximity to their caste fellows. Where, as in the case of Ayesha and her family, caste links were expressed in the unequal relationship of landlady–tenant, the caste bond embodied both symbiosis and inequality, both stability and potential stress. Inequality within the structure of caste was most visible in instances where well-to-do persons appeared as patrons of weaker members of their caste. Ayesha's tenant Balaji Bhikaji, for instance, was almost blind, while Mohammad Amin was no longer a practicing butcher but had taken to the humbler occupation of selling tea.[50] The experience of urban living tended to strengthen, rather than dissolve, the sense of caste. While being modified in certain ways, caste continued to be an intimate focus of identity that governed a network of received relationships.

Religion, in contrast to caste, linked a person to a wider world. It involved the conscious ackowledgement and conceptualization of the precepts of the religion, but in this, as we shall note, a subtle re-interpretation often took place.

Islamic Identity and the Deed

Muslim identity in some Indian communities, it has been suggested, often took shape as a reaction to counter-identity movements—the Arya Samaj conversion (*shuddhi*) campaigns of the late nineteenth century, for instance, setting off proselytization (*tabligh*).[51] A less obtrusive process of identity formation involved the appropriation of religious symbols in the conduct of everyday life. A dual movement is noticeable here. Autonomous acts were sanctified by means of a subconscious association with the tenets of the religion and religious symbolism was adopted in the praxis of mundane matters. The culture was thereby subtly modified and integrated. Islamic forms, or rather procedures perceived as Islamic, may have been adopted in such matters as the conveyance of property. This tendency may have accompanied upward social mobility. In trying to see what being Muslim may have meant to Sobhan Balaji and his family, we come upon a realm in which religious categories were invoked for a secular purpose.

Sobhan's circle of Muslim friends and acquaintances extended beyond his fellow butchers. This extension may have accompanied the improvement in his station in life. We mentioned Sheikh Ali Sheikh Mohammad, the person who used to teach the Quran to Ismail. His name suggests a higher lineage. Being literate and able to read the Quran must also have enhanced Sheikh Ali Sheikh Mohammad's position. As a contractor for road metal, that is, for the construction of metalled (tarred) roads, he may have been an employer both of capital and of labour. Then there was the Khoja magnate, Dharamsi Poonjiabhai, with whom the family had some contact. Ismail reported that his father had left an account book with 'Dharamsi Punji'. This may have been in keeping with a convention whereby influential creditors would have the books of their clients brought over to their own place for the debt to be entered.[52] But perhaps the act also suggested a relationship of trust. Dharamsi's son, Meerali Dharamsi, had advanced Ismail Rs 400.[53] Although we learn little else about this connection, the association with Dharamsi and perhaps with other Khojas may have influenced the family's values and strategies concerning property.

The person who played a leading part in affirming the family's Muslim identity through a deed of gift couched in a distinctly Islamic form was the elusive figure of Syed Husen bin Syed Ahmad Rafai. Ayesha said he 'was a friend of my husband's who used to visit the house'. Sheikh Ali Sheikh Mohammad corroborated Ayesha's statement. Referring to Syed Husen bin Syed Ahmed Rafai as 'Syed Saheb Rafai' or simply 'Rafai,' he said, 'Syed Saheb Rafai was a friend of Sobhan and used to visit the house. I knew Rafai well. He is now dead. I don't know when he died. He was a Pir, and a holy man. He knew Arabic.' Sheikh Ali Sheikh Mohammad had more to say about Syed Husen bin Syed Ahmad Rafai, whom he first knew eighteen or nineteen years earlier:

> Rafai lived in Gogari Mohla Street.... He was in the habit of writing deeds for people.... I knew him for about a year. He came from Bagdad. Where he went I know not. So far as I know he has not been here since 17 years. He acted as a Pir during the year he was here. He used to pray in the mosque and write for others.[54]

This account reveals both the range of Syed Husen bin Syed Ahmed Rafai's functions, and the cultural underpinnings of the deed he helped to execute.

We may consider the deed, which Ayesha produced in court to support her claim to the house, as evidence of the existence of a private legal culture, which resorted to religious categories, in this instance Islamic, for a non-spiritual objective—the conveyance of property. These categories were the language (Arabic), the citation of verses from the Quran, and the agency of a Muslim pir. The document, translated and read out by the court interpreter, was a deed of gift in Arabic executed by Sobhan Balaji, by which he gave the house, household furniture, gold, silver and copper pots to Ayesha, daughter of Bachubaba. It stated the boundaries of the house and the date, Friday, 5 December 1854. Sobhan put his mark on it. Then followed the names of the first three witnesses as written by Syed Husen bin Syed Ahmad Rafai, together with their marks. As we have noticed, the mark in each case was a pair of scales such as were generally used by butchers. These first three witnesses were Husen (Chandaji) Dhangar, whom Ismail identified as his father's partner, Bhau Ranoji Chogule, and

Kasam Ahmad Lamtari, Ayesha's nephew. The fourth witness was Sheikh Ali Sheikh Mohammad, who signed in his own handwriting. At the end was stated the name of the writer of the document, Syed Husen. Sheikh Ali Sheikh Mohammad, as one of the two surviving witnesses, and the only one who was literate, provided details of the manner in which the deed was drafted. Sobhan gave the instructions for writing the deed. 'He did not tell the Sayad what verses of Kuran to write, but only to write according to Mahomedan Law.'

What weight did such a private deed carry? When Ayesha presented it in court, the opposing counsel argued that the gift was invalid, as it was not followed by delivery of possession. On the other hand, Badruddin Tyabji declared, 'Ayesha was put in possession of the house in the only way in which a married woman could be put in possession.' Tyabji went on to state that the document was a genuine one, as the paper bore the watermark of the year in which it was executed, 1854. No questions were raised concerning the authenticity of the deed as an instrument of transfer. Moreover, this particular deed was not unique. We learn that Syed Husen bin Syed Ahmad Rafai used to write deeds, presumably private deeds, for various people. Kasam Ahmed Lamtari declared that Rafai had executed other deeds.

However indirectly, the episode has a bearing on the evolving culture of the colonial state. At this date, in a leading metropolis of the empire, private legal culture had not been wholly subsumed. Yet we become aware that this culture was under threat. This is apparent in Ayesha's interrogation concerning the status of the house. Viewed literally, she seemed to contradict herself and tie herself in knots. But her testimony may also be seen to reflect a real conflict in ascribed value between the deed, on the one hand, and the municipal bills, on the other, as tokens of legitimacy. Seen in this light, her answers are a tribute to her courage and intelligence.

For Ayesha the deed was the thing. She said, 'The house stands in my name. Formerly it stood in the name of my husband. It passed to me by the writing [that is, the deed].' Believing this was the case, she had no hesitation in admitting, 'The house stands in the Government records in my husband's name to this day.' At this point in the examination, the importance of the name that appeared in the bills gradually assumed primacy, pushing her to the wall. She claimed the bills were in her name, then pleaded her inability, being a woman, to know who had entered her name, and finally presented papers that negated her position. Ayesha declared:

> The bills for taxes used to come in my husband's name. They have come in my name since my husband gave me the writing. I don't know who had the bills altered to my name, because I am a woman. I have known they were in my name because the bill man used to call out my name when he brought the bills. He has called my name ever since my husband executed the writing. I have brought some of the bills.

Asked if she had kept account books of the rents she had received, she was quick to answer, 'There were no books and no occasion to keep any.' She had carefully kept the bills of the taxes that had been paid. Unfortunately for Ayesha, all the tax bills she presented in court were in Sobhan's name. We have noticed that in this instance private law, embodied in the deed of gift, was not displaced outright. Even the opposing counsel tacitly conceded the ground to Islamic law. But the trend of the questioning was unmistakably weighted in favour of official documentation. Had she got a second chance, Ayesha would perhaps have tried to have her name entered in the tax record and used that to assert her claim to the house.

The point need not be stressed that popular identities were affirmed, perpetuated, negated, and modified along a historical continuum. Explicit events, legal enactments or popular protests constituted one part of the process. Another part comprised the almost imperceptible moulding of popular culture in praxis as a response to the functioning of the organs of the state, especially the law courts. This may also have altered the pivotal position of the leaders who mediated that culture. In our narrative, Syed Husen bin Syed Ahmad Rafai was one such leader, who appeared not in person but in the evidence of the witnesses. The prefix of his name, 'Syed', betokened descent from the Prophet. He was believed to have come from Baghdad and wrote deeds for people. We learn of the subject matter of one such deed, Sobhan's deed of a gift to his wife drawn up in accordance with Islamic law.

Syed Husen's services included praying in the mosque. We are not told whether he simply led the prayers, or whether he also preached. Nevertheless, we do get a view of a man learned in Islamic tradition rendering essential service to a largely illiterate community. He may indeed have been one of a continuous stream of learned men drawn from the Arab world to India, where there existed a demand for their services from the time Islam came to the subcontinent. A few years before Ismail put in his petition, we meet another insolvent, Syed Rajub bin Syed Ebraheem

Rufaee, described as a 'Mahomedan fukeer or what is called a priest or beggar'.[55] Somewhat later we find the petition of the insolvent Jaanoola Abadin bin Syed Hismuddin Rafae, 'a Mahomedan priest'.[56] Such men, as the vagueness about Syed Husen's whereabouts suggests, were perhaps itinerant pirs, who lived on the support of their well-wishers. Syed Husen, we are told, was a friend of Sobhan's and used to visit his house. Sheikh Ali Sheikh Mohammad knew him well. It is not difficult to imagine that these people not only functioned as scribes but may also have exercised religious influence.

They may, in consequence, have acted as agents for conversion, especially among artisanal and service communities aspiring to higher social status. Dyers in Bombay, at the end of the century, reminisced that their ancestors had converted to Islam because they had had differences with the Saraswat Brahmin priests.[57] Dyers, who used urine in the process of dyeing, and butchers, who handled blood and flesh, would most likely be considered ritually unclean by the orthodox. A good deal of conversion may have taken place quietly in towns and kasbahs where artisans and service people were concentrated.

Syed Husen's supposed origin in Baghdad may have represented a part of the folklore of Indo-Muslim culture which, in common with nearly every other religious culture, located its spiritual anchorage in the place where the religion originated. This was in the Arab world. In other words, Syed Husen, as one learned in Islamic tradition, was associated by the community with Baghdad, an important seat of Islamic learning. But there was also perhaps a more tangible link. Baghdad was of course famous as the birthplace of the Sufi saint Abd al-Qadir al-Jilani, founder of the Qadiriyya order. However, the suffix of Syed Husein's name, 'Rafai' (Rifai, Rufaee, Rufae), connects him not with the Qadiriyya but with another order, the Rifaiyya—one of the most widespread and lasting of Sufi orders that originated in Iraq in the twelfth century.[58] Men such as Syed Husen bin Syed Ahmad Rafai, Syed Rujub bin Syed Ebraheem Rufaee, and Syed Janoola Abadin bin Syed Hismuddin Rafae open for us a window onto the influence of Sufism upon popular culture. They appear as 'barefoot' holy men who mingled with the people. Syed Husen prayed in the mosque and facilitated the material arrangements of the community by drafting deeds. While participating in the life of the people, did such men convey something of the humane message of Sufism?

The deed Syed Husen drew up legitimized the act of giving. It bound together the participants—the giver, receiver, witnesses, and writer—in a rite that was practiced in a specifically Islamic form, and enjoyed the sanction of the community. The ready availability of instruments of private law, beyond the all-powerful influence of caste elders and orthodox priests, may have attracted working people to Islam: people who, for instance, had acquired some wealth and wished to transfer it as they wished. Private law probably also had an extended function as a focus of community cohesion. Consequently, it is likely that any ground gained by official procedures and public law over private customary practices threatened that cohesion.

The cultural identity of this micro-community of butchers, with its strong sense of caste as well as of religion, embraced a spectrum that included moorings in Indian pastoral society and, at the same time, in the world of Islam beyond. Within this spectrum, the urban matrix served to transform culture in praxis through the selective appropriation and assimilation of concepts and institutions that were neither tribal nor Islamic, though in the record they might be termed 'Islamic'. Language, we shall suggest, mediated the transition to a new cultural synthesis.

In the actual encounter of such communities with official, colonial culture, and their concomitant encounter with the culture of other groups, we may postulate two simultaneous developments. While the former may have deprived the practice of Islam of some of its secular, mundane aspects, in that sense making it more narrowly 'spiritual', the latter perhaps allowed the appropriation of a wider range of cultural elements, some of which may also have had a practical value. This function was an attribute of the diversity of a city such as Bombay, where the range of cultural alternatives was relatively wide. At the same time, cultural choices may have been influenced by the given priorities, both material and spiritual, of particular communities. For suggestive evidence, we turn again to the most revealing of our witnesses, Ayesha.

'Like a Good Musalman'

Sobhan gave away his three houses, one each to his son, his brother Wali, and his wife. In addition, he gave Rs 1,000 to Wali. In referring to these gifts, Ayesha made the striking remark, 'Like a good Musalman he divided all his property during his lifetime.' Now, there is no clear precept in Islam enjoining a man to gift his property in the manner in which Sobhan had done so. There is, however, a rule of inheritance, and the usual practice is for a man's property to be divided according to this rule upon his death. Why then did Ayesha look upon her husband's acts as being virtuous in an Islamic sense? She may, of course, simply have equated 'a good Musalman' with 'a good man', who took this course in order to ensure that there was no dispute after his death. Nonetheless, the question comes to mind whether Sobhan's action, and Ayesha's view of it, may have had a more specific context.

Many Muslim communities of the west coast followed customs governing succession and property that were common to other people. So evident was this that in 1847 Chief Justice Sir Erskine Perry made the remarkable ruling, 'If a custom as to succession is found to prevail amongst a sect of Mahomedans and be valid in other respects, the Court will give effect to it although it differs from the rule of succession laid down in the Koran.'[59]

Practices other than Islamic were prevalent, especially among the Memons and Khojas. The latter converted to Islam three or four hundred years earlier. At first farmers and small traders in Sind and Kutch, they had spread to Kathiawar, and from there, in the last hundred years, as merchants to Bombay and to Africa, Arabia, Iran, and China. The well-known Khoja merchant Habibbhai Ibrahimbhai declared, 'We do not regulate inheritance in our caste by the Mahomedan law but according to the customs prevailing from time immemorial in our caste. I believe it is according to Hindu customs.'[60] Among these customs was one whereby a son could claim his share of family property during his father's lifetime. The institution lent itself to the requirements of trading communities, for it enabled sons to start independent businesses at an early age. This practice was widely prevalent among Khojas in Kutch and Kathiawar. Not surprisingly, it did not have unquestioned sway. Disputes were known to occur when a father was unwilling to grant his son's claim to his share of the family property. One such dispute involved the prominent Khoja merchant Ahmedbhai Habibbhai and his son, Cassumbhai. Among those actively engaged on Cassumbhai's side was his close relative Dharamsi Poonjiabhai.

The debate concerning the laws that applied to Khojas remained alive for almost half a century. It probably engaged the attention of other Muslims in the city, who were likely to be affected by a law governing inheritance. Indeed, Perry's landmark judgment of 1847, to which reference was made in the case of Ahmedbhai and Cassumbhai, embraced not only Khojas but all Muslim sects. Ayesha, active in managing her property, must have been familiar with the custom, and may also have been aware of the ongoing debate. Dharamsi Poonjiabhai, as we have noted, was known to her husband. Ayesha's remark seems significant not because it reflected juridical dichotomies, but because it perhaps mirrored a process of conceptualization that was opposite, one in which dichotomies were obliterated in the course of a continuous process of assimilation, precept and practice being linked in unbroken customary sequence. For Ayesha, 'a good Musulman' was one who did as other Muslims did. Since many Muslims followed the custom of dividing the family property while the head of the family was living, this custom was considered right. By implication, a man who divided his property in this manner could be looked upon as being 'a good Musulman'. Ayesha did not invoke either Quranic or Hindu precept, although the rule that she tacitly acknowledged was in fact derived from custom other than Islamic.

Language played an important role in the process of assimilation. It obscured dichotomies and enabled fresh synthesis to take place unselfconsciously. Ayesha's words suggest aspects of this structuring of popular culture. As we have noticed, the precept she tacitly acknowledged did not derive from Quranic text. And yet, in her view, her husband's action had been virtuous in an Islamic sense. By thus embedding a customary practice, she was subconsciously and creatively extending the meaning of what it was to be a good Musalman. And while the words she used mediated her interpretation, they were themselves modified in the process. To be a good Musalman, in her sense, was clearly different from being one who followed Quranic principles in the matter of property inheritance, although she herself may have been unaware of the distinction. Through the meaning attached to these words, a new synthesis had been achieved. Language and cultural formation were here locked in a synchronous, subconscious process. By contrast, official criteria were invariably bounded by dichotomies: Hindu/Muslim and customary/Quranic, to mention a few. Such criteria tended to marginalize not simply customary laws, but also the process of their evolution. The cultural process that Ayesha's words reflect must have been a part of folk tradition, wherein that tradition was continually enriched by the incorporation of new elements. It is likely that this enrichment was checked by bureaucratic attempts to codify and administer the laws.

Not that there was an overt design to distort the people's laws. In fact, an impressive feature of the official discourse was the painstaking endeavour to discover what the laws actually were.[61] So, too, was the realization that the bias of those who answered queries concerning custom—generally heads of castes or learned men—often obscured the truth.[62] In order to overcome this bias, Justice Jardine, for instance, urged that more weight should be given to the norms embodied in the wills and deeds of an earlier period.[63] Indeed, those who drafted the codes incorporated in those codes many customs as they perceived them. All the same, custom and its intrinsic processes were subtly sidelined. This was the result not so much of lack of knowledge about custom or of callousness on the part of the authorities, as it was of their overriding compulsion to systematize custom and render it manageable for the purpose of administration. In the event, notwithstanding ambiguities which still exist, a more uniform reality tended to gain precedence over a more multifaceted reality that accommodated opposing and contradictory elements. The codification project perhaps drew on the Enlightenment conviction that laws defined and written down somehow embodied the truth better than those left uncodified. By contrast, the basis of indigenous justice was its flexibility, grounded as it was in the personal participation of local elders, landowners, heads of castes, and community spokesmen in disputes over property and other matters. When, on the other hand, such cases came under the purview of the courts, the inevitable move was towards a uniform law which established its position through the accumulation of precedent. Older institutions were thereby displaced. Contemporaries noticed, 'To this day the Khojas dwelling under the Darbars of Cutch and Kathiawad have suffered less interference of Courts and law than the Khojas of Bombay.'[64] With codes and courts in place, there was now little room for the legal services of individuals such as Syed Husen. We cannot tell how the erosion of customary law may have unobtrusively affected the consciousness and confidence of local communities such as the butchers in our account. On the other hand, we do know that their fortunes reflected, in a tangible form, fluctuations in the commercial life of the city.

Commercial Boom and Crisis

The formative years of the family's business, we notice, coincided with an upsurge in the city's commerce. Cotton exports to Lancashire began to expand in the early 1850s, culminating in a boom during the American Civil War. It was in these years that Sobhan's business came into its own. He formed stable trading relations and enlarged his clientele to include prominent merchants—among them, Dharamsi Poonjiabhai and Limji Manockji, descendent of the famous eighteenth-century ship-owning Cawasji Banaji family. Sobhan gained a reputation as the biggest butcher in town. Prosperity led him to buy property and add an upper storey to the house. The family acquired the status of landlords. Then came the crash of the cotton trade. The crash hit not only those directly involved in the export of cotton, but also other traders as well as working people. Signs of this widespread effect were seen in the spate of insolvencies involving a wide section of the population that gripped the city well into the 1870s.

At the time of his death in 1868, as we have noticed, Sobhan's business was on shaky ground. Considerable sums were owed to him, while his own debts had piled up. The confidence of creditors, partners, and clients, which had sustained his business, showed signs of falling apart. Some of his clients had become bankrupt. Dharamsi Poonjiabhai's son, Meerali Dharamsi, from whom Ismail had borrowed money, petitioned as an insolvent in 1873.[65] Another important client, Limji Manockji, became insolvent a few years later.[66] He appears as a debtor to Ismail for Rs 815.[67] Dharamsi Poonjiabhai himself petitioned as an insolvent at a later date, 1886.[68] Three years afterwards, he was described as 'an old man broken in fortune, who had only recently passed through the Insolvency Court'.[69] Some clients may have felt the financial pressure that made them reluctant to settle accounts, while others may simply have exploited Ismail's discomfiture. He declared that customers owed him Rs 16,000: 'No one would pay me,' he said. Ismail may not have been an efficient manager, but his insolvency should be seen in the context of the commercial crisis of the city.

There were, of course, ways of overcoming the worst consequences of insolvency. Many insolvents whose debts were much larger than those of Sobhan and Ismail emerged from the crisis almost unscathed. They resorted to the law of trusteeship.[70] Sobhan knew that this was a way out. We have already seen how he tried, in vain, to persuade his principal creditors, Dorabji and Allarakhya, to become trustees of his estate. Even though he was not literate, Sobhan was familiar enough with the legal culture of the city. But being able to secure trustees was not always a simple matter. Persons who could pay in kind or in service may have found it easier to obtain trustees. Here, humbler citizens with businesses of their own were probably at a disadvantage compared to the bigger merchants and brokers, especially those with European connections.

A final decision on Ismail Sobhan's petition was postponed for a year. During this time he was not protected by the court. How Ismail fared during that year, we do not know. The court required him to pay the costs of the opposing creditors. This must have strained his resources. Without credit, his business had come to a standstill. He still earned half a rupee a day as a butcher, although, since filing his petition, he had not had a butcher's shop. He had to mortgage his house, which had given him a rental income, to his creditor, who sold it.[71] He no longer had his pleasure carriage.

It is conceivable that petitioning the High Court entailed hidden cost. The Official Assignee of the High Court, who dealt with the estates of insolvents, exercised enormous power. After the court had passed an order on an insolvent's petition, it was the Official Assignee who took the initiative in carrying it out. He could withhold the execution of the order if he wished. For the officials and employees of the court, the temptation to abuse power must have been considerable.

We do not learn whether Ayesha had to surrender her house for Ismail's debt. It seems, therefore, that she was able to keep it and, if that was the case, she may have provided both shelter and food to her son and his family. A year later, Ismail petitioned again, submitting a schedule of his finances that was considered to be in better order. In December 1874, the court granted him protection from arrest in respect of the debts mentioned in his amended schedule. Ayesha and Ismail's story ends for us at this date.

***

Historical writings concerning India's working people often represent them as oppressed and downtrodden. This is especially the case with accounts of women's lives. Invariably, these accounts are set in the period of colonial rule. Women are seen as victims of a cruel, male-dominated society whose bias was often reinforced by colonial law.[72] The marked emphasis on the abject position of women occludes a significant aspect of their lives, namely their role as agents in the societies in which they were placed. In this narrative, by contrast, an intimate view emerges of a particularly forceful, capable, and articulate woman—one who was mistress of her domain in the inner realm of family, work, and property. Ayesha arranged her daughter's marriage; worked at her husband's shop; and took the initiative in enlarging her house, managing the property, paying the taxes, and renting out a portion of the space. At the base of her position as homeowner was the customary law, put into effect by private agency, which made it possible for a married Muslim woman to be put in possession of property. Sobhan appears to have been a supportive husband who not only gave his wife a house, but who also attended to her wish to have it rebuilt. All this happened, we note, in the enabling environment of a leading colonial city whose commerce could embrace large merchants as well as smaller traders. Moreover, in their strategies of survival, Ayesha and her family could turn to people in the wider environment of the city. These included lawyer-politicians, such as Ismail's counsel, Badruddin Tyabji, then at the beginning of his legal career, who were adept in negotiating the labyrinth of the law and the courts. In turn, Tyabji's defence of the 'ignorant butcher' and his like may have helped Tyabji—the future president of the Indian National Congress—and his fellow lawyers to gain support among the people of Bombay. In the city, too, were traders and moneylenders with whom business arrangements could be made, as well as wealthy Khoja merchants who helped the family and whose customs of inheritance, some derived from Hindu law, may have influenced Ayesha and her family. Besides, the insolvency law provided relief to innumerable insolvent debtors, since the court gave protection to the vast majority of petitioners, and in so doing forged ties of dependence between ordinary people and the state. Ayesha's pastoral ancestors could not have imagined such a world. The remarkable fact is that she, a humble, unlettered woman, could make her way in it, albeit with some difficulty.

How many women in her time were as independent and self-assured as Ayesha; how many families placed as hers was? This narrative suggests that the records of insolvents may enable us to delve into to the lives of working people. The petitioners included several thousand people from a wide range of occupations, many at the subaltern level. The petitions tell us a good deal about individuals. In particular, we learn about their occupations and their material existence, what they earned and from what sources, and how they spent their money. We also learn about their personal and financial connections. It is true that Ayesha's story is indeed very richly documented. But much may be learned from these materials about other lives as well.

Notes and References

1. Sena Wakhta's evidence.
2. Ismail's evidence.
3. Ayesha's evidence. Elsewhere in the records, 'Dontad' is spelled 'Don Tar', as in the census of 1864, or 'Don Tarr' ('two palm trees'). Earlier, street names more often took after natural features than prominent personalities.
4. Ismail's evidence.
5. Jamnadas Nagardas's evidence.
6. Cadastral Survey, Bombay Collector's Records, 1915.
7. Khoja: A sect of Muslims at first located especially in Sind, Gujarat, and then Bombay.
8. Cadastral Survey, personal communication, Ruquia Lalljee, granddaughter of Abdullajabhai Lalljee.
9. Insolvency schedule 10683, 1875. All insolvency schedules refer to the records of the Bombay High Court and are cited by number and date.
10. Insolvency schedule 7562, 1871; Insolvency schedule 83504, 1883; Insolvency schedule 10746, 1875; Insolvency schedule 126, 1896.
11. Insolvency schedule 8373, 1872; Insolvency schedule 553, 1896; Insolvency schedule 135, 1889.
12. Insolvency schedule 18, 1882; Insolvency schedule 43, 1878. 'East Asian' generally referred to Indian Roman Catholics converted by the Portuguese who belonged to Bombay as distinct from Goa.
13. Insolvency schedule 353, 1880; Insolvency schedule 311, 1885; Insolvency schedule 504, 1880.
14. Insolvency schedule 215, 1881. We cannot be sure whether those who identified themselves as Portuguese were Europeans or Indo-Portuguese.
15. A haveli is a type of traditional dwelling used by middle- and upper-class urban residents in northern and central India, as well as in Gujarat and parts of the west coast. It usually consists of a central courtyard surrounded by rooms.
16. Ismail's evidence.
17. Dorabji's evidence.
18. Ismail's evidence.
19. Dorabji's evidence; Sena Wakhta's evidence.
20. Balaji Bhikaji's evidence.
21. Marwari(s): Specifically, inhabitants of Marwar in Rajasthan. The term is used in a general sense for Rajasthani moneylenders, traders, and businessmen. See T.A. Timberg, *The Marwaris* (New Delhi: Vikas Publishing House, 1978).
22. Purshotum Callianji Thucker, a real cloth dealer, complained that his creditors, Premjee Jeevun and Morarjee Gokuldas (the latter would become a

prominent industrial magnate), had confined him to his house and stationed 'their stout Bhayajee with their clubs' at his door. Purshotum Callianji alleged that the debt was on account of damaged cloth they had given him, which he could not sell (Insolvency schedule 4421, 1866). Premjee Jeevun, Hurjeevun Jeevun and Morarjee Gokuldas were wholesale dealers in imported cloth (Morarjee Gokuldas, autobiography, typescript). It turns out that a part of the cloth imported at about this time had been damaged by mildew (Annual Report, Bombay Chamber of Commerce, 1864–5). The term 'bhayajee' or 'bhaiaji' refers to persons from northern India who were often employed as guards and watchmen in Bombay.

23. Evidence of Nanabhai Vishwanath, clerk to superintendent of markets.
24. Dorabji's evidence.
25. Allarakhya's evidence.
26. Carriages were being made in Bombay, but the most fashionable citizens imported theirs from England. Wealthy townsmen, such as the Jejeebhoys, were helping their friends to import English carriages. See Jejeebhoy Letterbooks, Bombay University Library.
27. In Maharashtra, the Devnagri script used for the writing of Sanskrit, Hindi, and Marathi is also called Balbodh. It is a broken, as distinct from a running, hand. (Pandit Mahadevshastri Joshi, ed, *Bharatiya Sanskritikosh* [Pune, 1967].) Balbodh was often used for children's primers.
28. Sheikh Ali Sheikh Mohammad's evidence.
29. Gopal Sakharam's evidence.
30. Deshpande's evidence. An anna was equal to one-sixteenth of a rupee.
31. Deshpande's evidence.
32. Nanabhai Vishwanath's evidence.
33. The Modi script is believed to have been introduced in the thirteenth century by Hemadi Pant, chief minister of the Yadava ruler of Deogiri. As against Devnagri, it is a continuous hand suitable for rapid writing, and came to be widely used, especially in the Maratha dominions, from where it spread to other regions including Mysore and Madras (Joshi, *Bharatiya Sanskritkosh*).
34. While Ismail declared the total amount owed to him was Rs 16,000, the list of debts filed in his schedule amounted to only Rs 2,307.
35. Badruddin Tyabji (1844–1906) was a Suleimani Bohra, barrister at law, prominent nationalist, lawyer and politician, President of the Indian National Congress (1887), and judge of the High Court of Bombay.
36. Ismail's evidence.
37. Hilan Moosaji may himself have been a frequent petitioner to the insolvency court. Names closely resembling his appear three times: Hilal Moosajee in Insolvency schedule 3000, 1862; Hillel Moosjee in Insolvency schedule 7346, 1871; and Hillel Moosajee, Insolvency schedule 8815, 1872.

38. Insolvency schedule 572, 1890.
39. Insolvency schedule 62, 1887.
40. Timberg, *The Marwaris*.
41. Personal communication, Dr B.V. Subbarayappa, director, Centre for History and Philosophy of Science, Bangalore. K.P. Kulkarni, *Marathi Etymological Dictionary* (Bombay, 1946), p. 296, describes 'chowgula' as 'the peon of the village patil' (headman). See also James Thomas Molesworth, *A Dictionary, Marathi and English*. 2d ed., rev. and enl. (Bombay: Printed for government at the Bombay Education Society's press, 1857), p. 295.
42. Reginald Edward Enthoven, *The Tribes and Castes of the Bombay Presidency* (Bombay: Printed at the Government Central Press, 1920–2), vol. 1, pp. 311ff.
43. Insolvency schedule 254, 1887; Insolvency schedule 490, 1883.
44. Enthoven, *Tribes and Castes of the Bombay Presidency*, vol. 2, p. 163.
45. Mohammad Amin's evidence.
46. Mohammad Amin's evidence. The word in the original is 'zamatkhana'.
47. See F. Conlon, *A Caste in a Changing World* (Berkeley: University of California Press, 1977), pp. 118–22.
48. Almost all the butchers in our data used scales as their mark.
49. Balaji Bhikaji and Mohammad Amin's evidence.
50. Balaji Bhikaji and Mohammad Amin's evidence.
51. See Majid H. Siddiqi, 'History and Society in a Popular Rebellion: Mewat 1920–1933', *Comparative Studies in Society and History* 28, no. 3 (1986): 442–3.
52. Deshpande's evidence.
53. Ismail's schedule.
54. Gogari Mohla (mohalla: neighbourhood), with a population of 6,500 was, according to the census of 1864, the most populous street in the Bhuleshwar subsection. Peopled originally by immigrants from the port of Ghoga in the Gulf of Cambay, it retains to this day the character of a predominantly Muslim locality with different communities, each with its own jamatkhana.
55. Insolvency schedule 3927, 1865.
56. Insolvency schedule 657, 1891.
57. 'Musalman Classes: The Khatris or Rangaris', vol. 25, General Department, Maharashtra State Archives, 1896.
58. See A. Hourani, *A History of the Arab Peoples* (New York: Warner Books, 1991), p. 154.
59. Sir Erskine Perry, or cas 110, 1847, quoted by Justice Jardine in *Cassumbhoy Ahmedbhoy v. Ahmedbhoy Hubibhoy & c*, 1887. (M. Subramaniam and M.V. Krishnaswamy, eds, *The Law Reports of British India*. High Court [Chennai,

India], Great Britain, Privy Council, Judicial Committee [Madras: The Law Reports Office, 1913–15], pp. 200–1).

60. Ibrahimbhai Habibbhai's evidence in the Agha Khan case, 1847, quoted by Justice Jardine. (Subramaniam and Krishnaswamy, *The Law Reports of British India*, p. 200).
61. Prominent among official enquiries concerning customary law were: (*a*) Arthur Steel, *Summary of the Law and Custom of Hindoo Castes within the Dechun Provinces Subject to the Presidency of Bombay, Chiefly Affecting Civil Suits* (Bombay, 1887); (*b*) Borradaile's *Gujarat Caste Rules*, published with the sanction of the High Court of Bombay by Sir Mangaldass Nathoobhoy, in 2 volumes (vol. 1, Bombay, 1884, and vol. 2, Bombay, 1887).
62. See Justice Jardines's comments on Borradaile's report. (Subramaniam and Krishnaswamy, *The Law Reports of British India*, p. 207.)
63. Subramaniam and Krishnaswamy, *The Law Reports of British India*, p. 208.
64. Subramaniam and Krishnaswamy, *The Law Reports of British India*, p. 209.
65. Insolvency schedule of Meerali Dharamsi, 9414, 1873.
66. Insolvency schedule of Limji Manockji, 481, 1881.
67. Ismail's insolvency schedule.
68. Insolvency schedule of Dharamsi Poonjiabhai, 444, 1886.
69. Justice Sarjent, judgment in case of *Ahmedbhai Habibbhai* v. *Cassumbhai Ahmedbhai*.
70. See the cases of Tata Sons and Premchund Roychund.
71. Ismail's evidence.
72. See Ranajit Guha, 'Chandra's Death', in *Subaltern Studies V*, edited by Ranajit Guha (New Delhi: Oxford University Press, 1987).

Conclusion

This volume highlights the intensity of the commercial crisis that gripped Bombay upon the crash of the cotton trade in the late 1860s. Both the number of insolvencies and the dip in incomes show that event to have been cataclysmic. We have traced the effects of the crisis on a panoply of Bombay's people—not only merchants who were directly involved in the cotton trade, but also many working people who were not directly involved in trade and speculation. The severity of the crisis was the consequence both of commercial fluctuations and of the terms intrinsic to colonial trade, namely the manner in which capital was raised and accounts settled for the export market. As against the quasi-moralistic view which explains the crisis in terms of over-trading and reckless speculation—'share mania,' as it was termed—we see it as a crisis that was propelled by global events as much as by local business activity. Our study of 20,000 petitions by insolvents from a wide range of social, economic, religious, and professional backgrounds reveals the workings of complex and dynamic financial relationships among Bombay's people.

The crisis had a disastrous effect on the fortunes of wealthy and powerful Bombay merchants. As the American Civil War ended, American cotton again entered the global market, and the price of Indian cotton plummeted, many merchants saw their business empires crumble in a matter of months. Despite their misfortune, some of these merchants were saved from personal ruin by the insolvency courts. Starting in 1828, the British colonial government had introduced a series of acts for the relief of insolvent debtors. The government had no wish to see the traders and merchants who were the lifeblood of the economy languishing in prison. When the market crashed, many Bombay merchants were able successfully to petition for relief under the Insolvency Act of 1865. Passed through the influence of Bombay's merchants and financiers and their European counterparts, the Act protected debtors from imprisonment and facilitated the appointment of trustees who would superintend the liquidation of the debtors' estates. Our analysis of the income levels of petitioners shows that the crisis affected people with a wide range of incomes, over the course of many years. We find higher numbers of insolvents petitioning at the upper and lower ends of the range of incomes, a fact that suggests that the courts actively protected the poorest and the wealthiest insolvents.

Our study of the insolvency petitions of three wealthy and powerful Bombay merchants has revealed how differently they fared when faced with insolvency. Kahandas Narandas was ruined by the financial crises, whereas Jamshedji Tata and Premchand Roychund, both of whom he had business dealings with, were able to obtain the protection of the courts and eventually to recover. The sharp differences in how these merchants fared can be explained by their vastly different styles of doing business and the differences in their relationships with the colonial financial elite.

Kahandas Narandas came from an extremely wealthy, well-established family of traders based in Ahmedabad. His firm, Motichund Ragoonathdass, was involved in the jewellery trade as well as other traditional staples of trade: piece goods, tea, sugar, and cotton. The firm was also involved in the opium trade. Kahandas's affluence is evident in his style of living and his relaxed way of doing business. As we have seen, various entries in his accounts indicated that he had written off large sums. He did not himself monitor the details of commercial transactions, but rather left bookkeeping to his mehta. He conducted his financial affairs on the basis of trust and personal reputation. In his cultural milieu, generosity and lavishness indicated a person's means and credibility, which were essential to doing business. Of equal importance were personal relationships and friendships, which, along with reputation, assured the flow of credit. Kahandas's was a traditional way of doing business, and he appeared not to have fully grasped the workings of the emergent financial culture. Nor was Kahandas wise to the laws and legal processes governing trade and finance that the British colonial administration had introduced. The insolvency court ruled that he had failed to provide adequate evidence. We do not know why he did not appoint a trustee. Trustees were handsomely paid and he may have lacked the means to find one. He also lacked the personal support of the colonial financial elite, and perhaps this too explains why he foundered in the insolvency courts. His downfall cannot be attributed simply to his failings as a businessman; rather, it reveals the gap between the old and new modes of trade and finance.

Jamshedji Tata and Premchand Roychund were also bankrupted by the financial crisis, but unlike Kahandas, they were able to rebound and reconstitute their businesses. They emerged from the crisis relatively unscathed because they were better connected with the English banks and trading elite, and were more worldly about the functioning of the financial system and the courts. Faced with insolvency, they procured trustees, explained their finances in terms acceptable to judges, and successfully obtained relief from the insolvency courts.

Our analysis of the insolvency petitions of wealthy merchants yields a rich picture of trade in the mid-nineteenth century. It reveals a wide range of trade networks extending to the Middle East and China. As we have seen, enormous profits were being made in this period from the opium trade in addition to other commodities such as cotton. Our study suggests that the British administration loosened the regulations they had themselves instituted so that capital was more readily obtainable. An 1840 Act had required that loans be backed by 'hard' securities: government paper, bullion, imperishable goods, and suchlike. This provision was countermanded by an Act of 1863 that permitted the granting of loans against 'negotiable goods'. This could be a promissory note signed by one person. As we see in the case of Premchand Roychund, British bank officials followed Indian custom in advancing loans on the basis of personal securities. This loosening of regulation, combined with European firms' interest in maximizing their commissions regardless of the outcome of trading, created great instability.

Our study of insolvency records has afforded a rare glimpse into the lives of women from different social classes and milieus in Bombay during the mid-nineteenth century. Contrary to colonial stereotypes of Indian women as trapped in oppressive patriarchal relationships, weak, helpless, and submissive, we find that women had considerable agency. Many had independent incomes, owned property, and enjoyed power in the domain of home and family life. They were articulate, shrewd, and capable in their dealings with the insolvency courts. Women from wealthy merchant families actually owned much of the borrowed capital. At the same time, men controlled the financial transactions; so the extent of women's financial power is ambiguous. Women did exercise control over their incomes and could bequeath these incomes to their daughters.

We infer from the insolvency records that women who were not wealthy and worked also had considerable agency. In our study, about 38 per cent of the women who petitioned the insolvency courts for protections were dancing girls, courtesans, and prostitutes. This high proportion can be explained by the fact that women in these professions had independent incomes and were directly affected by the crash. It is striking that a number of the dancing girls and courtesans followed matrilineal customs of inheritance and bequeathed their property to their daughters rather than sons. We were able to glean information about the lives of these women from their petitions. While courtesans and dancing girls (the terms are more or less interchangeable) were generally better off than prostitutes, the incomes of women as a group of insolvents were low. At the same time, the incomes of dancing girls and courtesans varied greatly. Many dancing girls and courtesans were mistresses of men who gave them money, and they also earned incomes from their professions. Some dancing girls had been trained at some expense, were accomplished performers, and were paid well by their patrons. The social status of dancing girls and courtesans also varied depending on the standing of their patrons. Literacy levels for women insolvents were low regardless of their income and social status.

We were able to construct a relatively detailed account of the life and milieu of one woman, Ayesha, from court documents related to the petition of her son, Ismail, an insolvent butcher. Ayesha's strength of character, her independence, and her ability to manage her affairs come across in her testimony. She gave her testimony with self-possession in the English court, though she spoke no English and was illiterate. She had a house that her husband had transferred to her name, housed tenants and collected rent from them, paid taxes, and maintained custody of jewels and important papers. She supported herself and was not dependent on her son; indeed she arranged and financed the marriage of her daughter.

Our study of Ayesha and her family also sheds light on the commercial culture and social relationships in the neighbourhood near Mohammad Ali Road where she lived. This part of the city had a population that was heterogeneous with regard to religion, ethnicity, and occupation. The testimony of witnesses and the evidence indicates that Ayesha and her family had a wide circle of acquaintances from different communities. In this close-knit, urban milieu, the core categories of identity, caste, and religion took on new meanings.

As we have noted, insolvency records provide information about a wide range of Bombay's people, not just wealthy merchants. Among the people who made an appearance in the insolvency petitions were artisans, traders, prostitutes, managers, homemakers, domestic servants, and labourers. The documents tell us about types of professions, modes of self-identification, kinds and degrees of literacy, and income levels.

Taking signatures on documents as indexes of literacy—those who were not literate signed with marks of various kinds—we found that a surprisingly large number of petitioners were literate. We also found that the proportion of literate petitioners seemed to go up over the years, indicating a trend toward increasing literacy. This trend may be explained in part by the efforts of official, private, and missionary organizations in Bombay to spread literacy, which was traditionally the preserve of the upper classes and the upper castes. Literacy in English was valued especially highly and corresponds in our study to higher income levels.

Petitioners frequently identified themselves with reference to their religion and occupation as well as their origins. Our study shows that there was often a correlation between religion and occupation, and people of specific religions tended to follow particular occupations. We believe that a heightened sense of religious and regional identity is evident in the way petitioners identified themselves. This might have follow from the introduction of censuses that solicited personal information. Or a sense of separate identity might have been strengthened by the kinds of encounters between people from different communities in an urban milieu, encounters that at times precipitated clashes.

The study also enables us to observe certain features of colonial law. As was true of other areas of Indo-British jurisprudence, we notice in the laws of debt and insolvency an attempt to systematize and render definite what had been flexible. Earlier, debt obligations were tacitly looked upon as a matter of honour, involved the credibility of a person's dealings, and were enforced by the influence of those whose personal authority was acknowledged both by the debtor and the creditor. By contrast, the use of the instruments of the state, the law courts, and prisons moved debt obligations out of the private to the public domain. This was consistent with the ruthless endeavour to secure the sanctity of contract, no doubt with the object—as Justice Pinhey noted in the case of Sunderji Waghji to which we have referred—of 'protecting society generally and specially honest traders'.[1] We find that people whose conduct was grounded in customary codes of practice, which were relatively flexible and informal, had to negotiate the streamlining and codification of practices that the colonial government undertook.

Debtors' law and insolvency law together enhanced the power and presence of the state while at the same time they weakened the social basis of traditional institutions in relations of borrowing and lending between individuals and between commercial bodies. First by introducing the practice of imprisonment for debt, something that was foreign to Indian society, and then through the insolvency law, making provision for protection, the colonial state exercised immense power over the lives of individuals in the metropolitan cities of India. Had it not been for the insolvency law, thousands of people could have been sued by their creditors and put in jail. The practice of the courts to readily admit petitions for protection demonstrated how greatly people must have depended for their freedom on the instruments of the state. In a subtle way the law propagated a certain subservience. At the same time, dissatisfaction with the way in which the colonial state adjudicated business may have fed into emergent nationalist sentiments towards the later part of the nineteenth century.

This study looks at insolvency during a particularly eventful period of the history of Bombay. The law of 1848 applied also to Calcutta and Madras. An examination of the insolvency records of these cities would offer scope for comparative study.

Note

1. Insolvency schedule 9317, 1873. Hearing, 17 June to 26 August 1874, recorded in Justice Pinhey's notebook entitled 'Notes by Justice Pinhey', Insolvent Court, Bombay, 1873.

Index

About the Author

Asiya Siddiqi is an economic historian specializing in nineteenth-century India. She was born in Dalhousie, India, and grew up in Lucknow and Allahabad. After studying at Isabella Thoburn College in Lucknow and Allahabad University, she completed her BA from Somerville College, Oxford, and her DPhil from University of Oxford, UK. She has held positions as a reader at Aligarh Muslim University and University of Mumbai and as a visiting professor at the University of Southern California. She is a life member of Clare Hall, University of Cambridge, UK.

Asiya Siddiqi's early work was on the agrarian economic history of colonial India. At Oxford, she did research for her DPhil with May McKisack on transformations in the economy of Uttar Pradesh during the nineteenth century. She published her research as a book, *Agrarian Change in a Northern Indian State* (1973). After moving to Bombay in 1964, she shifted her attention to the mercantile history of Bombay. In 1995 she published an edited volume, *Trade and Finance in Colonial India, 1750–1860* (Oxford University Press , 1995). The present volume extends the study of Bombay's mercantile history to include the social history of a range of Bombay's residents in the latter half of the nineteenth century.

Asiya Siddiqi's research has been supported by grants from the University Grants Commission, India.